Gender, Change & Society: 3

Women and the State

Women and the State
International Perspectives

Edited by

Shirin M. Rai
and
Geraldine Lievesley

Taylor & Francis
Publishers since 1798

UK	Taylor & Francis Ltd, 1 Gunpowder Square, London EC4A 3DE
USA	Taylor & Francis Inc., 1900 Frost Road, Suite 101, Bristol, PA 19007

First published 1996

A Catalogue Record for this book is available from the British Library

ISBN 0 7484 0360 4
ISBN 0 7484 0361 2 pbk

Library of Congress Cataloging-in-Publication Data are available on request

Cover design by Amanda Barragry.
Typeset in 10/12 pt Times
by Best-set Typesetter Ltd, Hong Kong.

Printed in Great Britain by SRP Ltd, Exeter.

Contents

Contents

Acknowledgments

The editors wish to thank the contributors to this book for their commitment to the project. We have all shared an enthusiasm about the need to bring the question of Third World women's experiences in dealing with the state to the foreground of feminist debate.

We are also grateful for the support received from our editor, Comfort Jegede. Finally, we thank each other for not letting the pressures of work take away from the pleasure of working together.

Introduction

Shirin M. Rai and Geraldine Lievesley

This book explores the relationship between the state, women's struggles, and women's organizations. It is a multidisciplinary volume with perspectives from political science, sociology, law and political economy. The geographical areas covered by contributors include South America (Chile and Peru), Africa (Kenya, Zimbabwe and Botswana) and Asia and the Middle East (Bangladesh, China, Palestine, Lebanon and Algeria).

Taking the colonial experience as a starting point the contributors examine the processes and functioning of state institutions in exercises of power in various areas of public and private lives of women, and women's resistance to these intrusions. While taking into account the unique and particular cultural, economic and political histories of the various countries, all the contributors, who met for a workshop on the theme at the Centre for Studies in Democratization at Warwick University, argue from a perspective that combines a critique of structural explanations of the state with a recognition of the need for 'taking the state seriously'.

The major themes that emerge in the volume are of nationalism and the nation-state, economic modernization and its critique, an examination of state processes, capacities and institutions in the post-colonial context, and issues raised by women's struggles and participation in the public and political sphere.

Much of the volume speaks against the received wisdom regarding gender and state. The targets of opposition are different, and reflecting of the variety of historical contexts, and yet there is an overall perspective which regards the state (used throughout as a shorthand term for a network of contested power relations) as an uneven and fractured terrain with dangers as well as resources for women's movements. Women's struggles are also critically examined – the ways in which they are able to make claims upon and fight against state institutions leading to fundamental changes in gender relations at any given time; and also the way in which the threat of cooptation never leaves a successful women's movement. Struggle, therefore, is regarded not simply as a question of opposition to state institutions, but also one of critical self-examination by women's movements and organizations. While there is an engagement in the book with the dominant Western feminist discourses on the state, the contributions largely centre on the experiences of women in the

Third World (a term accepted by all contributors as a term of political opposition, as well as indicative of the colonial experience of these states).

In the first chapter, Shirin Rai argues that much Western feminist state theory has largely ignored the experience of Third World women. She discusses the fractured and constantly shifting formations of weak Third World states and their embeddedness in civil society. Those configurations construct the boundaries within which women act and are acted upon. In order to travel through previously prohibited political terrain, women must develop complex strategies. Rai concludes that the question of whether women should 'deal' with the state is actually a decision that women are not in a position to make. It is not they who approach the state but the state which approaches them. What feminist debate must be concerned with is women struggling against the Third World state, that is the process by which they take control of their lives.

Ann Stewart's discussion of the legal status of women in Kenya, Tanzania, Zimbabwe and Botswana focuses upon how women are located within the process of nation-building as it is shaped by the discourse between tradition and modernity. Women claiming recognition of their rights by the state are criticized for attempting to destroy traditional cultural practice as defended by customary law. Here, modern legal convention is identified as yet another form of imperialist intervention and women's rights activists as its collaborators. The tradition/modernity cleavage is, however, not so clear-cut. The colonial state penetrated the construction of customary law using it to underpin its own power and to uphold patriarchal structures. Modern African states use the rhetoric of the 'rule of law' in order to acquire legitimacy but their implementation of it is always arbitrary and often perfunctory.

Geraldine Lievesley's chapter on Peruvian women's activism investigates the relationship between the state and women and also the often problematic connections between different branches of the women's movement. She suggests that distinct types of activity and mobilization – career political, feminist, popular – must coexist rather than being regarded as mutually exclusive. Her account of Peruvian political history from 1968 to the present offers a possibly surprising paradox in that the opportunities for women's political organization appeared to be more fruitful under military rule than during the three civilian governments which followed the transition to liberal democracy in 1980.

Maria Holt compares the experiences of Palestinian and Lebanese Shi'i women involved in processes of state formation and state reconstitution respectively. She points to the role women have assumed in the provision of basic welfare services which their non-existent or non-functioning states are incapable of offering. She also discusses how the use of Islam – as both culture and religion – has been a significant factor in the creation of a 'Palestinian national entity' and a 'Lebanese national identity.' Islamism has been a radical, empowering ideology but it has also wanted women to repudiate their specific needs and demands.

Malika Mehdid continues the theme of women, nation-building and the state in her case study on Algeria. She argues that the nationalist discourse which emerged during colonial rule contained a strong defence of the family (and of women's traditional role within it) and of Arabo-Islamic values. After independence in 1962, the new Algerian state's commitment to socialist modernization existed in uneasy tension with conservative ideologies of the family and the nation. Women were expected to freeze their specific gender concerns in recognition of the overriding importance of national development. Algeria's collapse into 'civil war' since the military's decision to annul the fundamentalist election victory of 1992 has had serious consequences for women activists who have been targeted by Islamist terrorism.

Georgina Waylen presents an account of the government-created Servicio Nacional de la Mujer (SERNAM) in Chile. The institution's officials are recruited from women members of the political class, that is, individuals who are confident in their dealings with state bodies and expect positive results from these contacts. Waylen believes that the class origins and political attitudes of these women have damaging implications for their relations with poor Chilean women. She identifies the inherent weakness of such 'political' women which is that the success of their aims is dependent upon friendly male opinion within other state agencies and political parties. The consequence has been that legislative progress has been made in those areas regarded as least controversial whilst gender-specific issues have been effectively blocked.

Anne Marie Goetz focuses upon the working experiences of women development staff involved in state and NGO rural poverty reduction programmes in Bangladesh. Her concern is to discover how far it is possible to institutionalize women's presence in decision-making processes in such organizations and also if these women are able to promote oppositional – that is, women-centred – perspectives to deflect male-dominated bureaucratic cultures. She concludes that the common belief that NGO staff are more gender-sensitive, in both their relations with poor women and their implementation of projects, than state institutions is a misleading representation of the real situation. Her findings suggest that institutional and attitudinal obstacles impede qualitative 'development service delivery' to women by both NGOs and the state and that, indeed, some features of the latter's management systems may offer women staff better opportunities to develop 'oppositional' positions.

Tamara Jacka argues that the Chinese state has been compelled to accept the vital role played by the informal economy and the pivotal presence of women within this through the medium of 'domestic sidelines' or courtyard industries. The paradox here is that, despite the conventional perception that their involvement in the informal economy perpetuates women's marginalization in that it facilitates the maintenance of gender hierarchies within the family, 'domestic sideline' activities can elevate *some* women's status and opportunities, bestowing upon them greater independence than they would enjoy in larger-scale employment. Jacka concludes that the courtyard economy may be a viable route for improving Chinese women's socioeconomic status but that this will depend upon factors such as improved literacy and skills training, and organization in order to articulate and defend their interests vis-à-vis the state.

Annie Phizacklea brings the volume to a conclusion with her contention that we need to consider not only the relationship between women and the nation-state but also that between women, state and the international political economy. Her purpose is to disclose how the international market for women's labour continues to be mediated by the policies of individual states, thus making them complicit in the gendered division of labour. Taking a structuralist perspective which is that poor women are forced to migrate through economic necessity rather than personal volition, she investigates the traffic in prostitution and mail-order brides, domestic service and the clothing trade. In each case, she describes how national legal and political systems privilege the male thus leaving women without official status and often in precarious and dangerous circumstances.

All the contributors concur in a reading of Third World states as being open to mediation by women because of the existence of internal fissures within them. The state is not, as Tamara Jacka points out, a discrete institution pursuing its own interests which are, and must always be, inimical to women. There are opportunities for both progress and regression in the struggle for women's emancipation. Women are compelled to develop interactive programmes with regard to the state (that is, there is no mileage to be made out of a position which rejects such 'dealing') but are also aware of how frustrating this relationship will be and how slow and piecemeal changes in legislative and socio-economic conditions are. This notwithstanding, it is the belief of the authors of this book that women are repudiating the passivity historically assigned them and are now dynamic actors involved in societal transformation.

Chapter 1

Women and the State in the Third World: Some Issues for Debate

Shirin M. Rai

This chapter examines the debates on the state within the feminist literature. It stresses the importance of bringing the state back in to any discussion of women's lives in the Third World. I use the term 'the state' not as signifying a unity of structure and power. The state is used here as a shorthand term to describe a network of power relations existing in cooperation and also in tension. I do not regard these relations as based on a reductionist explanation of socio-economic systems but rather situate these power relations within a grid which is composed of economic, political, legal and cultural forms all interacting on, with and against each other. Such an approach allows us to examine the state within the context of social relations which are affected by systems of power, and which affect these systems through the struggles against these systems. Further, such an approach allows a space within which to give importance to the 'form' that states take in different historical contexts. One such historical context is that of colonialism, which has marked the development of Third World states. While accepting that the Third World encompasses countries with very different social, historical and economic traditions, this chapter raises some issues about the post-colonial states as they have emerged from struggle against imperialisms and colonial rule. The Indian colonial and post-colonial experiences form the basis of some general observations, firstly on the importance of the post-colonial state as a conceptual and political category for Third World women and secondly on the implications of this understanding for the strategies available to women in their struggle against and negotiations with post-colonial states.

I will begin by examining some recent interventions in feminist state theory. I argue that Western feminist state theory has largely ignored the experience of Third World women under the post-colonial state. The assumptions made are West-centred but the theorizing takes on a universalizing language. Similarly, theories of the 'developmental state' (as opposed to 'theories of development' in general) have developed in gender-blind and sometimes Orientalist ways (Joseph, 1993, p. 26), and therefore ignore the particular relationship that women in the Third World find themselves in vis-à-vis the post-colonial state. Both tend to overlook the processes of state and class formations in the Third World, and therefore the relations of exploitation operating in the economic and the socio-political terrain. This further leads to assumptions about the nature of struggle and the strategies that can be included or are to be excluded from the ambit of struggle. There is now a growing literature on women and the state in the Third World, which seeks to challenge the universalizing language of the Western feminist and developmental state discourses about women, the state, and struggle. I will argue that what we need is a continuing and more focused debate about women and the post-colonial state as Third World women come to experience not only national but international economic and political power in the era of economic restructuring and institutional (rather than necessarily political) democratization. Such a focus will also allow us to examine the growing and diverse arenas of women's political activities which include not only opposition but negotiation, not only struggle but also strategic bargaining in spaces that are intersections of the private and the public spheres.

Western Feminist Interventions in State Theory

The state, as a concept and as a network of power relations, evokes deep suspicion, anger, fear, and hostility among feminists. This suspicion of the state has more recently been supported by poststructuralist explanations of power. Indeed, since the 1970s, the concept of the state has been so reduced in status that its very existence has been brought into question. 'Where the concept remains in everyday use, it is used descriptively, mostly by the "practitioners" of social policy and social welfare' (Pringle and Watson, 1992, pp. 54–5). However, during the 1970s and 1980s there was also a growing sense of the power of the state as the welfare state became more important in the lives of individuals – regulating, defining, providing and monitoring. Women began to enter the arena of local politics and legal disputes in order to represent their own interests (Pringle and Watson, 1992).

There have developed in Western feminist theory two very different approaches to the question of the state. Historically, both have roots in the experience of women's movements in different contexts. In countries with strong class affiliations and a tradition of class-based political action like Britain, feminist writing was dominated by the Marxist analysis of the state as an oppressive instrument of the ruling (capitalist) class. Marxist feminists added the 'woman question' to the class question in capitalist societies by emphasizing the role of the state as a mediator between the two different but complementary systems of patriarchy and capitalism (Wilson, 1977; Eisenstein, 1979). In countries with a strong tradition of welfare state politics, there has been less resistance to dealing with the state. In Australia and Scandinavia for example, a positive value has been place on state intervention, and the state has been more clearly seen as an arena for bargaining among interests (see Hernes, 1987). Women's interests have been regarded as one among others, and feminists have insisted that they must be articulated within that space. Not only has the question of interest articulation been seen in a positive light, but also that of participation in state functioning. The 'femocrat' is the creature of this strategy of influencing the state in the interests of women by infiltrating it (see Franzway *et al.*, 1989). Though the Marxist feminist and the institution-based approaches took very different views of the state, both acknowledged the state as a reference point in feminist politics. Both also spoke of the state in institutional and functionalist terms. In sum, both took the state seriously.

The other Western feminist approach towards the state has been inspired by poststructuralism. Within this category too there are differences. Some would regard politics as a 'set of debates and struggles over meaning', and the state as 'erratic and disconnected rather than contradictory'. They would point out that what 'intentionality there is comes from the success with which various groupings are able to articulate their interests and hegemonize their claims: it is always likely to be partial and temporary' (Pringle and Watson, 1992, pp. 61, 63). Further, poststructuralist feminists would argue that the focus of our analysis of public power should not be an impossible unity of the state, but micro-level organizations and institutions that affect individual lives daily. Unlike the Marxist feminists, they do not see the state, in its dispersed sense, as simply reflecting and bolstering gender inequalities, but consider that 'through its practices, [it] plays an important part in constituting them; simultaneously, gender practices become institutionalized in historically specific state forms. It is a two way street.' (Pringle and Watson, 1992, p. 64). A more radical feminist response to the issue of the state asks the question 'whether the state is a specifically problematic instrument or arena of *feminist* political change' (Brown, 1992, p. 8). This poses the dilemma that the poststructuralist feminists discussed above have not acknowledged in full. 'If the institutions, practices, and discourses of the state are as inextricably, however differently, bound up with the prerogatives of manhood in a male-dominated society . . . what are the implications for feminist politics?' (*ibid.*). The answer given to this question by postmodern feminists would be to suggest that for women to 'be "protected" by the very power whose violation one fears perpetuates the specific modality of dependence and powerlessness marking much of women's experience across widely diverse cultures and epochs' (*ibid.*, p. 9). The state in this analysis is a regulating, constraining, structuring network of power, and interaction with it can only have one outcome – the production of 'regulated, subordinated, and disciplined *state* subjects' (see also Smart, 1989 and 1992; Allen, 1990).

These debates among Western feminists are on-going. What is particular about this debate, and unsurprising, is that it has focused almost exclusively on Western state formations and processes. While some postmodern feminists do point to how the 'process of decentering and diversifying politics has helped increase the visibility of historically marginalised interests and perspectives, for example, feminist, postcolonial and "Third World" interests' (Weedon, 1993), questions such as whether the post-colonial state poses any particular problems for women, whether Third World women can relate such a West-centred debate to their own lives, and whether an analysis of Third World states by feminists might throw up questions for feminists theorizing and debating the state, have not been asked. Are there any particular features of the post-colonial state that challenge or problematize Western perspectives of the state? Which of these features need to be taken into account by Third World women when they consider their own relationship with the state?

The Colonial State and its Legacy

We cannot understand the various constituting power relationships of the post-colonial state without reflecting on the legacy of colonialism in the Third World. This legacy has been material, cultural and political. The relationship between the colonial powers and the colonies, while based on economic exploitation of one by the other, encompassed a complex set of changing relationships.

The colonial powers' bargaining with important political groups within colonial societies as well as the introduction of new socio-economic arrangements brought about different results for men and women. The process of privatization that took place during colonial rule is a case in point (see Agarwal, 1992). With increasing control over common land, the colonial state was able to refashion the relationship of men and women to natural resources. Needed to supply the demands of the British colonial navy, for example, the monopolization of forest resources led to significant deforestation in India. The commercialization of agriculture as a means of extraction of economic surplus also led to a curtailment of the customary rights of local populations to common lands. Given the greater dependence of women on the forests as well as on common grazing areas and village wells, the impact on the quality of their lives and on their economic positioning within the community was significantly affected (Agarwal, 1992). However, the colonial powers refashioned gender relations within colonized countries through the exercise of not only material but also discursive power.

The colonial interventions in the traditional systems of economic production were paralleled by reinterpreting and reinventing the social and political histories of the colonized countries as means of supporting a modernizing ideology which at the same time delegitimized the traditional societies that were now subjugated.

> Perhaps one of the most important aspects of any relationship that is defined by a significant imbalance of power is how the narrative of the one is given legitimacy over the narrative of the other. This is the case not only when the more powerful is defining itself, but also when it is defining the other. (Liddle and Rai, 1992)

The image of the colonized societies created in the Orientalist discourse was a complex one. On the one hand there was a recognition of 'lost glory' of past civilizations, on the other hand the image of barbarity and decline. While explaining the fall of ancient cultures this discourse also legitimized colonial rule within the framework of modernity. Exoticism and degradation – both are images that we recognize today as signifying the Third World – were used as explanatory and legitimizing devises to construct a hegemonic discourse that was rooted in the Western philosophical and historical traditions of the Enlightenment.

Orientalist discourse used highly emotive images of social evils to mark the colonized societies as barbaric and in need of the civilizing hand of the colonizing powers. In creating this discourse women's bodies were particularly important – in sati, child marriage, footbinding, clitoridectomy – as symbolic of the condition of the societies in which they live. On the one hand, we find a construction of colonial women as 'naturally' libidinous and out of control (as opposed to the placid and controlled Victorian woman), on the other, they are victims of a vicious, though male population, needing the protection of the civilizing colonial state. Not only were women's bodies symbolic in this discourse, men too were normalized as either effeminate or 'martial' – products of social practices that impacted on the genetic pool of a whole population.

The nature of colonial interventions was, however, not uniform. Concerns of administrative and political control, developing of an infrastructural network supporting economic extraction as well as suppressing opposition to colonial rule, bargainings with traditional authority structures, and the strength of local and national oppositional movements, meant that colonial states intervened in socio-economic systems of their colonies in unsystematic ways. Not always were laws made to reflect the dominant power relations in the colonial countries. For example, in India, the matrilineal traditions that were widely prevalent in some southern states were abolished through the imposition of patriarchal legal arrangements that had their basis in English property law. While matriliny was deemed 'immoral' the colonial government continued to accept the Muslim practice of polygamy.

Another feature of colonial intervention was an attempt to simplify traditional social and economic arrangements in order to be able to introduce new rules and regulations and laws that were needed to formalize their power relationships as well as support the need for surplus extraction. The complex and different socio-economic arrangements got in the way of the standardization of procedures required for administration. This simplification of traditional social codes also allowed the colonial powers to reproduce hegemonic discourses and give them legal force. This process of simplification in India, for example, privileged the social practices of the educated, upper-caste Brahmins, which were codified in laws governing all Hindus in India, while practices of marriage, property rights, access to social spaces etc. varied enormously from one caste to the other, one state to the other. 'Official discourse . . . had palpable material consequences, of which the constitution of personal law from [dominant] religious texts is perhaps most significant from the point of view of women' (Mani, 1989, p. 91).

Shirin M. Rai

The Nationalist Discourse: Ideological Foundations of the Post-Colonial States

The nationalist opposition to colonialism was mounted largely within the modernizing parameters that were privileged by the colonists. However, as Sarkar has pointed out, colonial subjugation produced not a 'full-blooded bourgeois modernity' but a 'weak and distorted caricature' (Sarkar, 1975). In this context Mani's work on debates on sati in colonial India is valuable. She contends that the conception of tradition that the modernizing nationalists attacked and the traditionalists defended is one 'that is specifically "colonial"' (Mani, 1989, p. 89). This implies the normalizing of the colonial modernist and Orientalist discourse within the indigenous elites who were to take over the reins of power upon decolonization.

If the colonial powers used women's bodies as symbolic and real reference points to legitimize colonial rule, nationalist opposition also used images of women to symbolize the new nation. Veena Mazumdar has pointed to the different strategic positions taken by the 'conservative' and the 'modernizing' sections of the Indian nationalist leadership on the question of women's political participation (Mazumdar, 1975). The traditionalists saw women's participation in the nationalist movement as important to contain the on-rush of Western values. The concept of *Bharat Mata* (Mother India) was specifically used to link women to traditional roles within the (Hindu) Indian society, while challenging the power of the Western colonizer. The 'modernizers' saw the participation of women in the national movement as signifying modernity, – as a break with tradition that was constructed in terms similar to the Orientalist discourse. Women were granted the right to vote, to stand for elections, and to be elected; they were given the right to work. However, the needs of capitalist production, of a patriarchal hegemonic culture and practices, and the universalizing language of modernism meant that prevailing gender relations were not questioned despite the significant refashioning of these by the colonial power. Gandhi's position was an interesting one in this context. He based his argument on two different premises – the first was to do with representation and legitimacy, both modernist concerns; the other was more complex. On the one hand it centred on women's historical experience of oppression; on the other it privileged women's 'natural submission' to social convention and made them 'natural leaders' of a non-violent movement. Gandhi sits uncomfortably between the polarities of tradition and modernity. In most decolonizing countries in the 1950s and 1960s, modernizers had the upper hand. While this provided women with opportunities, it also placed them within the modernizing agenda that a largely male political leadership constructed. The strains that inevitably developed as a result make up the subject of the rest of this chapter.

One of the important strains between the women's movements that developed during the nationalist struggles and after decolonization was to do with the priorities of these modernizing nationalist elites. The prioritization of goals is an important heavily implicated process. Writing about the positions that women occupied during the Algerian revolution, Helie-Lucas writes:

> It would have seemed so mean to question the priority of the liberation of the country, and raise issues which would not be issues any more after the liberation: we believed that all the remnants of women's oppression would disappear with independence.

Overarching projects of first the nationalist movement, and then the post-colonial state, 'prioritize out' issues that are potentially challenging of the modernist developmental conceptions of the new nation-state. Helie-Lucas continues:

> We are made to feel that protesting the name of women's interests and rights is not to be done NOW ... not during the liberation struggle ... not after independence, because all forces had to be mobilised to build up the devastated country.... Defending women's rights 'now' – this now being ANY historical moment – is always a 'betrayal': of the people, of the nation, of the revolution, of Islam, of national identity, of cultural roots.... (1991, pp. 57 and 58)

In the next section I discuss interventions by Third World feminists on the complex relationship between the colonial and post-colonial states and the construction of the 'woman question' that takes into account the historical experience of women in colonized countries as well as during movements of national liberation. Modernity has been problematized by most Third World feminists at a conceptual level, while at the same time being used as a resource to challenge the construction of tradition by nationalist elites.

Third World Feminist Perspectives

In the writings of Third World women analysts of the state, we find that the state – especially the post-colonial state – is regarded as of critical importance in women's lives both public and private. Mernissi, for example, even speaks of the 'feminization' of the male in the post-colonial state (her own being Morocco) as the traditional role of the economic provider is no longer the exclusive concern of the man in the family, and as the modernizing state draws women into the public arena through both law and public provision such as education (see Mernissi, 1991). Similarly, in India we find a considerable emphasis placed upon the power (or lack of power) of the state to formulate, legislate and enforce laws regarding equality between men and women (see, for example, Kapur and Cossman, 1993). Many women's groups have, for example, been involved in the drawing up of the *National Perspective Plan for Women 1988–2000* (Ministry of Human Resource Development, 1988) which 'recommends certain special interventions for women as transitory measures to ensure that they catch up with the mainstream by 2000 A.A.' (p. ii). There is thus an implicit setting up of a binary opposition between the state and patriarchal forces in society (Mehdid, 1992).

Other women writers in this area point conversely to the symbiosis between the state and patriarchy: 'Whereas the traditional exercise of patriarchal authority tended to rest with particular men – fathers, husbands and other male kin – the communalization of politics, particularly when backed by state-sponsored religious fundamentalism, shifts the right of control to all men' (Kandiyoti, 1991, p. 14). However, neither group argues for an abandonment of the state either as a concept or as an arena for struggle. Furthermore, emphasis is laid by all on questions of women's access to the public sphere in both the economic and political fields (see Kandiyoti, 1991; Mehdid, 1992). Secularization, democratization and modernization of the state and of the political sphere are regarded as relevant to the lives of women while at the same time there is an acknowledgment of the state's penetration by the community. As Alvarez argues in the context of Brazil, 'feminists should neither dismiss the State as the ultimate mechanism of male social control nor embrace it as the ultimate vehicle for gender-based social change. Rather, under different political regimes and at distinct historical conjuctures, the State is potentially a mechanism either for social change or social control in women's lives' (Alvarez, 1990, p. 273; see also Chhachhi, 1991).

Finally, in the writing of feminists like El-Saadawi the presence of international capitalism looms large. She argues, together with others, that the penetration of international capitalism in Third World states brings about a general social crisis that leads to the impoverishment of whole communities and that women suffer most in this context of exploitation (see also Rosa, 1987; Longrigg, 1991). Kandiyoti points out, however, that the impact of capitalism on women's lives is not entirely negative. Capitalism, while exploitative, also leads an attack upon traditional patriarchy in the countries of the Third World, creating new opportunities for women in the public sphere. This on-going work on Third World states is an important alternative perspective that the universalizing debates among Western feminists largely neglect to take into account.

In the next section I examine two theoretical approaches to the post-colonial state that became very influential in the 1960s and 1970s in explaining the models of governance and economy that the decolonized nations were constructing. The first was influenced by the analysis of economic dependency of the post-colonial state in the context of international capitalism on the one hand, and relative autonomy of the post-colonial state from indigenous social classes on the other. This theoretical model was based on the dichotomy between base and superstructure that characterizes much of structural marxism and is therefore of limited value given the analytical framework of this chapter. Further, it is a deterministic paradigm in examining the relation between international capitalist centres and the economic periphery of the

Third World. The second examined the nature of the post-colonial state in terms of its capacity to deliver its projects, and secure its boundaries. Starting from a Weberian model of rationalized bureaucracy, this model explored the relations between the state and 'peak interest groups' of society. Neither of these paid attention to issues of gender; the first privileged class, the second functional and institutional systems. So why examine these models here? I argue here that while these interventions are in themselves problematic, they raise important issues about the processes and workings of the post-colonial state that have been largely ignored by feminist writing in the area, but can be crucial in order for women's movements to devise strategies of struggle and negotiation.

The Post-Colonial State: Autonomy and Capacity

In his study of the Indian state, Anupam Sen has argued that a feature of the Indian state that indicated its relative autonomy from social classes was its ability to promote and develop a cultural environment hostile to private capital and conducive to state capital (Sen, 1982, p. 160). While seemingly anti-capitalist, this was a modernizing state wanting to build a modern capitalist economy while at the same time securing the privileged position of its own elites. However, Sen's analysis falls short of acknowledging the relative autonomy of the political. The rhetoric of socialism is cast as a legitimizing instrument in the hands of the state. Its potential of being used by oppositional groups as a means of holding the state organizations accountable, and of delegitimizing state fractions when there is a lack of such accountability, is not analysed. This is because there arises an expectation born of anti-capitalist rhetoric that social justice must inform a welfare state; this despite the existing and supported patterns of redistribution of wealth, and lack of resources that constrains its welfare functions. Taking the relative autonomy of the political seriously would also invite an examination of the democratic processes and functioning in the country for the last forty-seven years. To dismiss this feature of the Indian political system as a 'charade' as Alavi did (1972, p. 63), and many others subscribing to such analysis continue to do, is to fail to see how important this very uneven, pitted and sometimes dangerous political terrain is for mobilization of opposition by various groups, including women.

The second intervention in post-colonial state theory focused on the question of state capacity. Gunnar Myrdal (1968) distinguished between the 'strong' state – in this case his native Sweden – and the 'weak' or 'soft' state – India. The defining features of the 'strong' state in this literature have been 'state capacity' to 'implement logistically political decisions throughout the realm' (Mann, 1984, p. 189); a high degree of bureaucratic autonomy from institutions and groups in civil society; and corporatism, either democratic or authoritarian. In the soft states these features were absent, as a result of which there was a 'general inclination of people to resist public controls and their implementation' (Myrdal, 1968, p. 209) The focus was therefore on the levels of successful implementation of decisions achieved by particular states. A discussion therefore arose about factors that would enhance or reduce this capacity (see Charlton and Donald, 1992). Mann distinguished between 'despotic' – non-negotiated and non-institutionalized – and 'infrastructural' – co-ordinated and institutionalized – power (1984). This distinction is important to emphasize that there exists no direct, linear correlation between 'state autonomy' and 'state capacity' (Onis, 1991, p. 123). The first will not automatically lead to the other.

While the dependency theorists pointed to the relative autonomy of the post-colonial state from social classes, the state capacity literature saw a close cooperation between the state and the 'peak interest groups' in civil society as a feature of strong states. This cooperation was conceptualized as the state's 'embeddedness' in civil society. The concept of 'embeddedness' has been imported into the developmental state debate from the work of Karl Polanyi in which he argues that 'The human economy, then, is embedded and enmeshed in institutions, economic and non-economic' (Polanyi, in Lie, 1991, p. 220). Johnson used this concept to study Japan where state-society (read 'peak interest groups') cooperation was established for pursuing the single goal of economic development. This model was used to study other east Asian countries like South Korea, Taiwan, and Singapore to establish that strong states are needed in order to secure capitalist development in the decolonized world. What was obscured by this model's explanation of the success of the strong east Asian states was the extraordinary levels of American investment that went into these economies, together with their particular geographical and demographic (small areas and populations) situations and the political context of external threat as a unifying element that the political elites could use for establishing state interventionist approaches to capitalist development. The fact that most Third World states cannot be characterized as 'strong' states needs to take these particular conditions in the east Asian states into account.

Further, while the use of the concept of 'embeddedness' implicitly challenges the Weberian wisdom of the need for a 'rational bureaucracy' as a prerequisite of a modern state, it does not provide a cultural and historical context within which 'embeddedness' operates. Given its unitary model of the state, it does not examine how different fractions of the state relate differently with 'peak interest groups', and does not allow that 'embeddedness' while supporting the goal of economic development can and does act against the interests of the politically marginalized groups of which women are one. In 'weak' states the fragility of their infrastructure leads to a greater infiltration by the dominant gendered interests which impacts on the framing of issues, and policies by state institutions. For the women in the Third World the state and civil society are both complex terrains – fractured, oppressive, threatening, while at the same time providing spaces for struggle and negotiation. State embeddedness, as well as state autonomy, therefore embody complex gendered relations that work against women, as well as providing resources for negotiation and struggle.

In the light of the discussion about the writing on the state within feminist theory, and the particularities of the developmental state that affect women in the Third World in ways that are different from those in Western societies, can we begin to construct explanations of state practice and the complex strategies that women create, and continue to employ in their interactions with the states in the Third World?

Negotiating the State

As we have seen above in our discussion of the various feminist approaches to the state, strong cases have been made by those who argue for working in and through the state, and those who are furiously opposed to this. However, what I want to explore now is whether the particular features of the developmental state we have discussed above allow us to form a judgment about the various possibilities and strategies of action available to women in the context of such a state.

Three features of post-colonial states are of relevance at this point. First, nationalist elites in most post-colonial states saw themselves as agents of social and economic transformation. Through their constitutions, laws, and legislation, these states created a framework within which they sought to change and develop societies marked by the experience of colonial exploitation. Whether on the basis of liberal secularism, as in India, or one of religious identity as in Pakistan, these states tried to significantly refashion and remodel their societies. Indeed, as pointed out above, much of the writing about the 'woman question' in India, as in many other Third World countries, acknowledges this transformative role of the state. The rhetoric of change on the one hand, and the relative autonomy of state institutions from dominant social classes on the other, can create spaces for both institutional and political initiatives and struggles. In India, for example, since the 1980s the Supreme Court has taken a social interventionist approach in its judgments claiming that 'in a developing society judicial activism is essential for participative justice. . . . Justices are the constitutional invigilators and reformers [who] bring the rule of law closer to the rule of life' (P. N. Singh, cited in Cooper, 1993, p. 6).

Second, the infrastructural capacity of the state is varied within both the global and the national context. The ability of a state to enforce its laws and regulations impacts upon the transformative project of the state as well as the subversive agendas of political and social movements. Where the 'infrastructural power' of the state is weak, the implementation of directives can become a hostage to random factors outside the control of the state institutions. Thus, the implementation of directives, however radical, could be contingent upon the personal attributes of enforcers rather than the capacity of the state to ensure the implementation of its laws. 'Good' or 'bad' judges/

bureaucrats thus become important as independent factors in the lives of people, but as such do not fit into the structural network of the state. This unpredictability of the state can also be a resource for social movements as they try to negotiate their way through the state's institutional terrain and the success of which could depend upon targeting the 'soft', sympathetic institutions, and even individuals in official positions (see Rai, 1995).

Corruption, the third feature that I want to discuss here, then becomes an important variable particularly in the functioning of a 'weak' state, affecting the lives of different people differently. Women, of course, are affected in different ways from men; the 'favours' asked for are not just financial, but can also be sexual. As implementation of rules is undermined by endemic corruption working with(-in) the state is not always possible. Protest has to replace petition, and support mobilized outside the institutions and corridors of state power. This can bring women into confrontation with the state. At this stage the rules of the political game can change significantly as the state no longer feels able to contain the demands of groups. The strength of the opposition as well as the mobilization of state power against the opposition will be important factors in the political struggle at this point. Visibility in confrontation is one thing that states try to avoid; gaining visibility is important for oppositional (women's) groups. By becoming visible they force the coercive arm of the state – the police – to become visible too, thus exposing it to public scrutiny and media interest. Here, of course, the space provided (or not) by the civil society to organize is an important variable.

What we begin to piece together from our study of women and the state is that it is a highly complex picture, and one that is radically different from the reality faced by Western women. In the next section I want to explore some of these differences and themes.

In and Against the State?

There are two different standpoints that we have to keep in mind when we discuss the question of the state vis-à-vis women's movements. The first is that of the daily lived realities of women's lives. Here we have to consider both the nature of national state formations, as well as the different social and political variables that affect their dealings with the state. The second is the standpoint of the feminist response to the state. Whether as strategy or as critique the options before feminists have to be read distinctly despite obvious overlaps in order that we might be in a better position to understand both. The relationship between theory and practice has to be foregrounded once again to be able to address the question of the political role that women can and need to play in the arena of public power. I will come back to this later.

One of the most startling differences between the women in Western liberal states and those in the Third World is the extent to which they are directly 'touched' by the regulatory power of the state. Women in Third World countries are more removed from the state in all its manifestations than are Western women. This is because the state in the Third World is unable to provide the kind of safety network that the Western liberal state does with its welfare provision. Neither upper-class women nor those of the lower classes fall within the ambit of state functioning. In health, education, childcare and employment the upper-class women have traditionally depended on the private sector, and so too have the poorest women – the first group because of access to private, non-state resources, the second because the state can provide them with very little support.

Second, as most Third World states can be categorized as 'weak' states, women in these states do not become aware of many areas of state legislation and action. The dissemination of information about new legislation is extremely varied and patchy. Illiteracy and exclusionary social practices further exacerbate this isolation from the processes of the state. The lack of political will to disturb traditional family values is one manifestation of the 'weak' patriarchal state. Political expediency overrules the rhetoric of social justice fairly easily when the state perceives the threat to its continuance. Further, the lack of infrastructural power of the state means that its laws are altogether ignored in many parts of the country. So even though Indian women have constitutional rights of inheritance, divorce, and maintainance, for example, the enforcement of these rights is at best patchy.

However, another feature of the Third World states is a weak system of internal regulation resulting in relatively high levels of state violence. The women's movement in India, for example, is rooted in women's opposition to police brutality (Spivak, 1987) in the 1970s. Rape, murder and beatings in police custody continue to be a common feature of state operation especially in rural areas. At this time, depending upon their race, class and caste situation, most Third World women have fewer resources to withstand the violations of the state. The lack of education, economic vulnerability, weak infrastructural social support and unavailability of information leave women in these states more dependent upon their own resources which in themselves are meagre. These also determine to a large extent the options that women have, and think that they have, available to them in their dealings with the state.

The civil society is not an uncomplicated 'space of uncoerced human association and . . . of relational networks – formed for the sake of family, faith, interest and ideology – that fill this space' (Walzer, 1992, p. 89). The civil society is a deeply fraught space with hidden and explicit dangers that lurk there in the garb of national, religious, and ethnic identities as fashioned by male-directed movements of various kinds. In this context, the 'embeddedness' of the state in the civil society cannot be regarded in the positive light in which many developmental economists see it: 'This idea that "bureaucratic capacity and social connectedness may be mutually reinforcing rather than in opposition" in turn becomes "the key to the developmental state's effectiveness"' (Charlton and Donald, 1992, p. 7). For women the reinforcing of bureaucratic capacity by social norms can be a terrifying combination threatening any attempt to change their lived reality. In this context, however, the fracturing of the state becomes important.

One of the most significant contributions of poststructuralist argument to the theorizing of the state has been its insistence that there is no unity that we can point to as 'the state'. However, precisely because of this fluidity and dispersal of power we cannot regard the 'touch' of the state as universally polluting as many Western feminists would have us believe. We cannot simply argue, as Wendy Brown does, that an appeal to the state for protection 'involves seeking protection *against* men *from* masculinist institutions' (Brown, 1992, p. 9). This is not only because one of the implications of the poststructuralist arguments about the dispersal of power is the acknowledgment of the varied forms that power takes and the uses to which it is and can be put. If we add to this reading of power relations our understanding of the complexity of the civil society in which women operate, taking simply an 'against the state' position becomes positively dangerous. The civil society is as deeply masculinist as is the infrastructure of state relations. Third World women (and for that matter Western women) cannot look to one to oppose the other. Both spaces – of informal and formalized networks of power – are imbued with masculinist discourses; neither is 'uncoerced', however different the forms and mechanisms of coercion.

This takes me back to the question of theory and practice that I raised at the begining of this section. For most women in the Third World, as we have discussed above, the state figures only marginally in their lives. It looms large only when women transgress the boundaries set by the state in various areas of public and private life that it has jurisdiction over. Therefore, for the majority of women the question is not whether or not to approach the state. *It is they who are approached by the state*, in many instances in a brutal and violent way (Rai, 1995). In that context, can one argue that 'to be "protected" by the very power whose violation one fears perpetuates the specific modality of dependence and powerlessness marking much of women's experience across widely diverse cultures and epochs' (Brown, 1992, p. 9)? In the face of the exercise of violent state power, the 'protection' given by a court order prohibiting that violence can make the difference between life and death to individual women (see Williams, 1991).

Second, the question surely is not one of simply 'seeking protection', but of *fighting* state violence. The forms that this struggle might take may vary from country to country, state formation to state formation. But to focus simply on the regulating, structuring, constraining power of the state and to overlook the struggle against all these is to sell short the daily lives of millions of women. Worse, it is the road to inaction and nihilism. Women are routinely aware of not only the state's huge importance to their immediate existence, but also of its corruption and its violence. Women's movements and organizations are also aware of the limitation of the protection offered by legislation and court orders. They wage their struggle on many different fronts in order to *create* a protection for themselves that could not be ensured simply by administrative or judicial directives. This they do by making themselves heard in the public arena, not simply directly in their own voices but also in others' words. Thus, when Brown writes 'Just as microelectronics assembly plants in Third World "Free Trade Zones" do not simply employ women workers but produce them – their bodies, social relations, sexualities, life conditions, genders, psyches, consciousnesses – the state does not simply handle clients or employ staff but produces state subjects, *inter alia*, bureaucratized, dependent, disciplined and gendered ones' she completely ignores the tremendous struggle that Third World women carry on daily in the 'Free Trade Zones' to resist the multinationals and their own states taking over all meaning in their lives (see Rosa, 1987). She also, of course, portrays Western women in an entirely passive light.

Finally, I would argue that the question of 'in and against' the state has to be looked at afresh. Ehrenreich and Piven (1983) make a case for increasing women's involvement with the state by pointing to the radical potential of such a project for women both as individuals and as a growing collective. The London Edinburgh Weekend Return Group in their influential book *In and Against the State* make a different point: 'The state, then, is not "our" state. It is "their" state, an alien, oppressive state' (1980, p. 53). However, they remind us that 'we have made positive gains [under this hostile state] not by "winning power" in any formal sense but by taking a degree of control, counter-posing our forms of organisations to theirs' (*ibid.*, p. 147). I would argue, not in opposition but from a different standpoint, that if we do not regard the state as a unity we cannot look upon struggle as a unified strategy either. My concern in this chapter has been to point to the lack of intentionality of a unified state structure, and also to point to the spaces that are available, and can be created for and through struggle for retrieving, reconstructing and regaining control over the meanings and signifiers in women's lives. They do this in different ways taking into account their own experience, needs, and situations, and they approach the various forms of state differently – in opposition, in cooperation, through subversion not simply of rules but of articulated intentions of state forms, and through negotiations. And they do all this actively, if not always with a coherence and intentionality of their own. It is on these struggles that we must focus to understand the relationship that women construct with states.

Bibliography

ALAVI, H. (1972) 'The State in Post-Colonial Society: Pakistan and Bangladesh', *New Left Review*, 74 (July–August), p. 63.

ALLEN, J. (1990) 'Does Feminism Need a Theory of the State?', in WATSON, S. (Ed.) *Playing the State*, London, Verso.

ALVAREZ, SONIA E. (1990) *Engendering Democracy in Brazil: Women's Movements in Transition Politics*, New Jersey, Princeton University Press.

BARRETT, MICHELE and PHILLIPS, ANNE (Eds) (1992) *Destabilizing Theory: Contemporary Feminist Debates*, Cambridge, Polity.

BROWN, WENDY (1992) 'Finding the Man in the State', *Feminist Studies*, Vol. 18, No. 1 (Spring).

CHHACHHI, AMRITA (1991) 'Forced Identities: The State, Communalism, Fundamentalism and Women in India', in KANDIYOTI, DENIZ (Ed.) *Women, Islam and the State*, London, Macmillan.

CHARLTON, ROGER, and DONALD, DAVID (1992) 'Bringing the Economy Back In: Reconsidering the Autonomy of the Developmental State', paper presented at the Annual Conference of the Political Science Association, Belfast, April 7–9.

COOPER, JEREMY (1993) 'Poverty and Constitutional Justice: The Indian Experience', *Mercer Law Review*, Vol. 44.

DAVIS, K., LEIJENAAR, M. and OLDERSMA, J. (Eds) (1991) *The Gender of Power*, London, Sage.

DAVIS, MIRANDA (Ed.) (1987) *Third World, Second Sex*, London, Zed Books.

EHRENREICH, B. and PIVEN, F. F. (1983) 'Women and the Welfare State', in HOWE, IRVING (Ed.) *Alternatives: Proposals for America from the Democratic Left*, New York, Pantheon.

EISENSTEIN, ZILLAH R. (Ed.) (1979) *Capitalist Patriarchy and the Case for Socialist Feminism*, New York, Monthly Review Press.

ELSON, DIANE (1992) 'Gender Analysis and Development Economics', paper presented at ESRC Development Economics Study Group, Annual Conference, March.

EVANS, HARRIET (1992) 'Monogamy and Female Sexuality in the People's Republic of China', in RAI, SHIRIN, PILKINGTON, HILARY and PHIZACKLEA, ANNIE (Eds) *Women in the Face of Change: The Soviet Union, Eastern Europe and China*, London, Routledge.

FRANZWAY, S., COURT, D. and CONNELL, R. W. (1989) *Staking a Claim: Feminism, Bureaucracy and the State*, Cambridge, Polity.

GUHA, RANJIT (1982–87) *Subaltern Studies: Writings on South Asian History and Society*, Delhi, Oxford University Press.

HELIE-LUCAS, M. A. (1991) 'Women in the Algerian Liberation Struggle,' in WALLACE, T. and MARCH, C. (Eds) *Changing Perceptions: Writings on Gender and Development*, Oxford, Oxfam.

HERNES, H. (1987) *Welfare State and Women Power. Essays in State Feminism*, Oslo, Norwegian University Press.

HOWE, IRVING (1983) *Alternatives: Proposals for America from the Democratic Left*, New York, Pantheon.

JOSEPH, SUAD (1993) 'Gender and Civil Society', *Middle East Report*, No. 183 (July–August).

KANDIYOTI, DENIZ (Ed.) (1991) *Women, Islam and the State*, London, Macmillan.

KAPUR, R. and COSSMAN, B. (1993) 'On Women Equality and the Constitution:

Through the Looking Glass of Feminism', *The National Law School Journal* (Special Issue on Feminism), Vol. 1.

LIDDLE, J. and RAI, S. (1992) 'Feminism and Orientalism', in KENNEDY, M. LUBELSKA, C. and WALSH, V. (Eds) *Making Connections: Women's Studies, Women's Movements, Women's Lives*, London, Taylor and Francis.

LIE, JOHN (1991) 'Embedding Polanyi's Market Society', *Sociological Perspectives*, Vol. 34, No. 2.

LONDON EDINBURGH WEEKEND RETURN GROUP (1980) *In and Against the State*, London, Pluto.

LONGRIGG, CLARE (1991) 'Blood Money', *Amnesty*, February/March.

MANI, L. (1989) 'Contentious Traditions: The Debate on Sati in Colonial India', in SANGAN, K. and ZAID, S. (Eds) *Recasting women: Essays in Colonial History*, New Delhi, Kali for Women.

MANN, MICHAEL (1984) 'The Autonomous Power of the State', *Archives Européennes De Sociologie*, Tome XXV, No. 2.

MAZUMDAR, V. (1975) *Women's Participation in Politics*, Occasional Paper, New Delhi, Centre for Women's Development Studies.

MEHDID, MALIKA (1992) 'Feminist Debate on Women and the State in the Middle East', in CHERIET, B. (Ed.) *The Middle East Report*, Vol. 22, No. 1 (Jan–Feb).

MERNISSI, FATIMA (1991) *Women and Islam*, Oxford, Basil Blackwell.

MOHANTY, MANORANJAN (1990) 'Duality of the State Process in India', in *Capitalist Development: Critical Essays*, Bombay, Popular Prakashan.

MOUFFE, CHANTAL (1992) *Dimensions of Radical Democracy: Pluralism, Citizenship, Community*, London, Verso.

MYRDAL, G. (1968) *Asian Drama: An Enquiry into the Poverty of Nations*, Vols. I–III, Harmondsworth, Penguin.

ONIS, ZIYA (1991) 'The Logic of the Developmental State', *Comparative Politics*, Vol. 24, No. 1 (October).

The Pioneer (1992) 'Janpath Hawker Women Win Legal Battle', 2 October.

PRINGLE, ROSEMARY and WATSON, SOPHIE (1992) 'Women's Interests and the Post-Structuralist State', in BARRETT, M. and PHILLIPS, A. (Eds) *Destabilizing Theory*, Cambridge, Polity.

RAI, SHIRIN (1995) 'Women Negotiating Boundaries: Gender, Law, and the Indian State', *Social and Legal Studies*, Vol. 4, No. 3 (September), pp. 391–410.

RISSEEUW, CARLA (1991) 'Bourdieu, Power and Resistance: Gender Transformation in Sri Lanka', in DAVIS, KATHY *et al.* (Eds) *The Gender of Power*, London, Sage.

ROSA, KUMUDHINI (1987) 'Organising Women Workers in the Free Trade Zone, Sri Lanka', in DAVIS, MIRANDA (Ed.) *Third World, Second Sex*, London, Zed Books.

SARKAR, S. (1975) 'Rammohun Roy and the Break with the Past', in JOSHI,

V. C. (Ed.) *Rammohun Roy and the Process of Modernization in India*, Delhi, Vikas.

SAID, EDWARD (1979) *Orientalism*, New York, Vintage Books.

SEN, ANUPAM (1982) *The State, Industrialisation, and Class Formation in India*, London, Routledge and Kegan Paul.

SMART, CAROL (1989) *Feminism and the Power of the Law*, London, Routledge.

SMART, CAROL (1992) 'The Woman of Legal Discourse', *Social and Legal Studies*, Vol. 1, No. 1 (March).

SPIVAK, GAYATRI C. (1987) 'Draupadi', in *In Other Worlds: Essays in Cultural Politics*, London, Methuen.

WALZER, MICHAEL (1992) 'The Civil Society Argument', in MOUFFE, CHANTAL (Ed.) *Dimensions of Radical Democracy: Pluralism, Citizenship, Community*, London, Verso.

WATSON, SOPHIE (Ed.) (1990) *Playing the State*, London, Verso.

WEEDON, CHRIS (1993) *Feminism and Postmodernism*, paper presented at the Women's Studies Network (UK) Conference, July.

WILLIAMS, PATRICIA J. (1991) *The Alchemy of Race and Rights*, London, Harvard University Press.

WILSON, ELIZABETH (1977) *Women and the Welfare State*, London, Tavistock.

Chapter 2

Should Women Give Up on the State? –
The African Experience

Ann Stewart

Introduction

I want to introduce you to four women, Wambui Otieno, who lives in Kenya, Holalia Pastory in Tanzania, Molly Muchabaiwa in Zimbabwe and Unity Dow in Botswana. The first wanted to bury her husband, the second to sell her land, the third's father wanted compensation for her seduction and the fourth wanted her children to be Botswanan citizens. These desires all aroused great public controversy.

Wambui Otieno[1] was married for over twenty years to a prominent criminal lawyer, Silvanus Melea Otieno. They lived an urban lifestyle in Nairobi. Mr Otieno, a Luo, died in 1986. Mrs Otieno, a Kikuyu, wanted to bury him on their farm just outside Nairobi. Mr Otieno's brother and the representatives of the Umira Kager clan wanted to bury him in clan lands according to Luo custom. Wambui Otieno sought a court order allowing her the right to bury her husband where she and, it seemed, he wanted. After highly publicized hearings in the High Court and Appeal Court, he was buried, 154 days after he had died, in Luo clan land following customary practice.

> This was the single most significant event in the daily life of the Kenyan people as a whole, in the year 1987. It must have been one of the events most keenly followed in Kenya during the first quarter-century of independence. It moved the society. (Ojwang and Mugambi, 1989, p. 3)

Holalia Pastory[2] was a poor widow in rural Tanzania who had inherited clan land. Her husband's relatives sought a court order to prevent her selling it, arguing that, according to Haya customary law, as a women, she had no power to sell this land although she could use it for her lifetime. A male member of the clan can sell clan land but if he sells it without the consent of the clan members, other clan members can redeem it. The land returns to the clan and becomes the property of the man who repays the purchase price. Despite a previous higher court judgment to the contrary, the High Court in 1989 decided that she could sell it on the same conditions concerning redemption as a male clan member. The Court relied on international legal instruments prohibiting sex discrimination and national constitutional measures ensuring equality. This ruling generated considerable confusion and hostility.

Molly Muchabaiwa's[3] father went to court in 1984 relying on customary law to claim damages against the man who had seduced her and therefore reduced the amount of roora/lobola which might be payable to him on her marriage under customary law. The Supreme Court in Zimbabwe held that a father could not make such a claim because his daughter was 21. The Legal Age of Majority Act enacted in 1982 had given all citizens in the country aged 18 the right to vote and also to become legal subjects. Prior to this, African women had been permanent jural minors unable to take legal action in their own right. 'Few people in Zimbabwe could have failed to notice the uproar that this decision created . . .' (Stewart, 1986, p. 168).

Unity Dow[4] went to court in Botswana because female Botswanan citizens who married non-citizens were prohibited from passing citizenship to their children or naturalization privileges to their spouses. The 1984 Citizenship Act provided that male Botswanan citizens who married non-citizens would automatically pass Botswanan citizenship to their children and allow for naturalization of their wives. The Court of Appeal held that this gender-discriminatory legislation was unconstitutional.

> The Dow judgment sent the government reeling . . . While women's rights activists have won the battle in the courtroom, the war still rages throughout the country. Nearly two years after the Court of Appeals handed down the judgment, the Botswana government refuses to enforce the decision. (Dow, Stumbras and Tatten, 1994, p. 12)

Some suggest that the government planned to hold a referendum to amend the Constitution of Botswana in order to legalize sex discrimination and that, if this were done, they would be likely to win the vote (Dow, Stumbras and Tatten, 1994, p. 13).

What is it about women's wishes which, when translated into particular forms of legal action, arouses so much anger and confusion? What does it tell us about women's relationship with law in these African states?

There are a variety of ways in which the actions of these women can be understood. The sections which follow offer four different possibilities. These are separated out for ease of argument but in practice overlap. Each section introduces us to an approach and then considers the implications of this approach for the women's stories.

Modernity and the Fully Acting Subject

Arguing with Rights

The four cases can all be seen as women's attempts to be treated as 'fully acting subjects' rather than as objects (Whitehead, 1984; Freeman, 1990).

Wambui Otieno argued that her Christian marriage and urban lifestyle took precedence over Luo customary practice, that her husband, although of Luo origin, was not, as it were, a practising Luo, and that the wishes of her husband and herself should govern the decision, not customary practice. The Kenyan Court of Appeal disagreed. It upheld the High Court judgment which considered that there was neither statute nor relevant common law inherited from colonial times to decide the issue and therefore Mr Otieno, having been bred a Luo, remained a member of the Luo tribe and subject to the customary law of the Luo people.

Wambui Otieno did not succeed in convincing the court that she had the capacity as a widow to deal with her husband's body.

> there was not a word in the Otieno judgment about the wishes of the widow in the burial saga. . . . The only moment when the Court of Appeal came close to even considering the widow was when they mentioned s66 of the Law of Succession Act which gives the widow a priority right to administer her husband's estate. However, they quickly went on to find that this particular widow, Mrs Otieno, had not got her grant of administration yet. . . . (Cotran, 1989, pp. 162–3)

The other three women fare differently. The right to be treated as adults was granted to black Zimbabwean women in 1982 by the enactment, shortly after independence, of the Legal Age of Majority Act. In Molly Muchabaiwa's case, the court used this statute to change the basis of customary marriage which takes the form of a negotiation between the families of the prospective spouses and an agreement to pay lobolo (gifts given to the bride's family by the bridegroom's family). The payment of lobolo signifies a valid marriage. The court held that:

> Over the years, legislative and judicial moves have been made to loosen the legal disabilities of African women. . . . Parliament's intention [in the Legal Age of Majority Act] was to create equal status between men and women and, more importantly, to remove the legal disabilities suffered by African women because of the application of customary law. African women now have full legal capacity. An African women can contract a marriage without the consent of her guardian because she no longer needs a guardian. She may allow her father to ask for roora or lobola from the man she wants to marry her, but this is her choice. Roora is not a prerequisite to a lawful marriage. (Katekwe v Muchabaiwa SC 87/84 at 112)

The 1982 Act has been used to suggest that the widow can now inherit her husband's estate. The customary practice has been such that the widow is not entitled to be the heir to her husband's property. Among patrilineal tribes, the eldest son of the deceased inherited his father's estate or in the event of there being no son some other male relative inherited. The widow depended on her former husband's family for her future although custom recognized their obligations to her. There have now been a number of challenges in the courts on inheritance. One Supreme Court judgment allowed the daughter of the deceased father to succeed to her father's estate on the basis that the only reason why women had been unable to inherit in the past was because of the lack of legal capacity, now removed by the 1982 Act.[5] It followed from this line of reasoning that a widow could also inherit although the Court has subsequently moved back from this position, finding that the requirements of customary law presented an independent obstacle to women's inheritance.[6] The case law is clearly in a state of flux and open to challenges. Generally, women's individual legal capacity to be fully acting subjects seems to be increasingly recognized.

Although there had been a previous judgment in the Court of Appeal which had considered it contrary to customary law for women to sell clan land,[7] Holalia Pastory did convince the Tanzanian court that she should be a fully acting subject despite the fact that her right to sell would have far-reaching consequences for communitarian clan land policy.

> From now on, females all over Tanzania can at least hold their heads high and claim to be equal to men as far as inheritance of clan land and self-acquired land of their father's is concerned. (Mwalusanya, J., p. 13)

Unity Dow finally managed to persuade the Court of Appeal by a majority of three to two that the Botswanan constitutional guarantee of sex equality must prevail over the discrimination in the Citizenship Act 1984 and that she had as much capacity as a male citizen of Botswana. The Botswanan government had argued 'that discrimination on the grounds of sex must be permitted in Botswana society as the society is patrilineal and therefore male oriented' (Human Rights Watch, 1994, p. 2).

The International Framework

All four cases used the framework of liberal democratic rights to argue against practices drawn from custom. They can be seen as a product of the international women's rights movement. Women have struggled very hard over many years to achieve recognition of their needs by coming together in organizations throughout the world and pressurizing the bodies which represent the international community. Eventually, this has led to the international recognition of the disadvantages which women have suffered and to measures addressing the specific needs of women. These are now incorporated into the United Nations Convention on the Elimination of All Forms of Discrimination Against Women which came into being in 1979 and into force in 1981. (See Pietila and Vickers, 1994 for further discussion of the UN system.)

The convention has an aspirational aspect but those countries which have ratified the convention must also comply with its provisions. (See Tomasevski, 1993 and Freeman, 1993 for further discussion on the convention.) Its terms should therefore be incorporated into national constitutional contexts to support provisions on equality. National legislation should be compatible with the terms of the convention and the provisions can then be used in court proceedings to support arguments on behalf of women who are arguing for their rights. Women's groups can also use the convention as a lever for further changes in their country's legal system. This process can thus be characterized as a trickle-down theory of law.

This process can been seen in both Unity Dow's and Holalia Pastory's cases. Tanzania, having signed the Convention in 1980 and ratified in 1985, has been obliged to review its domestic laws to try to bring them into conformity. It established a Ministry for Women and Community Affairs which submitted a well-considered report on the position of women to the international monitoring committee in 1990. In addition in 1984 the Constitution was amended to incorporate a Bill of Rights. Article 13(4) prohibits discrimination against women. The judge in Pastory's case took the international laws including the Convention and the bill of rights seriously. He reviewed the impact of these international and constitutional provisions which are based on concepts of equality and rights very carefully and found sufficient justification to cast aside customary law in favour of a woman's individual right to sell land on the same basis as a man.

Even though Botswana has not ratified the convention, the judge there was strongly influenced by the international framework.

> Botswana is a member of the community of civilized states which has taken to abide by certain standards of conduct, and unless it is impossible to do otherwise, it would be wrong for its Courts to interpret its legislation in a manner which conflicts with the international obligations Botswana has undertaken. (Attorney General v Unity Dow, quoted in Human Rights Watch 1994, p. 7)

From Rights to Development

The last section described briefly the political contribution of the international women's rights approach. When presented within a development framework, proponents of the women and development approach[8] argue for legal reforms which abolish discriminatory laws and policies to facilitate women's economic and social development (Dengu-Zvogbo *et al.*, 1994, p. 19).

Since the mid 1980s, international development policies have been dominated by the market-driven economic structural adjustment programmes of the World Bank and the IMF. With the collapse of the communist bloc, these policies and those of Western donor governments have linked economic policies to political changes and now emphasize the importance of good govern-ance, democratization and the rule of law.

The World Bank has incorporated a perspective on the position of women within its policies. 'The distortions in resource allocations which result from . . . discrimination carry high development costs – too high to remain invisible in current and future economic development strategies' (Martin and Hashi, 1992a, p. 5; see also Martin and Hashi, 1992b and 1992c). The emphasis is on removing the legal barriers to economic 'empowerment' and encouraging the development of 'civil society'.

> Although efforts to reform laws have been made since independ-ence, most have not fully eliminated historical constraints. . . . For example, land reforms acts might define land rights in terms of the family, which has come to mean that men control use and effectively have entitlement to the land; statutes aimed at improving a woman's right to property in a marriage will allow property to descend in accordance with custom or bar a women from defending her property rights against her husband. (Martin and Hashi, 1992a, p. 4)

Although the outcomes desired by the World Bank and the women's lobby might not be the same nonetheless they both seek to make progress through state-sponsored legal reforms. The assumption is that the state can be persuaded to introduce laws which will seek to ensure equality and overcome past discrimination.

Impact and Interpretation

There has been a variety of responses to the development of the women's rights approach. Those generated within the women's movement itself have concentrated on the lack of effectiveness of the measures (see Byrnes, 1991), the limitations of the framework for tackling issues defined as private such as violence against women (Rao, 1993) and the universalist and essentialist ap-proach to women's needs and rights enshrined in the Convention (Armstrong *et al.*, 1992; Bunting, 1993) although the 'woman' constructed by these interna-tional rights looks suspiciously Western despite various provisions aimed at supporting the claims of rural women (Nesiah, 1993).

More generally, however, there is a view from within the societies that women who attempt to enforce their rights are an urban Westernized elite. Thus a widow seeking to bury her husband is portrayed as championing this type of lifestyle and denying custom.

> It matters not that the deceased was sophisticated, urbanised and developed a different lifestyle. It seems to us quite unsustainable on the grounds suggested by [counsel] that a different formal education

and an urban lifestyle can affect adherence to one's personal law. At present there is no way in which an African citizen of Kenya can divest himself of the association with the tribe of his father if those customs are patrilineal. (extract from the Court of Appeal judgment quoted in Cotran, 1989, p. 160)

Women are seen as in an unholy alliance not only with Western women and their perspectives on the world but also with the international bodies who are responsible for draconian economic policies. This apparent association between the women's rights movement and the international financial bodies increases antagonism in countries where externally imposed adjustment programmes have been very economically and socially painful for the mass of the population and indeed for women in particular (Vickers, 1991; Commonwealth Expert Group, 1989; Tanzania Gender Networking Programme, 1993). Women resorting to the courts are seen as putting their specific interests above those of the beleaguered mass of the population.

So a young woman in Zimbabwe is seen as undermining her father's traditional economic recompense for childrearing in the pursuit of self-determination. A widow in Tanzania can be seen by many in the rural area as self-seeking, unmindful of tradition, eager to commodify rural land. The judge in the Pastory case saw the matter differently while illustrating the wider point:

It has taken a simple, old rural woman to champion the cause of women in this field but not the elite women in town who chant jejune slogans years on end on women's lib but without delivering the goods. (Mwalusanya, J., p. 14)

The emphasis within this approach has been on the ability of international and national legal provisions to improve women's position. Those resisting these changes seek to argue that the activities are generated by external influences which are alien to custom and tradition, divisive and not in the interests of the mass of women. It is to the arguments over the construction of the customary that we now turn.

Legal Pluralism and the Resisting Subject

Challenging Tradition

All four women live in legally pluralistic societies. Under colonialism, the colonialists' activities would be governed by 'metropolitan' laws imported with variations, while the African population would retain customary law unless it was 'repugnant to morality or public policy'. On independence, governments often retained most of the previous laws but africanized them to regulate the activities of the entire population.

Thus the division between customary and common law became constructed partly as one of choice and lifestyle: if the person concerned lives a 'traditional' lifestyle then the customary law applies. The distinctions also reflect the world of the market and the realm of personal activity, in particular the family. Thus, the public/private split takes a particular legally structured form. It is also gendered: women's activities are regulated through customary law because of their position within the family and clan but also through work in the subsistence and informal economies. It equally divides those who live urban, middle-class, market economy lives from those who live in rural areas.

Although in practice these distinctions are far from clear-cut, the dichotomies are powerfully constructed, particularly in legal discourse. Part of the job of legal method in post-colonial societies involves deducing lifestyle and defining custom for the purposes of the law. State law is seen as separate from customary law which itself must be clearly definable.

Our cases demonstrate the way in which contests are constructed in plural legal systems. Wambui Otieno was caught up in a battle to establish the legitimacy of customary law in Kenya.

I have no doubt that the Otieno Case constitutes a landmark for customary law. It is I think the first time in Kenya's post-independence history that the highest Court in the land has attempted to find the real place of customary law in Kenya's legal system. (Cotran, 1989, p. 159)

Cotran, a Kenyan judge and legal academic, sees the decision as moving away from the 'old colonial notion' that an educated, westernized African can deny his/her personal law (i.e., the customary). Wambui Otieno found out that burial customs and practices are defined legally as personal matters, not the concern of the international community nor the state, leaving her with the customary practices of the Luo people which did not recognize her wishes or those of the nuclear family. In the binary categorization, 'modern' or 'traditional', the court decided there was no choice.

In Zimbabwe we see the contest constructed between a statute which symbolized the success of the independence struggle and customary law. The Legal Age of Majority Act was relatively uncontroversial when seen as a civil and political rights issue. Its extension into the area of customary and family matters, moving into the private realm, has caused considerable anxiety and hostility. This concern is particularly voiced in rural areas where the legislation is seen as contributing to the breakdown of social structures and leading to 'lawlessness' among young adults generally.

In both the Zimbabwean and Tanzanian cases, the issue was whether the state courts had the power to change customary law. Although the judge in Holalia Pastory's case quoted Hamlyn J. in 1968[9] as saying 'It has frequently been said that it is not for the courts to overrule customary law. Any variations in such law as takes place must be variations initiated by altering the customs of the community where they originate', he held that the bill of rights took priority over customary law. Thus having constructed a distinction between customary and state law any perceived interference by the courts with the customary is controversial.

Constructing and Resisting Tradition

There is a considerable body of literature on the relationship of custom and tradition to legal pluralism which reveals the way in which these dichotomies are constructed. One analysis of legal pluralism, dominant in the 1970s, linked it to theories of underdevelopment which analysed African economies as exploited by the international capitalist economy. (I shall return to the political economy approach later.)

However, the work of anthropologists and historians has produced more grounded accounts of the relationship between customary law and the state, a few of which have also incorporated a gendered analysis (Hay and White, 1982; Chanock, 1985; Parpart and Staudt, 1989). Chanock (1982) questioned the whole idea of a separate customary law which embodied traditional culture. Rather he demonstrated through his work in what is now Malawi and Zambia that this customary law was a product of the relationships between male clan elders and the colonial state anxious to prevent social unrest and in particular to curb the activities of women who were finding ways under colonialism to avoid traditional forms of authority (see also Parpart, 1988; Mbilinyi, 1988). Thus not only has customary law been made by husbands, fathers, uncles, headmen and chiefs (Dow, Stumbras and Tatten, 1994) but it has also developed within the context of particular state laws.

To give an example which is relevant to Holalia Pastory's case, Chanock, in discussing the construction of the customary law of land tenure in East Africa, argues:

> Assertions about the nature of what could legitimately be done with land could only be made by Africans during the colonial period if presented in terms of what had been sanctioned by custom. Only in this way could the assertion be heard as valid by the colonial rulers, and in this way too it could summon up reserves of ideological support in African communities. (1991, p. 72)

Customary land law was a product of resistance and negotiation with the colonial state. Inalienability of land was argued in the context of the white land grab. However, colonial administrators enabled clan leaders/chiefs to distribute land on an individual basis within the clan, not through the construction of rights but rather through administrative discretion. What was 'mine' and what was 'ours' depended on contexts and the particular relations of power.

> An indigenous system of land tenure did not exist under colonial conditions but its shadow was summoned into existence by both colonial and postcolonial states, essentially to retard the establishment of freehold rights for Africans in an economy which was otherwise becoming increasingly capitalist. (*ibid.*, p. 82)

Thus the construction of customary land tenure is very much a product of the power relations within the colonial and post-colonial state and is not necessarily based on rights or regulation by law but on administrative fiat dictated by the particular state priority at the time. (See Shivji, 1994 for the contemporary Tanzanian situation.)

A growing literature shows however that women are not passive victims in these relations of power, but resisting subjects. Women exploited the fissures in regulation by the clan and the colonial state to maximize their ability to control their lives. Women avoided traditional marriages by running away to the towns or to the mining compounds (Mbilinyi, 1988; Bujra, 1982). Once married they would use the colonial courts set up in part to regulate indigenous marriages to increase their bargaining power within marriage and on divorce by using arguments which would be recognized by the colonialists (Parpart, 1988). Conversely, O'Rourke demonstrates how in present-day Kenya 'Mandinka, Kikuyu and Kipsigis women have found that through employing the discourse of "tradition", as an authorized vocabulary, they have managed to facilitate positive change on their own behalf' (O'Rourke, 1995, p. 93).

Impact and Interpretation

Legal pluralism constructs dichotomies between the customary and the state legal system which many see as the colonial system still in operation. By appealing to the state legal system to gain rights, women are seen as denying custom and therefore as anti-African. In gaining rights women are seen as engaged in a broader attack on the traditional. However, the customary land tenure system which Holalia Pastory is seen as challenging and damaging is itself a construct of power relations. In this analysis state law and customary law are products of each other and of colonial power relations. Despite the discourse of law in relation to both, regulation in the colonial and post-colonial state was and is based more on executive action than the rule of law. Nonetheless tradition born out of resistance to and accommodation with the colonial state still represents the constructs of those who would maintain power. Women, by resort to whatever power state law may have in post-colonial states, are seeking to use its power to resist customary constructions of their lives.

Political Economy, the African State and the Rule of Law

I have considered two approaches. The first sees women achieving equality with the assistance of legal reforms which will remove barriers to progress and grant rights. Women will make progress through state-sponsored and state-enforced law. This process assumes a benign, liberal state which is open to the issues presented to it by its citizens, a state which is not only willing but able to bring about social change. It further assumes that the rule of law exists and that the judiciary is independent and able to adjudicate between competing claims.

The second approach requires us to consider the legacy of the colonial state in the post-colonial states of Africa but concentrates on the way in which the colonial state managed to extend its tentacles into many aspects of African relationships, in particular into the construction of customary laws and gender relations. It suggests that law has a power to construct meanings and that this power has been used to resist colonial constructions but also to construct and resist gendered constructions of customary law under colonialism.

The Analysis

Neither approach directly considers the nature of law and state in post-colonial Africa. The dominant analysis of the state in Africa has come from the perspectives of political economy (Fatton, 1989; Ghai, 1993; Shivji, 1993, 1995).

Ghai suggests that those who obtain state power on independence have an 'insecure base in the economy, which is dominated by foreigners or immigrants' (1993, p. 68). The regimes are made more vulnerable by external factors. The state itself can be seen to be contingent on international economic and political pressures because of its dependency on the 'outside world for economic and military aid, trade and technology' (Ghai, 1993, p. 71; see also Himbara and Sultan, 1995). Corruption is an integral part of this economic system, 'woven into the very fabric of the state apparatus' (Ghai, 1993, p. 69). It is also necessary for political survival. Public accountability cannot be tolerated and 'resistance is met with principally by coercion' (*ibid.*, p. 69).

Shivji argues that

> In liberal democratic states, the boundary between the use of legal/ legitimate use of power and the illegal/illegitimate abuse of power is set by the Rule of Law. This Rule of Law is not simply a composite concept embracing certain principles and procedures of exercise of power but also an ideology through which the exercise of power is legitimated. (1993, pp. 80–1)

He characterizes a state where the use of state power is in accordance with the Rule of Law as intra-legal and where it is not as extra-legal. But he emphasizes that 'the fact that the state is extra-legal does not mean that it does not use law. Rather that the state rules *through* law but not *within* it' (Shivji, 1993, p. 83). Legitimacy has not been based on the rule of law, rather on the ideology of independence, modernization and development. Not surprisingly law has a very low status 'in the eyes of politicians, the bureaucracy and the public' (Ghai, 1993, p. 73).

As Parpart and Staudt point out, (1989) there has not been much discussion of gender in these analyses of the state.

> In both mainstream political science and classical marxism, state action has been explained in terms of state-society interaction. . . . Women fit uneasily in either view. . . . In both of these conceptions, theorists pay little heed to the dominance of men in state structures. . . . Yet such dominance matters enormously for women, as states institutionalize male control over female sexuality and labor in varying degrees. (Parpart and Staudt, 1989, p. 4)

Equally the dominant analysis of customary law within this approach which saw it as a 'semi-feudal system strongly supported, if not created, by capitalism to sustain social relations in the traditional rural sector which subsidised the cost of labour power in the capitalist sector' (Dengu-Zvogbo *et al.*, 1994, p. 19) ignored the gendered nature of these relations.

The End of History?

Africa experienced profound economic crises in the 1980s. As we have seen earlier, the response of the international community came in the form of economic structural adjustment programmes with their emphasis on economic liberalization and the freeing of the market from the state. In the 1990s, the World Bank and other international agencies have incorporated a political science perspective into their approach. Their analysis of the malaise of some African states seems to be similar to that of the political economists. The state is corrupt and overblown. State bureaucracy hinders entrepreneurial capacity and the development of markets. Their solution is 'good governance' programmes which have encouraged the development of multi-party democracies and the strengthening of the rule of law in an attempt to make the state more accountable. As Ghai points out, 'good governance thus requires the rehabilitation of the very concept of law itself' (1993, p. 72).

Ways of Seeing Women – Interpretation

If we consider the actions of our women within this perspective we can see the ways in which their actions might be seen. If the state is not based on the rule of law but none the less state power is exercised through law, women who resort to constitutional or state law which has such little legitimacy are going to find it an unrewarding and haphazard experience. A strategy based on legal reform to bring about change in circumstances where there is scant institutional support is not likely to be successful.

Unity Dow has discovered this even in Botswana which probably falls into Shivji's intra-legal category. She won her case in the highest court in the land but when she and several other women applied for citizenship for their children her application was rejected and the others ignored. The immigration authorities continue to prevent Botswanan women married to foreign men from travelling in and out of the country with their children because the children are denied citizenship.

In societies where the state resorts to the rhetoric of law to bolster legitimacy with external agencies but relies on other sources of legitimacy with its population such as Africanism and tradition, women who seek to enforce legal rights can be seen as using the policies of agencies like the World Bank against the interests of the masses. Thus the government was able to argue in Unity Dow's case that 'the appellant accepts that the citizenship act is discriminatory but this was intentionally made so in order to preserve the male orientation of the Botswana society' (Human Rights Watch, 1994, p. 2). Commentators adopting the political economy approach see the women in our cases as colluding with the external forces which represent a new phase in the exploitation of Africa in the world markets.

Dow *et al.* summarize the position well.

Upholding custom and tradition are compelling arguments for a society that has been subjected to colonial dominance and imperialist interests for over a century. The constitutional rhetoric of the urban centred elite may serve powerful interests in giving the system 'an appearance of liberal economic and social order'. While appeasing the international community with a facade of democracy, however, the Botswana government appeals to its citizenry with promises to maintain customary practices and halt further deterioration of the traditional order – all to the detriment of women's advancement. (Dow, Stumbras and Tatten, 1994, p. 14)

However, as Gaidzanwa points out, there is another way of looking at the activities of these women: 'The new democratic movements and politics which are emerging in Africa demonstrate the fact that the initiative can be seized from the nationalist leaderships that have formed governments' (1992, pp. 122–3).

In the next section we will develop this link between gender and nationalism further.

Nationalism, Identity and Tradition

Collective Development

Gender theorists have been analysing the issue of the legitimacy of the 'women's question' in nationalist struggles and in post-colonial societies (see generally Yuval-Davis and Anthias, 1989; Moghadam, 1994). The work has analysed the interaction between feminism and nationalism in Asian and Islamic societies (Kandiyoti, 1991; Shukrullah, 1994; Yeganeh, 1993; and *Feminist Review* No. 44 (1993) generally). Some have reassessed the legacy of the nationalist projects in the context of rising fundamentalism (Chhachhi, 1989).

Jayawardena (1986) shows the close alliance between feminism and nationalism in Asia in the nineteenth and early twentieth centuries: 'The movement towards women's emancipation was acted out against a background of nationalist struggles aimed at achieving political independence, asserting a national identity, and modernizing the society' (Moghadam, 1994, p. 3).

All the examples from Asia, despite different contexts, show that feminism and nationalism were 'complementary, compatible and solidaristic' (Moghadam, 1994, p. 3). This has changed.

> Today feminists and nationalists view each other with suspicion if not hostility, and nationalism is no longer assumed to be a progressive force for change. . . . In addition, the nationalist project increasingly assigns to women the rather onerous responsibility for the reproduction of the group – through family attachment, domesticity, and maternal roles. (*ibid.*)

Separate Development

There has been less discussion of the impact of the women's question on the struggle to decolonialize Africa (see, however, Obbo, 1989). However, as we have seen in the previous section, feminism has instead been linked with imperialism and been seen as divisive.

In Zimbabwe, women were heavily involved in the anti-colonial struggles in ways which changed perceptions of gender roles. These changes were reflected in the Legal Age of Majority Act 1982 (which as we have seen prevented Molly Muchabaiwa's father obtaining seduction damages) and other model enactments for women (although not in the constitution). But as soon as 1983 there were round-ups of women and the re-establishment of more 'traditional' roles for women described by Gaidzanwa (1992) as redomestification – a move back to a family, work and society model with men as heads and women as dependents. Yet at the same time, the economic policies of structural adjustment have resulted in increased numbers of female-headed and female-managed households which undermine this model of society.

Hassim (1993) and McClintock (1993) have pointed to the strong emphasis on familial values and motherhood within Afrikaner and Zulu nationalism in South Africa. There has been a similar emphasis on motherhood in the African National Congress. Although McClintock argues that 'Over the decades, African women nationalists, unlike their Afrikaans counterparts, have transformed and infused the ideology of motherhood with an increasingly insurrectionary cast, identifying themselves more and more as the "mothers of revolution"' (McClintock, 1993, p. 75), she argues further that in recent years a 'transformed African discourse on feminism has emerged, with black women demanding the right to fashion the terms of nationalist feminism to meet their own needs and situations' (1993, p. 73). Thus African women in South Africa are contesting the claim that feminism is imperialist, a product of the West and divisive of nationalist struggles. Their argument is that there is nothing wrong with feminism. It can be as progressive or as reactionary as nationalism (McClintock, 1993, p. 76). However, McClintock points out that the theoretical and strategic analyses of South Africa's gender imbalances have not run deep and that it is the newly returned ANC women's leadership who champion the cause of an anti-imperialist feminism. Gaidzanwa makes a similar point in relation to the vulnerability of the discourse of gender equality in Zimbabwe (1992).

The contest between feminism and tradition is considered by Walker (1994) in the context of the state reconstruction programmes to redistribute land to women in South Africa. She describes a rural patriarchy which becomes legitimized as 'tradition'.

> Not only do key institutions in rural society have to be radically transformed, including the institutions of local government (the chief and traditional and tribal authorities), customary law, polygyny, and the male-dominated homestead, but also the legitimating discourses of 'tradition', 'custom' and 'African culture'. Together these interlocking systems of authority constitute what I describe as 'official rural patriarchy', as distinct from the more amorphous, contradictory and fluid patriarchy of ordinary relationships and popular culture. (Walker, 1994, p. 347)

Walker assumes that the state through its structures and law can be used to counter this rural patriarchy.

> The [Rural Development Plan] requires the democratisation of chieftaincies as a matter of priority at all levels as well as legislation empowering all women, regardless of their marital status, to enjoy secure access to land and to inherit property in their own right. (Walker, 1994, p. 356)

Not only does this approach have strong echoes of the World Bank one discussed earlier, although the objectives are different, but it shares all its practical difficulties. Walker recognizes that such a programme will require major investments of resources in popular education as well as monitoring and enforcement on the ground. Where are these investments coming from 'in a resource starved isolated and frequently disorganised and divided communities' (Walker, 1994, p. 356)?

Interpretation

The independence struggles within Africa, particularly those in Mozambique, Zimbabwe and South Africa, changed the gender relations within society and resulted in the post-colonial governments introducing legislation to reflect these changes such as the Legal Age of Majority Act in Zimbabwe. However there has also been a strong tendency to see feminism as divisive to the struggle for independence and national identity within Africa. This feminism is characterized as a Western bourgeois implant benefiting the urban elite and antithetical to the traditions of Africa. Vulnerable post-colonial governments have sought to rely on the discourses of tradition and Africanism to maintain their positions in dire economic and political contexts. The women in our stories seeking to achieve their wishes have found themselves caught within these complex discourses.

Conclusions: Women and the Rule of Law

It is now possible to address the question why these four cases caused so much outcry. Many African countries since independence have experienced a considerable lack of economic self-determination, being vulnerable to externally defined policies and dependent on externally granted support. The state, lacking legitimacy with its population, has sought legitimacy through resort to constructions of tradition and Africanism as well as constructions of independence and development.

Women resorting to state law to enforce rights as women can be seen as anti-African, as imperialists, supporting a Western generated and supported philosophy of feminism, part of a tiny privileged minority who have the capacity to undertake such alien activities at the economic and cultural expense of their country and heritage.

African legal systems lack popular legitimacy because of the nature of the state which is seen as using law in arbitrary ways against the populace. The rule of law is not a mechanism for supporting civil society. However, in using the law women can also be seen as supporting another externally generated set of policies on the rule of law and good governance. Women's rights could be seen as one way to try to destabilize patrimonial states, to use the new international movements to mobilize opposition to such governments. For women this creates possible space to manoeuvre but also dangers. Crudely, they may find themselves championed by international agencies but vulnerable to criticisms from their compatriots.

There are those who have a strong interest in constructing dichotomies between traditional, customary law and state law. Legal method reinforces this dichotomy. Thus when women argue for individual rights they are seen as opposing custom and tradition. In the context of the state law courts, state law is powerful and is a threat to the traditional constructions of power. Women can then use the judgment to try to change power relationships in 'traditional' settings. Their success will depend on the conditions prevailing – enforcement of a legal decision is not easy and can lead to considerable resistance. Enforcing decisions in the context of a structurally corrupt state is going to be haphazard and not dependent on the merits of the decision.

The question is therefore do women give up on the state and law? The answer is no – not least because it will not give up on women. We have seen that the authoritarian and closed nature of the state has forced women, or they find it more conducive, to operate at arm's length from the state. Women become the objects of various public order or morality campaigns, round-ups of 'prostitutes', clampdowns on illegal trading and so on, which affect the way that all women are constructed within the society. These activities have to be challenged.

A strategy for empowerment based on legal concepts of equality is of limited value if the dominant sources of legitimacy in society lie elsewhere. This problem is not, of course, limited to women's empowerment issues alone, but it causes particular difficulties when we consider the sources of legitimacy in society. Women need a strategy which strengthens their legitimacy and authenticity in lobbying the state to achieve greater justice within society.

The question then is how? There is a need to build on the insights gained in the work on customary law and practice in colonialism. There is a need to plot and understand the complex and varied responses of rural women and men to 'tradition' and the choices being offered them through various development or reconstruction programmes. The analysis must be open, it must recognize differences between women and between men, it must value women's own assessment of needs and priorities and choices. It involves an engagement with the constructions of tradition and recognition that custom is a site for power relations and resistance.

Recent work of African women legal scholars and activists provides us with further insights because they concentrate on the relationships between the various regulatory regimes and women's position within them. I will take as an example the action research undertaken by the Women and Law in Southern Africa project and its newer sister project, Women and Law in Eastern Africa. These projects are conducting research to establish what practices exist in relation to specific aspects of women's lives and what women want. There is a determined effort to listen to a wide variety of women. The first WLSA research project looked at maintenance provision in the six countries covered by the project (Armstrong, 1992). The research covered rural and urban areas and produced new understandings of women's varied engagement with the various regulatory regimes.

The second research project in WLSA and the first in WLEA has considered inheritance patterns (Dengu-Zvogbo *et al.*, 1994). Researchers have discovered the dynamic interaction between the various regulatory regimes, between families, customary and state laws. These are not separate; justifications or approaches within one sphere are translated into another and used in the negotiations. The customs associated with inheritance are changing within the construction of the customary. The researchers argue that the customary is best seen as processal rather than substantive: a dispute resolution process. They have listened carefully and considered the sense of identity and legitimacy which is brought by tradition and custom to women and men and the variations between women.

They stress the need also to consider the existing institutional structures (those described by Walker as the rural patriarchy). While recognizing the relations of power within the traditional institutions they find some flexibility, some pressures for change responded to; and they ask in the end what alternative there is other than a massive state bureaucracy which lacks legitimacy and will not deliver. A model of state-generated rights which rural women must be educated to want has been tried and found wanting for too long. The objective is to find ways to strengthen women's position within the existing contexts. There is considerable evidence, of course, that women have always done this. We have seen it in the discussion of the colonial period and in the present contexts. There is evidence from many countries that seemingly non-traditional activities can soon become so.

Parallel with and overlapping this research work, African women are developing their own legal scholarship which is breaking down these constructed dichotomies through investigation of the relationships between them and actively seeking to understand the ways in which the power of tradition and custom can strengthen women's position. These activities have started to unburden women legal activists of some of the complaints levelled against them such as their denial of custom and tradition. Such an approach which starts with a recognition of the complexity of women's lives and their many identities, as mothers, farmers, daughters, citizens, wives, city-dwellers and rural residents will in time create the legitimacy which women need to bring about legal changes without creating so much controversy.

Notes

1 Virginia Edith Wambui Otieno v Joash Ochieng Ougo and Omolo Siranga (H.C.C. no. 4872 of 1986 Nairobi).

2 Bernardo Epharahim v Holalia Pastory and Another (PC) Civil Appeal no. 70 of 1989 (unreported).
3 Katekewe v Muchabaiwa SC 87/84.
4 In re Attorney General v Dow, Court of Appeal, no. 4/91 (Ct App. 1992) (Bots.).
5 Chihowa v Mangwende SC 84/87.
6 Murisa v Musira S-41-92.
7 Deocras Lutabana v Densi Kashaga [1981] TLR 122 held that a woman had no more than a life interest in the clan land she had inherited and that she could not sell or bequeath the land. Because of the doctrine of precedent whereby decisions in a higher court should be followed in lower courts, it could be argued that the Pastory case is not a 'good authority' because it contravenes the earlier ruling. However, higher court decisions can be distinguished because of different circumstances. Here Judge Mwalusanya argued that the introduction of the Bill of Rights in 1984 in which discrimination against women is prohibited changes the circumstances.
8 See Karl, 1995, ch. 5 for further discussion of the different development strategies adopted in relation to women.
9 Bi Verdiana kyabuje v Gregory s/o Kyabuje (1968) HCD n 499.

Bibliography

ARMSTRONG, ALICE (1992) *Struggling Over Scarce Resources: Women and Maintenance in Southern Africa*, Harare, University of Zimbabwe Publications for Women and Law in Southern Africa.

ARMSTRONG, A. *et al.* (1992) 'Uncovering Reality: Excavating Women's Rights in African Family Law', *International Journal of Law and the Family*, Vol. 7, No. 3.

BECKMAN, B. (1993) 'The Liberation of Civil Society: Neo-Liberal Ideology and Political Theory', *Review of African Political Economy*, Vol. 58, pp. 20–33.

BUJRA, J. (1982) 'Women "Entrepreneurs" of Early Nairobi', in SUMNER, C. (Ed.) *Crime, Justice and Underdevelopment*, London, Heinemann.

BUNTING, A. (1993) 'Theorising Women's Cultural Diversity in Feminist International Human Rights Strategies', *Journal of Law and Society*, Vol. 20, No. 1.

BYRNES, A. (1991) *Building on a Decade of Achievement*, Minneapolis, International Women's Rights Action Watch.

CHANOCK, MARTIN (1982) 'Making Customary Law: Men, Women and Courts in Colonial Northern Rhodesia', in HAY, M. J. and WRIGHT, M. (Eds) *African Women and the Law: Historical Perspectives. Boston University Papers On Africa VII*, pp. 53–67.

CHANOCK, M. (1985) *Law, Custom and Social Order*, Cambridge, Cambridge University Press.

CHANOCK, M. (1991) 'Paradigms, Policies, and Property: A Review of the Customary Law of Land Tenure', in MANN, K. and ROBERTS, R. (Eds) *Law in Colonial Africa*, Portsmouth, Heinemann.

CHHACHHI, A. (1989) 'The State, Religious Fundamentalism and Women: Trends in South Asia', *Economic and Political Weekly*, 18 March, pp. 567–78.

COMMONWEALTH EXPERT GROUP (1989) *Engendering Adjustment*, London, Commonwealth Secretariat.

COTRAN, E. (1989) 'The Future of Customary Law in Kenya', in OJWANG, J. B. and MUGAMBI, J. N. K. (Eds) *The S.M. Otieno Case: Death and Burial in Modern Kenya*, Nairobi, Nairobi University Press.

DENGU-ZVOGBO, K. *et al.* (1994) *Inheritance in Zimbabwe*, Harare, Women and Law in Southern Africa Research Trust.

DOW, U., STUMBRAS, S. and TATTEN, S. (1994) 'The Time Has Come .... Looking at Women's Empowerment Initiatives from a Grassroots Level. ... A Botswana Example' Presented at conference on Human Rights in Africa, Lagos, Nigeria.

FATTON, R. (1989) 'Gender, Class, and State in Africa', in PARPART, J. and STAUDT, K. (Eds) *Women and the State in Africa*, London and Boulder, Lynne Reiner.

FREEMAN, M. (1990) 'Measuring Equality: A Comparative Perspective on Women's Legal Capacity and Constitutional Rights in 5 Commonwealth Countries', *Commonwealth Law Bulletin*.

FREEMAN, M. (1993) 'Women, Development and Justice: Using the International Convention on Women's Rights', in KERR, J. (Ed.) *Ours By Right*, London, Zed Press.

GAIDZANWA, R. (1992) 'Bourgeois Theories of Gender and Feminism and their Shortcomings with Reference to Southern African Countries', in MEENA, R. (Ed.) *Gender in Southern Africa: Conceptual and Theoretical Issues*, Harare, SAPES.

GHAI, YASH (1993) 'Constitutions and Governance in Africa: A Prolegomenon', in ADELMAN, S. and PALIWALA, A. (Eds) *Law and Crisis in the Third World*, London, Hans Zell, pp. 51–75.

HASSIM, S. (1993) 'Family, Motherhood and Zulu Nationalism: The Politics of the Inkatha Women's Brigade', *Feminist Review*, No. 43, pp. 1–25.

HAY, M. J. and WHITE, M. (Eds) (1982) *African Women and the Law: Historical Perspectives*, Boston University Papers on Africa, Vol. vii.

HIMBARA, D. and SULTAN, D. (1995) 'Reconstructing the Ugandan State and Economy: The Challenge of an International Bantustan', *Review of African Political Economy*, No. 63, pp. 85–93.

HIRSCHMAN, O. (1970) *Exit, Voice and Loyalty*, Boston, Harvard University Press.

HUMAN RIGHTS WATCH/AFRICA HUMAN RIGHTS WATCH WOMEN'S RIGHTS PROJECT (1994) *Botswana: Second Class Citizens: Discrimination Against*

Women Under Botswana's Citizenship Act, New York, Human Rights Watch, Vol. 6, No. 7.

JAYAWARDENA, K. (1986) *Feminism and Nationalism in the Third World*, London, Zed Press.

KANDIYOTI, D. (1991) 'Identity and its Discontents: Women and the Nation', *Millennium: Journal of International Studies*, Vol. 20, No. 3, pp. 429–43.

KARL, M. (1995) *Women and Empowerment: Participation and Decision-making*, London, Zed Press.

LOVETT, M. (1989) 'Gender Relations, Class Formation and the Colonial State in Africa', in PARPART, J. and STAUDT, K. (Eds) *Women and the State in Africa*, London and Boulder, Lynne Reiner.

MARTIN, D. M. and HASHI, F. O. (1992a) *Law as an Institutional Barrier to the Economic Empowerment of Women*, World Bank Working Paper No. 2, New York, The World Bank.

MARTIN, D. M. and HASHI, F. O. (1992b) *Gender, the Evolution of Legal Institutions and Economic Development in Sub-Saharan Africa*, World Bank Working Paper No. 3, New York, The World Bank.

MARTIN, D. M. and HASHI, F. O. (1992c) *Women in Development: The Legal Issues in Sub-Saharan Africa Today*, World Bank Working Paper No. 4, New York, The World Bank.

MBILINYI, MARJORIE (1988) 'Runaway Wives in Colonial Tanganyika: Forced Labour and Forced Marriage in Rungwe District 1919–1961', *International Journal of Sociology of Law*, 16, pp. 1–29.

McCLINTOCK, A. (1993) 'Family Feuds: Gender, Nationalism and the Family', *Feminist Review*, No. 44, pp. 61–80.

MOGHADAM, V. (Ed.) (1994) *Gender and National Identity*, London, Zed Press.

MWALUSANYA, J. Bernardo Epharahim v Holalia Pastory and Another (PC) Civil Appeal, No. 701 of 1989 (unreported).

NESIAH, V. (1993) 'Towards a Feminist Internationality: A Critique of U.S. Feminist Legal Scholarship', *Harvard Women's Law Journal*, Vol. 16 (Spring), pp. 189–210.

OBBO, C. (1989) 'Sexuality and Economic Domination in Uganda', in YUVAL-DAVIS, N. and ANTHIAS, F. (Eds) *Woman – Nation – State*, Basingstoke, Macmillan.

OJWANG, J. B. and MUGAMBI, J. N. K. (Eds) (1989) *The S.M. Otieno Case: Death and Burial in Modern Kenya*, Nairobi, Nairobi University Press.

O'ROURKE, N. (1995) 'Land Rights and Gender Relations in Areas of Rural Africa: A Question of Power and Discourse', *Social and Legal Studies*, Vol. 4, pp. 75–97.

PARPART, J. (1988) 'Sexuality and Power on the Zambian Copperbelt (1926–1964)', in STITCHER, K. and PARPART, J. (Eds) *Patriarchy and Class: African Women in the Home and the Workforce*, Boulder and London, Westview.

PARPART, J. and STAUDT, K. (Eds) (1989) *Women and the State in Africa*, London and Boulder, Lynne Reiner.

PIETILA, H. and VICKERS, J. (1994) *Making Women Matter – The Role of the United Nations*, London, Zed Press.

RAO, A. (1993) 'Right in the Home: Feminist Theoretical Perspective on International Human Rights', in *Feminism and the Law*, National Law School of India Journal.

SHIVJI, I. G. (1993) 'The Changing State: From an Extra-Legal to an Intra-Legal State in Tanzania', in MTAKI, C. K. and OKEMA, M. (Eds) *Constitutional Reforms and Democratic Governance in Tanzania*, Dar es Salaam, Freidrich Naumann Foundation and University of Dar es Salaam, pp. 79–90.

SHIVJI, I. G. (1994) *A Legal Quagmire: Tanzania's Regulation of Land Tenure (Establishment of Villages) Act, 1992*, London, International Institute for Environment and Development.

SHIVJI, I. G. (1995) 'The Rule of Law and Ujamaa in the Ideological Formation of Tanzania', *Social and Legal Studies*, Vol. 4, No. 2, pp. 147–74.

SHUKRULLAH, H. (1994) 'The Impact of the Islamic Movement in Egypt', *Feminist Review*, No. 47, pp. 15–32.

STEWART, J. E. (1986) 'The Legal Age of Majority Act Strikes Again', *Zimbabwe Law Review*, Vol. 4, pp. 168–72.

TANZANIA GENDER NETWORKING PROGRAMME (1993) *Gender Profile of Tanzania*, Dar es Salaam, Tanzania Gender Networking Programme.

TOMASEVSKI, K. (1993) *Women and Human Rights*, London, Zed Press.

VICKERS, J. (1991) *Women and World Economic Crisis*, London, Zed Press.

WALKER, C. (1994) 'Women, "Tradition" and Reconstruction', *Review of African Political Economy*, 61, pp. 347–58.

WHITEHEAD, A. (1984) 'Women and Men, Kinship and Property', in HIRSCHON, R. (Ed.) *Women and Property – Women as Property*, London, Croom Helm.

YEGANEH, N. (1993) 'Women, Nationalism and Islam in Contemporary Political Discourse in Iran', *Feminist Review*, No. 44, pp. 3–18.

YUVAL-DAVIS, N. and ANTHIAS, F. (Eds) (1989) *Woman – Nation – State*, Basingstoke, Macmillan.

Chapter 3

Stages of Growth? – Women Dealing with the State and Each Other in Peru

Geraldine Lievesley

Introduction

This is a study of the different types of political mobilization undertaken by Peruvian women and how these activities respond to and are affected by the state. The three forms of organization I look at are the popular women's movement, political women (that is, those pursuing advancement within traditional party politics) and feminist women. Their experiences are set against a historical background since 1968 of military rule, democratic transition and increasingly authoritarian civilian government. My intention is to explore the idea that just as the state assumes various identities depending upon changing political junctures and as its power is manifested in different ways at both national and local levels so too must women's activism take multiple routes. That is to say, it would be inappropriate and indeed counterproductive for one mode of activity to be held up as correct and others to be denied relevance. There has been a tendency within the Peruvian context to give priority to the feminist perspective and to downgrade the impact of the activities of popular and political women.

To illustrate this, it may be valuable to introduce the notion of a feminist reworking of W. W. Rostow's 'stages of growth' paradigm which exerted such an influence upon Western developmentalist thinking in the 1960s and 1970s. In *The Stages of Economic Growth: A Non-Communist Manifesto*, published in 1960, Rostow identified five categories of growth, key amongst which were the concepts of 'preconditions for take-off', 'take-off' and the 'drive to maturity'. Without experiencing these stages, no society could claim to have modernized on the model of Western Europe and the United States. Rostow's highly schematic view of development was hierarchical (based on a crude darwinist view of history) and inherently ethnocentric (the undeveloped regions of the world would strive to become more 'like us'). It is not difficult to transfer this 'stages of growth' model to the debate about and between women both in the relationship between First and Third World women's movements and, within the latter, between feminists and popular and political women. It could be presented as the placing of different types of mobilization on an evolutionary scale with a major distinction being made between the consciousness of popular and political women (regarded as not being able to reach the 'preconditions for take-off', the former because of their inability to rise above practical demands and the latter because they subscribe to the male world of politics) and feminism (regarding itself as already on the 'drive to maturity'). An example of this kind of attitude can be taken from the proceedings of the fourth Encuentro Feminista Latinoamericano y del Caribe (Meeting of Latin American and Caribbean Feminists) held in Taxco, Mexico in 1987. During intense debates, veteran feminists complained that their space was being invaded and the level of theoretical discussion diluted by the increased representation of the *movimiento de mujeres* (popular women's movement) at such fora. The notion of the wonderfully termed *feministómetro* (literally a yardstick or measure) was invoked, the idea being that the 'veterans' had the right to define what was and was not legitimate feminist activity. The irony here was that the tremendous growth in the size and diversity of the Latin American women's movement in the 1980s appeared to be creating a problem for some feminists (Saporta Stembach *et al.*, 1992, p. 228).

I am not suggesting that this is a universally held position, and certainly many feminists acknowledge it as a problem. Clearly there are considerable differences of education, job opportunities and cultural possibilities filtered through the lenses of class and ethnicity between Latin American women and these necessarily exert a strong influence upon the nature of their perceptions and types of mobilization. However, there is a need to establish norms of best practice in the dealings of feminists (typically middle-class and professional) with poor women. A sustainable women's movement with the ability to intervene in national politics cannot, arguably, be founded upon unequal relations between its constituent parts. Feminist groups focus upon issues of gender identity and sexuality and these are undoubtedly of fundamental importance but it would be unfortunate if this leads them to undervalue both the dynamics of class and race (and how these affect women's status within society and their relations with each other) and the priority survival strategies that the vast majority of women must pursue.

One starting point is the rather obvious assertion that there is no identikit 'woman' and that each individual's class position and ethnic identity, compounded by gender, will force women into distinct and sometimes contradictory roles (contradictory in the sense that one set of interests may conflict with another). In her study of Peruvian women peasant unionists, Sarah Radcliffe found that respondents regarded themselves as women, as mothers, as members of the peasant class, as members of the poor, as defenders of the land, as Indians fighting racism and as producers responsible for the reproduction of life for the sake of both their families and their communities. For these women, there was a felt need to organize alongside men in their collective struggles at the same time as trying to prevent union leaderships from marginalizing women's concerns and compelling their male colleagues to treat them as equals (Radcliffe, 1990, pp. 234–7). Such multiple identities require complex strategies. The construction of these strategies will also depend upon how women conceive their power with respect to the state.

Women and the State

An assessment of how viable women's activism can be will be coloured by how one characterizes the official political arena orchestrated by the state. A liberal democratic theory would presume the state's neutrality, arguing that it would be as open to women's demands as to those of any other articulate interest group. In this reading the state would not be prejudiced against women: rather, it would have no gender identity. It would, therefore, be willing to embark upon legislative and welfare programmes and would accept women working and rising within its institutions. This has obviously been an incentive for those women who have aspired to being career politicians. On the other hand, taking a structuralist approach – grounded in marxist theory – the state would be seen as constituted on the basis of class power, an important element of which would be patriarchy as reproduced through its ideological structures. This definition, taken to its zero sum conclusion, would mean that women could expect to obtain nothing from the state and should rather work for its overthrow.

I would argue that we need to tread a path between these idealized alternatives. The first thing must be to recognize that the state is not a static entity; rather, it responds to pressures and its formations change under the impact of the interplay of political competition between governing elites and the representation of different economic and social interests. This process can present opportunities (the Spanish word *apertura* – meaning opening or space – is a useful conceptual tool) which may be taken advantage of by various groups normally excluded from demand-making and political influence. These *aperturas* produce their own dilemmas with respect to organization and strategy, the question of alliance and, most pertinent, how short-term gains can be transformed into sustained achievements. Such opportunities will also be shaped and constrained by the political environment in which these groups operate.

Let me develop this idea with reference to what appears to be a paradox of recent Peruvian history. This is that, perversely, the period of military rule (1968–80) and particularly that of the transition process (1977–80) offered more opportunities for women's mobilization than the civilian regimes that have followed it. The Revolution of the Armed Forces government led by General Velasco (1968–75) was distinctive in that, unlike other military regimes of the period, its use of repression was very limited and it initiated a wide-ranging programme of structural reforms. These were intended to deepen the capitalist nature of the economy and, through income redistribution, preempt social unrest (Lauer, 1978; Booth and Sorj, 1982; McClintock and Lowenthal, 1983). The regime endorsed a philosophy of 'full participation' as a means of achieving a Peruvian 'third way' which would be neither capitalist nor communist (Delgado, 1974). The creation of a corporatist network of mass organizations, each representing a particular social sector, aimed to destroy traditional class and party allegiances and to create a controlled mobilization of the population which would grant the regime legitimacy (Cotler, 1975). However, this policy backfired. First, the military was itself divided on the nature and intensity of the reforms and the risks involved in encouraging mobilization. This led to the institutional coup of General Morales Bermúdez in 1975, the defeat of the military 'radicals' and the establishment of a far more conventional military government. Second, a growing economic crisis stimulated by the regime's indebtedness resulted in IMF-imposed restructuring. The retraction of the state sector, price hikes and galloping inflation accompanied by increasingly aggressive labour practices by management produced deindustrialization, high unemployment and a rising incidence of poverty and deprivation. A wave of popular protest – manifested in strike action and demonstrations – indicated that the regime was losing political control. From early 1977, Morales attempted to stage-manage the military's withdrawal from government.

The regime's problems were compounded by the fact that Peruvians had begun to take the idea of participation seriously. The mass organizations were caught up in mobilization against the military and formed links with increasingly militant unions and other popular groups. The fragmented left parties, hitherto marginalized from mainstream politics, were compelled – under the weight of popular pressure – to initiate unity discussions in order to contest elections for a Constituent Assembly in 1978 and a general election in 1980. The military had not appreciated that trying to create a political culture of controlled mobilization for inherently anti-democratic purposes in a hostile economic climate and with a regime lacking internal coherence was a precarious and ultimately futile strategy.

Women acquired greater public prominence during the period of military rule and were active in the opposition to the regime. One of the military's corporatist organizations was the Comisión Nacional de la Mujer Peruana (CONAMUP – the National Commission of Peruvian Women) which was founded in 1975. Its brief was to build up women's identification with the regime. It sponsored meetings between women from a wide variety of backgrounds: the parties, the Church, the universities, the professions, the arts and non-governmental organizations. It would prove to be a seed-bed for many women activists in popular, political and feminist groups. Women were also made visible through their involvement in community self-help projects in the shanty towns (Collier, 1976) as well as their increased economic input in the burgeoning informal sector. Women trade unionists acquired a particularly high profile during the epic six-month teachers' strike in 1979 although unionization of traditional women's work – such as domestic service – proved difficult. These were all opportunities fraught with problems of organization and sustainability, but nevertheless this period offered dynamic possibilities for women.

In theory, the restoration of civilian government in 1980 under centre-right President Belaúnde should have presented more possibilities for women's advancement. Parties, including those of the left, were to function normally, institutional arrangements for holding elections and parliamentary procedures were in place, civil rights would be protected by the rule of law and the military, authors of the crisis of the previous three years, had retired to their barracks. However, the democracy established over the last fifteen years has proved to have many negative features. The 1980s have been described as 'the lost decade' for Latin America as governments struggled with the on-going debt crisis, restructuring programmes were universally applied and the socio-economic consequences of these were felt, particularly by the poor. Peru was no exception to this experience. To its continuing economic problems were added the constraints upon political life imposed by Sendero Luminoso's insurrection which was launched in 1980. With states of emergency imposed in many areas of the country and intensifying political violence, the military assumed an increasing influence over government. The opportunities for ex-pression and activity were circumscribed, particularly for those involved in organizations of the left, trade unions and the popular movement who risked being branded as *senderistas*. There was a growing trend towards authoritarian and personalist government which culminated in President Fujimori's dissolu-tion of Congress in 1992. Political parties of both left and right have gone into what seems terminal decline.

These factors have adversely affected women's opportunities. Thus as the state's role as provider of services has been cut back so poor women have had to assume ever more responsibility for this function which has made collective activities (particularly outside their neighbourhoods) ever more difficult. The career possibilities for political women will inevitably contract as the tradi-tional parties are marginalized and 'anti-politics' politicians dominate the scene. In such an atmosphere, feminists may decide that engagement with popular women, with unions, or with the left is unproductive and withdraw from such interactions. In sum, formal democratization has not been friendly to women.

I want now to turn to the first of my case studies on women's mobilization which is that of popular women.

Popular Women's Organization

Patron-client relationships have been a constant feature of Peruvian life. They are based upon perceptions of dominant and subordinate status between actors and the exchange of material favours for political support at all levels of society. Poor people living in inner-city districts and shanty towns are the typical subjects of clientelism. They are the recipients of provision from the state (via both government departments and municipalities), from political parties, from the Church and from external donors. In return, they are ex-pected to accept prevailing structures and hierarchies and ways of acting politically. They are not regarded as independent actors; they function simply to acknowledge 'the gift' by their performance in the voting booth. There is a long tradition of paternalistic charitable activities by prominent politicians, often fronted by their wives, and the promise of land titles and infrastructure – although no surety that such promises would be kept (Collier, 1976).

Government, parties and the Church come into poor neighbourhoods and sponsor diverse activities such as mothers' clubs, food distribution, skills training, literacy campaigns and small-scale workshops. All these endeavours work to agendas set outside the neighbourhood. Thus the Catholic Church has been responsible for a great deal of development work within shanty towns which has been of enormous benefit to their inhabitants. However, it has wanted to control the terms of debate, encouraging women, for example, to subscribe to traditional notions of their roles as wives and mothers but blocking discussion of 'unsuitable' subjects such as reproductive rights, abortion and sexuality.

Over time women leaders emerge within neighbourhood groups, their role being to assume the 'official' voice of their specific constituency in dealing with formal bodies. This has frequently resulted in a passive membership and some degree of dependency upon the leader who is expected to resolve problems and deliver the goods. Organization by women in poor neighbourhoods and shanty towns has been obstructed by the pervasiveness of clientelist practices by parties across the political spectrum which have undercut the forging of horizontal links between local groups. As Barrig wryly states, 'all political parties act as though women's organisations are a political resource to be used for political ends' (Barrig, 1986, p. 167).

Women's groups have been riven by partisan conflicts. Thus, in the 1980s, divisions within the Izquierda Unida (the United Left, the umbrella organization representing the majority of left parties) permeated the Federación Popular de Mujeres de Villa El Salvador (the Popular Federation of Women of Villa El Salvador – this is the largest of the shanty towns surrounding Lima) severely constraining its effectiveness (*NACLA*, Vol. XXVIII, No. 4 (1995), p. 24). In 1983, Izquierda Unida's mayor of Lima, Alfonso Barrantes, introduced the Vaso de Leche (glass of milk) programme which aimed to fight infant malnutrition through the provision of daily milk to children under 6 years old (later extended to children up to 13 and to nursing mothers). The municipality also supported the spread of *comedores populares* (communal dining rooms) (Barrig, 1989, pp. 134–9). Important as these initiatives were, local women had to constantly guard against being subsumed by the front's national political agenda.

In her study of a poor Lima neighbourhood, Cecilia Blondet describes how women may, over time, acquire the confidence to leave the confines of the family unit and join with others to press for improved services from the state and also to engage in collective self-help activities. Traditional forms of organization based upon clientelism may be challenged as women become more assertive and independent (Blondet, 1990). The economic recession beginning in the late 1970s forced poor women into collective responses as they struggled with high prices and food scarcities. Virginia Guzman has described this as the 'feminisation of poverty' (1987, pp. 4–5). Women came to play an increasingly high-profile employment role – albeit in poorly paid, unskilled and non-unionized jobs in the informal sector – as they attempted to keep their families together. They were also at the forefront of community projects such as building schools, nurseries and pharmacies, demanding the provision of infra-structure, protesting price rises, supporting strikes and organizing training in health and nutrition, in childcare and literacy. Popular women were mobilizing on the basis of need, driven by immediate practical concerns.

Since 1980, the civilian governments of Belaúnde, García and Fujimori have continued to reduce the welfare role of the state. Fernando Belaúnde (1980–85) adopted neo-liberal economic principles including a commitment to privatization, a process which Alberto Fujimori (1990–present) has consoli-dated. Although Alan García (1985–90) resorted to more interventionist, populist measures (Crabtree, 1992) these still had a debilitating impact upon poor women. For example, the establishment of the Programa de Apoyo al Ingreso Temporal (PAIT – Temporary Income Support Programme) in 1986 attempted to reduce unemployment by offering three months' work at the minimum wage in schemes such as road and building repair. This was unskilled labour which offered no prospects of permanent employment. However, given the seriousness of their financial plight, many poor women joined the scheme – leaving the *comedores* and other community efforts as a result. The govern-ment – under the aegis of Señora García – also created a network of mother and child clubs, crèches and workshops and offered loans and equipment. Its clear objective was to break up independent, collective action by poor women and re-establish patron-client relations in the shanty towns.

Involvement in survival organizations by popular women adds immensely to their already heavy daily tasks. Caroline Moser has talked of the triple functions poor women have to perform. These are reproductive (childcare, keeping the family going), productive (income generation) and community management (the collective provision of infrastructure) (Moser, 1993). It has been argued that these activities merely confirm the traditional gender divi-sion of labour. That is, women are principally regarded as providers and sustainers and as their daily schedules make political activism outside the locality very difficult, they are unable to break out and have an impact upon national politics (Cedamanos *et al.*, 1990). Carol Andreas has criticized femi-nists who took this position: 'Feminism came to be identified as the province of those who could afford to be "pure" in their opposition to men as exploiters and who were dedicated to pursuing goals separated from ongoing neighbour-hood and community struggles' (Andreas, 1985, p. 200).

Women face many problems in making the transition from being organ-ized to organizing themselves including their lack of knowledge about the official male world of institutions and politics, their vulnerability to manipula-tion and the many pressures in their lives which obstruct sustained activism. Popular organizations experience a high level of membership turnover as women try to balance domestic and community demands. Notwithstanding the inevitable setbacks popular women's mobilization endures, there are many positive consequences. Women cease being passive subjects, they move into spheres of activity hitherto mysterious to them and they develop confidence in themselves as individuals and as a social force. By engaging in local struggles, they will both begin the slow transformation of daily life and come into contact with other sectors (unions, human rights and ecological groups, NGOs and feminists). This will contribute to a broadening of perspective, with the private beginning to impinge upon the public world.

It would be incorrect to suggest that popular women are solely concerned with practical issues such as food, money and shelter; matters such as reproductive rights and domestic violence also have a presence in their lives. However, they may come lower on their list of priorities because of the pressing concerns of everyday survival. It would be inappropriate to regard grass-roots mobilization as inherently inferior. The feminist movement needs to be grounded in broad mass struggles in order to enable it to acquire the critical mass to put pressure upon the state. Popular women need the strategic and long-term inputs which feminists can offer. In this sense, their 'stages of growth' should be a mutual rather than mutually exclusive process.

Political Women

In using the category of political women I intend those who have taken the upwardly mobile route – that is, the official, male journey – in political parties and trade unions as well as seeking public appointment. Such women may gain position and influence within existing state institutions but their progress will always be dependent upon the state and its attendant bodies. The aim of women power-seekers is to use party, bureaucratic or governmental appointment to affect policy-making and implementation processes and to permeate institutional cultures in order to give women's issues a higher profile.

Political parties of the centre and right in Peru have, in recent years, made a point of spotlighting high-flying women in order to demonstrate their 'pro-women' sensibilities. APRA (the Alianza Popular Revolucionaria Americana – the American Popular Revolutionary Alliance, Peru's oldest political party) has an ethos which has always acknowledged the importance of women within its tradition of family dynasties and the sustenance of an alternative *aprista* culture through its periods of persecution since 1924. However the terms of acceptance of women achievers is that they should not rock the boat, that is, they should avoid controversial issues such as abortion (here all parties, including those of the left, regard this as a political liability given the Catholic Church's opposition to legislation), and also that they should accept that a women's agenda must always take second place to the party's programme.

In the 1980s, most parties created women's commissions and women were appointed to publicized roles (for example, in 1982 the Secretary of Acción Política de la Mujer was elected to the party's national executive although with

no real power). The parties sponsored access programmes in political education and training. García, when *aprista* President, created commissions on
women's issues in both the Ministry of Justice and the National Planning
Institute and appointed women to the Ministries of Education and Health.
Despite these apparent successes, political women suffered continued com-
partmentalization. Thus García established a Comisión 'de la familia' rather
than 'de la mujer' ('of the family' rather than 'of women'). Women did not
occupy positions of power within party hierarchies and those who acquired a
certain media visibility might be regarded as tokens. Mercedes Cabanillas,
congressional deputy and indeed APRA's presidential candidate in 1995, in-
advertently admitted as much in an interview in 1986. Questioned on why,
despite his pledge to increase women's representation, the electoral lists only
had a 30 per cent quota and no woman was granted ministerial status in
García's first government, she responded that a Cabinet 'had to possess certain
characteristics which would inspire respect for those important measures it
would need to begin implementing' (*Viva*, November 1985, p. 18). The clear
inference was that women ministers would not possess sufficient gravitas to
inspire that respect.

A fascinating contemporary case of a political woman with ideas above
her station is that of Susana Higuchi, wife of President Fujimori. Since the
summer of 1994, her revelations about executive corruption and what she sees
as the illegitimate status of the regime have engaged the nation's attention.
Their very public estrangement followed by her hunger strike and then her
abortive attempt to register a new party, Harmonia 2000, have been followed
as avidly as any soap opera. This is definitely not the usual role performed by
presidential wives who are expected to immerse themselves in non-threaten-
ing charitable concerns rather than washing their spouses' dirty linen in public
(*Peru Update*, October 1994, p. 2).

It would be wrong to dismiss the impact of political women. Clearly
positive results such as improved legal status, the opening up of educational
and job opportunities, welfare legislation and the publicizing of issues cannot
be repudiated. However, these activities should not be seen for more than
what they are. Although they may produce advances, they are not challenging
underlying structures of oppression. Political women will believe that they are
infiltrating the state but the latter has the upper hand in defining what issues
it recognizes as important, how far it will compromise and where it will draw
the line. However, the state also needs to be seen to be paying attention
to women's concerns, and this does give political women some room for
maneouvre. Women will continue to perform certain public roles but the
likelihood is that these will be in areas traditionally recognized as being
feminine (health and education are prime instances). It is unlikely that we will
see a Peruvian woman Minister of the Economy or of Foreign Affairs in the
near future. There is the additional possibility that political women become
progressively isolated from other women, particularly those without their
educational and socio-economic advantages. They will undoubtedly be ex-

pected where they do have contact with such constituencies to tame demands in exchange for what may be very limited piecemeal reforms.

In the 1990s all traditional parties have lost a great deal of political influence. The three front runners of the 1995 presidential campaign (Fujimori, Perez de Cuellar and Alejandro Toledo) were all 'anti-politics' politicians operating outside established political channels. The election results were dismal for parties of the left, right and centre who only garnered 6 per cent of the national vote between them (*Peru Update*, April 1995, p. 27). In this climate, political women will find it even harder to pursue their ambitions.

Left-wing parties have appeared to be more prejudiced against political women than their conservative rivals. This is because their class-based analysis of Peruvian society has led them to regard activism directed at gender concerns as irrelevant. From the mid 1970s, women militants began to criticize this state of affairs. Women's demands were, they said, either completely neglected or at best peripheralized and women militants were treated as second-class citizens within party culture. In 1978, women within Vanguardia Revolucionaria (Revolutionary Vanguard, an eclectic party formed in 1965 and a prime mover in the left unity discussions of 1977–80) condemned a party leadership which was imbued with 'sterile and arrogant intellectualism' and had no real idea as to how to improve its relationship with the popular movement including women (Vanguardia Revolucionaria, 1978). They contended that the party had to democratize itself in order to build real links with the latter. Rather than being a party of cadres, it had to become a mass party. The myth of the supremacy of 'the Party' was damaging and must be discarded in favour of greater interaction with the people. The adoption of a 'mass line' went hand-in-hand with the recognition of women's importance (Vanguardia Revolucionaria, 1982).

Other left parties experienced similar dissent. They responded by creating commissions and holding conferences but there was little commitment to change. Party hierarchies held to the view that feminism diverted energy from the class struggle and that specific gender concerns could only be addressed under socialism. Carol Andreas has wanted to make an exception of Sendero Luminoso, arguing that men and women have fought equally in the guerrilla struggle and pointing to the high incidence of women within the party's leadership (Andreas, 1985, p. 178). However, Sendero's authoritarian structure, its rejection of popular political involvement except under its rigid control and its repudiation of any other form of activism tend to undermine this characterization (Scott Palmer, 1992). Virginia Vargas has highlighted its assassination of Maria Elena Moyano, deputy mayor of Villa El Salvador and a strident critic of its attempts to dominate shanty town organization as an example of Sendero's hostility to the real needs and demands of poor Peruvian women (*NACLA*, Vol. XXVII, No. 1, July–August 1993, p. 46).

By the late 1970s, many women had decided to leave their parties, frustrated by the lack of progress and angered by the condescension of male colleagues who talked disparagingly of *las locas* ('the mad women'). They became involved in setting up autonomous feminist groups, although most retained attachments on the left. Other women resolved to stay within their respective parties but to continue the debate and attempt to change attitudes and behaviour. Relations between these two currents – subsequently termed *independientes* and *políticas* – are discussed below.

The Feminist Movement

The contemporary feminist movement has its antecedents in earlier pioneer struggles for university reform, for the suffrage and, in the 1960s, against discriminatory legislation (such as property laws). There was an eruption of activity in the 1970s, with 1973 being particularly noteworthy for the establishment of two self-defined feminist organizations, the Alianza de Mujeres del Perú (ALIMUPER – the Alliance of Peruvian Women) and the Grupo de Trabajo Flora Tristán (the Flora Tristán Study Group, named after a much revered early militant). ALIMUPER initiated the first feminist demonstrations such as that against the Miss Peru contest in 1973. A set of coincidental circumstances contributed to the growth of the movement. The first was that the Velasco government created CONAMUP in 1975 as part of its corporatist strategy. It sponsored dialogues between different types of women and unwittingly – as with the other official mass organizations – provoked the very thing it intended to prevent which was the development of independent activity and consciousness. The second element was that 1975 was also the inaugural year of the UN's Decade of Women which, given its possibilities for publicity and funding, gave a certain legitimacy to women's initiatives. Lima hosted the third Seminario Latino Americano de Mujeres in 1974; this was a preparatory meeting for the NGO forum which would accompany the UN conference in Mexico City the following year. Government, church and party women attended but the profile of the representatives was overwhelmingly urban, middle-class and hispanic with no indigeneous delegates (Miller, 1991, p. 201). The other factors were the debates and later departures of women militants from left parties and women's involvement in the intense mobilization against military rule. Feminists were concerned to be part of the wider movement for democratization but also to establish a niche from which they could launch a discourse attacking patriarchy.

The organizational 'lift-off' came in 1979 with the emergence of four autonomous feminist groups who decided to coordinate their activities under the aegis of ALIMUPER. These groups – the Movimiento Manuela Ramos, Mujeres en Lucha (Women in Struggle), the Frente Socialista de Mujeres (Socialist Women's Front) and the Centro de Mujeres Peruanas Flora Tristán – were devoted to academic research and cultural studies and campaigns both on feminist issues and in solidarity with strikers. They rejected dependency upon 'any organization which considers the struggle for women's liberation as a secondary activity' (Barrig, 1986, p. 158). This was an extremely ambivalent approach in that many autonomous feminists (the *independientes*) continued to reaffirm their socialist identity and maintained contacts with the left fronts FOCEP and the UDP (the Frente Obrero Campesino Estudiantil y Popular (Worker, Peasant, Student and Popular Front) and the Unidad Democratica Popular (Popular Democratic Unity)) which grouped trotskyists and maoists during the unity discussions of 1977–80. They were subsequently close to Izquierda Unida, particularly during its periods of municipal government. This was at the same time as *independientes* were complaining that left parties were attempting to take them over.

A similar paradox was that whilst autonomous feminists routinely disparaged any relationship with the official world of politics, in 1984 ALIMUPER announced the need 'to penetrate the institutions of public power'. The following year, two *independientes* – Virginia Vargas and Victoria Villanueva – stood for election to Congress, as deputy and senator respectively. The candidates aligned themselves with Izquierda Unida, declaring that despite its being 'very patriarchal and *machista*' it was still the organization best capable of representing women! Villanueva stated that they would ally with 'anyone' who sponsored women's rights and if elected would promote the creation of an all-party women's front in parliament (Sala, 1985, p. 15). Their campaign slogan – 'Vota por ti mujer' ('Women vote for yourselves') – aimed to attract women irrespective of class or ethnic background. Receiving no support whatsoever from Izquierda Unida, Vargas and Villanueva were trounced. This episode was a bizarre volte-face in terms both of their erstwhile eschewal of male politics and of their ingenuous belief in a homogeneous constituency of women. As Barrig has noted, feminists fail when they try 'to universalize the priorities of gender for all women' (Barrig, 1989, p. 120). The *independientes* were sending out confused messages indicating uncertainty with respect to their strategy vis-à-vis the state.

During the 1980s, *independientes* engaged in a debate with *políticas* who argued for the so-called 'double militancy' of feminism and socialism. *Políticas* criticized *independientes* for isolating themselves from broad political and social processes and exhibiting elitist attitudes towards popular women. The issues of sexuality and gender relations distracted attention from mass organizing and also created divisions based upon class and cultural differences. *Independientes* responded by attacking the *políticas'* acceptance of continued male dominance within their parties and their sanguine belief that women's issues would eventually be taken seriously. Each side, for example, accused the other of being 'bad' feminists at the second Encuentro Feminista Latinoamericano y del Caribe which was held just outside Lima in 1983 (Saporta Stembach *et al.*, 1992).

Fortunately many feminists came to appreciate that there could not be such a simplistic either/or answer ('we're right, you're wrong') to this dialogue. Indeed this type of response was itself the product of decades of introspective thought on the left with respect to the nature of 'the Revolution' which had singularly failed to take account of changing political environments and the complex interplay of social, economic and cultural factors. It was evident that the feminist movement as a whole was often guilty of replicating some of the least pleasant characteristics of Peruvian marxism, particularly its sectarianism and intellectual superiority. Virginia Vargas acknowledged the persistence of this psychological baggage:

> We conceived of ourselves as a group ... who were holders of the truth. ... We regarded our mission as the transmission of 'correct' knowledge to all other women. ... Women were regarded as virgin lands where the seeds of wisdom could be sown. (quoted in Stoltz Chinchilla, 1992, p. 48)

The legacy of the left has resulted in tentative advances bedevilled by organizational weakness and fragmentation (with ALIMUPER, amongst others, disappearing by the mid 1980s). The feminist movement has not been able to establish a strong identity because of its continued strategic confusion as to whether it should be involved in the broader political sphere or concentrate upon autonomous development. In the increasingly difficult political climate of the last ten years, the tendency has been to opt for the latter course. The creation of hierarchies of better and lesser women – which reflects my suggested 'stages of growth' metaphor – has inhibited the development of a strong and permanent relationship with the *movimiento de mujeres*.

Conclusion

My discussion of popular, political and feminist women's mobilization in contemporary Peru has suggested that each type of activism has its own set of problems, and that each operates at a different level of interaction with the state and for different purposes. The popular women's movement is confronted by both practical and cultural constraints as well as by the difficulty of making the transition from local to national politics. Women seeking advancement within political parties or governmental office risk being subsumed by these institutions rather than transforming them. Feminists who take the autonomous route will distance themselves from the socio-political processes which affect the lives of the majority of Peruvians, women and men.

The authoritarian tendencies of recent political history and the progressive weakening of left parties, trade unions and social movements lead to the conclusion that no oppositional group has the power to stand alone. In this situation, no strategy can claim to be exclusively 'correct'; rather such groups must act together or at least in implicit collaboration. They can only do this if old dogmas and perceptions which produce static viewpoints are jettisoned. In this sense, the contradiction between *independientes* and *políticas* and between *feministas* and *movimiento de mujeres* is as spurious as debates which have raged for decades on the left about reform or revolution. The political, institutional and structural odds are stacked so high against women that there has to be an acceptance of multiple forms of struggle and of coalitions which pursue varied goals.

It is true that government needs to be seen to be taking a positive approach towards women – to demonstrate its democratic credentials and to win votes – and women may therefore be able to take advantage of this despite the non-feminist motives behind the state's actions. Sonia Alvarez contends that 'State policies affecting women's status are sometimes quite contradictory and feminist strategies can often exacerbate those contradictions by taking the struggle into the heart of the state apparatus' (Alvarez, 1990, p. 196).

This is a difficult strategy which brings with it the danger of institutionalization. It is, however, a necessary programme of action so long as it is not the only one. Similarly neither popular women's mobilization nor feminist organization should be privileged to the exclusion of others. Rather the limitations of each form have to be recognized but, this notwithstanding, the long-term, cumulative effect of all women's activities – political lobbying, community work, party political and autonomous feminist – may be significant. Valerie Bryson calls for a 'realistic assessment of power': 'different forms of action can be seen as complementary rather than alternative for changes in one structure may both determine and be determined by others' (Bryson, 1992, p. 230).

If one accepts that the state is a complex apparatus and that it organizes different types of sustaining and defensive structures within civil society then activities directed at subverting its power must be as equally complex. Above all, it is important not to adopt a 'stages of growth' mind set which can only result in elitism and thus impotence. The Peruvian women's movement – as with all others – must be grounded in the experience of the vast majority of its members: 'Power is not only about the struggle for State power . . . rather it is present in all social discourse, in all social and interpersonal relations . . . in all daily life' (Vargas, 1986, p. 12).

Bibliography

ALVAREZ, SONIA E. (1990) *Engendering Democracy in Brazil – Women's Movements in Transition Politics*, Princeton, New Jersey, Princeton University Press.

ANDREAS, CAROL (1985) *When Women Rebel – The Rise of Popular Feminism in Peru*, Westport, Connecticut, Laurence Hill and Co.

BARRIG, MARUJA (1986) 'Democracia Emergente y Movimiento de Mujeres', in BALLON, EDUARDO (Ed.) *Movimiento Sociales y Democracia: La Fundación De Un Nuevo Orden*, Lima, DESCO.

BARRIG, MARUJA (1989) 'The Difficult Equilibrium Between Bread and Roses: Women's Organizations and the Transition from Dictatorship to Democracy in Peru', in JAQUETTE, JANE S. (Ed.) *The Women's Movement in Latin America: Feminism and the Transition to Democracy*, Boston, Unwin Hyman.

BLONDET, CECILIA (1990) 'Establishing an Identity: Women Settlers in a Poor Lima Neighbourhood', in JELIN, ELIZABETH (Ed.) *Women and Social Change in Latin America,* London, Zed.

BOOTH, D. and SORJ, B. (1982) *Military Reformism and Social Classes: The Peruvian Experience, 1968–80*, London, Macmillan.

BRYSON, VALERIE (1992) *Modern Feminist Thought: An Introduction*, London, Macmillan.

CEDAMANOS, G., HAWORTH, L. and TAMAYO, G. (1990) 'Genero y Ciudadania', *Viva*, December.

COLLIER, D. (1976) *Squatters and Oligarchs: Authoritarian Rule and Policy Change in Peru*, Baltimore and London, Johns Hopkins University Press.

COTLER, J. (1975) 'The New Mode of Political Domination in Peru', in LOWENTHAL, A. (Ed.) *The Peruvian Experiment: Continuity and Change Under Military Rule*, Princeton, Princeton University Press.

CRABTREE, J. (1992) *Peru under García*, London, Macmillan.

DELGADO, C. (1974) *La Revolución Peruana: Un Nuevo Camino*, Lima, Centro de Estudios de Participación Popular, SINAMOS.

ESCOBAR, ARTURO and ALVAREZ, SONIA E. (Eds) (1992) *The Making of Social Movements in Latin America*, Boulder, Colorado, Westview Press.

GUZMAN, VIRGINIA (1987) 'Cambios en el Trabajo Femenino', *Viva*, February–May.

GUZMAN, VIRGINIA and PORTOCARRERO, PATRICIA (1985) *Dos Veces Mujer*, Lima, Mosca Azul Editores.

LAUER, M. (1978) *El Reformismo Burgués, 1968–76*, Lima, Mosca Azul Editores.

McCLINTOCK, C. and LOWENTHAL, A. (Eds) (1983) *The Peruvian Experiment Reconsidered*, Princeton, Princeton University Press.

MILLER, FRANCESCA (1991) *Latin American Women and The Search for Social Justice*, Hanover and London, University Press of New England.

MOHANTY, C. T., RUSSO A. and TORRES, L. (Eds) (1991) *Third World Women and The Politics of Feminism*, Indiana, Indiana University Press.

MOSER, C. (1993) 'Adjustment from Below: Low-Income Women, Time and The Triple Role in Guayaquil, Ecuador', in RADCLIFFE, SARAH A. and WESTWOOD, SALLIE (Eds) *'Viva' – Women and Popular Protest in Latin America*, London and New York, Routledge.

RADCLIFFE, SARAH A. (1990) 'Multiple Identities and Negotiations Over Gender: Female Peasant Union Leaders in Peru', *Bulletin of Latin American Research*, Vol. 9, No. 2.

RADCLIFFE, SARAH A. and WESTWOOD, SALLIE (Eds) (1993) *'Viva' – Women and Popular Protest in Latin America*, London and New York, Routledge.

ROSTOW, W. W. (1960) *The Stages of Economic Growth: A Non-Communist Manifesto*, Cambridge, Cambridge University Press.

SALA, MARIELLA (1985) 'Feminismo y Elecciones en el Perú' *Viva*, March.

SAPORTA STEMBACH, N., NAVARO-ARANGUREN, M. and ALVAREZ, S. E. (1992) 'Feminisms in Latin America: From Bogotá to San Bernardo', in ESCOBAR, ARTURO and ALVAREZ, SONIA E. (Eds) *The Making of Social Movements in Latin America*, Boulder, Colorado, Westview Press.

SCOTT PALMER, D., (Eds) (1992) *Shining Path of Peru*, London, Hurst.

STAUDT, K., EVERETT, J. and CHARLTON, S. E. M. (Eds) (1989) *Women, the State and Development*, New York, State University of New York Press.

STOLTZ CHINCHILLA, N. (1992) 'Marxism, Feminism and the Struggle for Democracy in Latin America', in ESCOBAR, ARTURO and ALVAREZ, SONIA, E. (Eds) *The Making of Social Movements in Latin America*, Boulder, Colorado, Westview Press.

VANGUARDIA REVOLUCIONARIA (1978) 'El Emperador esta Desnudo'.

VANGUARDIA REVOLUCIONARIA (1982) 'El Partido Revolucionaria de Masas y la Mujer'.

VARGAS, V. (1982) 'El Movimiento Feminista en el Perú: Balances y Perspectivas', Lima, mimeo.

VARGAS, V. (1986) 'El Poder en Cuestión', *Viva*, September – October.

VARGAS, V. (1992) 'Women: Tragic Encounters with the Left', *NACLA*, Vol. XXV, No. 5, May.

Chapter 4

State-Building in the Absence of State Structures: Palestinian Women in the Occupied Territories and Shi'i Women in Lebanon

Maria Holt

The 'Middle East' is frequently portrayed as a labyrinth of insoluble problems and implacable hatreds. To the general Western public, it is an area where politics are coloured by religion, where Islam controls everyday life and where women's rights are routinely disregarded. It is also seen as a region of violence. Iran and Iraq, for example, fought each other for most of the 1980s, in a war that appeared incomprehensible to the outside world; in 1990, Iraq invaded its Arab neighbour Kuwait; a civil war between former North and South Yemen erupted in 1994; in 1995, Turkish troops entered northern Iraq to wage war against separatist Kurdish groups; and the Arabs and Israelis have been locked in belligerency for more than half a century.

Yet, in the recent past, in this region of apparent unreason, two events have occurred which give the casual observer hope that peace might at last be taking root. The first was the ending, in 1990, of the seemingly interminable civil war in Lebanon, coupled with the determination of all Lebanese factions that the country should remain undivided. This heartening conclusion is evidence of a shared commitment to the rebuilding of a war-shattered land and its institutions.

It is likely that many of the organizations which sprang up in Lebanon during the war years to keep alive as best they could the services that a government would normally be expected to provide (such as health and education) will remain, adapting themselves to new conditions. Although a large share of such responsibilities has always fallen on the private sector, one could argue that the institutions forged by the exigencies of war are bound to be qualitatively different to those emerging from peacetime wealth and choice.

The second startling event took place on 13 September 1993, when Yitzhak Rabin, the Prime Minister of Israel, and Yasser Arafat, Chairman of the Palestine Liberation Organization (PLO), shook hands on the lawn of the White House in Washington. Their mutually agreed Declaration of Principles (DoP), which had been secretly hammered out in the Norwegian capital Oslo, seemed to signal the opening of a new chapter in Palestinian history. Here at last was an opportunity for the Palestinians to start working towards the creation of a state of their own. They do not, of course, come to the business of state-building completely unprepared. Over the years, Palestinians in the West Bank and Gaza Strip, together with international agencies, have established a broad range of non-governmental organizations (NGOs) to cope with the needs of everyday life, as well as responding to the abnormal conditions caused by Israeli military occupation.

In this chapter, I will consider, first, how Palestinian women in the occupied territories have lived without formal state structures in a world of nation-states and, since September 1993, have adapted their NGOs to meet the requirements of an embryonic state. Second, I will discuss the implications for Lebanese Shi'i women of transforming their sectarian organizations, forged out of war and resistance, into elements of a functioning Lebanese state. I propose to examine, in particular, the alternative forms of organizations that have taken the place of such structures for the Lebanese and the Palestinians, how efficient these have been, and how they might translate into future state institutions. It seems clear that women have cooperated in male-led organizations and also made use of traditional frameworks, such as religion, the family and charitable societies, in order to meet basic needs.

Islamism and New Nation-States

I am arguing that Islam, as a culture and a religion, is a significant factor in the construction of a Palestinian national entity and a Lebanese national identity, and I want to develop this argument by drawing both parallels and contrasts between the experiences of the two communities of women. In each case, Islam has acted as a tool of legitimization, although the background conditions and the apparent outcomes are very different. However, by taking into account the oppressive nature of the Israeli occupation of Palestinian territory and the Lebanese civil war, I would like to suggest that 'Islam' – in the loosest sense – has been utilized to fill the gap which would normally be the preserve of state responsibilities. At the same time, it should not be forgotten that 'Islam', in this context, is somewhat removed from straightforward religious piety; it has been formalized into a full-blown political ideology, with a clearly defined mandate for radical change.

Both case studies considered here contain an element of Islamic revivalism (or Islamism). The quest for liberation from Western capitalism and Soviet-style communism, 'for indigenous solutions to indigenous problems, for an end to the state of dependency, and for economic, cultural, and political self-sufficiency is not an invention of Muslim revivalists, although it is now expressed through Islamic terminology and symbolism' (Hunter, 1988, p. xiii). There has been an upsurge in this brand of religious ideology in recent years.

Islamism, which is defined as 'twentieth-century movements for political Islam, usually aiming overtly or covertly at an Islamic state that would enforce at least some Islamic laws and customs, including those related to dress, sex segregation, and some economic measures and Qur'anic punishments' (Keddie, 1988, p. 15), embodies a response to marginalization, economic deprivation, political mismanagement and defeat. By no means a monolithic entity, it shapes itself to fit the history and characteristics of specific states and situations and is far from uniform in its modes of expression.

Indeed, the existence of Islamist strands in the Lebanese and the Palestinian cases has created two quite distinct tensions. For Palestinian women in the occupied territories, a conflict has arisen between the activities of well-established women's organizations, which tend to be secular in nature, and the more recent element of Islamist anger and activisim. In Lebanon, in contrast, tension occurs between the traditionally sectarian character of women's organization and the urgent new need for state-building along national lines.

While the two case studies are significantly different, they have much in common. Chief among shared characteristics is the violence which has accompanied the Palestinian struggle against Israeli occupation and the Lebanese Shi'i Muslim struggle against Maronite Christian hegemony, external interference and internal fragmentation. It is important to note both the negative and damaging effects of this sort of violence on women – together with the Islamic component of women's responses to violence within a traditional society – and, at the same time, the sorts of organizations which emerge and are nurtured by extreme adversity. Are they, for example, capable of sustaining themselves once the immediate threat has receded?

In addition, elements within both the Palestinian (Palestinian Muslims – like the vast majority of Muslims worldwide – belong to the Sunni branch of Islam; the Shi'a are a minority Islamic sect) and the Lebanese Shi'i communities have seized upon Islam as a powerful tool in the quest for liberation. Used in this way, 'Islam' has come to be associated with protest and even violent rebellion. But one should distinguish between *Islam* as a religion to which the majority of the population adheres and *Islamism* as a modern political movement. It is important to appreciate the differences between those who seek to make sense of an apparently hopeless situation from within the comfort of their religion, believing that fidelity to it can bring relief from intolerable pressures, and those who deliberately opt for participation in an activist movement based on an idealized form of early Islam.

State-Building and Islam

If we examine the attributes of the modern Western-defined state and the ways in which Islam is said to 'interfere' with the development of such a state and its typical structures, we will see that we need to discover more creative ways of thinking about and describing the process of state-building.

One of the explanations for the shape of a state is the way in which it came into being. For example, the Algerian state was created in the 1960s as a result of a violent and destructive struggle between French colonialism and Algerian nationalism, in which many thousands of people suffered or were killed. The ensuing state was based – at least in part – on a recognition of authenticity, in the sense of traditional Islamic values. But, as aspirations failed to be satisfied, the state itself rapidly became unstable. Eventually, a backlash occurred, in opposition both to the perceived corruption within the ruling regime and to the evident lack of democracy.

This raises the question of whether Islam and democracy are compatible and of course there is no single or simple answer. Much depends, firstly, on how 'democracy' is defined and, secondly, on individual circumstances. According to one commentator, 'Islam and democracy, though different in some respects, share a set of governing values in common' (Al-Akim, 1993, p. 78). Where they differ is on the question of sovereignty since, as far as Islam is concerned, 'Almighty God is the only sovereign' (*ibid.*). Democracy, on the other hand, 'rejoices in hotchpotch, melange, and controversy, for that is how novelty enters the world. Democracy loves indeterminacy and change-by-conflict-and-compromise. It fears and resists the absolutism of the Pure, the Grand Ideology. Defined in an ideological way, Islam potentially clashes with this basic feature of democracy because Islam itself is a special type of religion' (Keane, 1993, pp. 28–9). In some cases, Islam is held to be a perfected version of democracy, whereas elsewhere democracy is regarded as irrelevant in a situation where Qur'anic practices are respected.

To talk about 'state-building' when no state – or at least no functioning state – exists is to find oneself addressing, on the one hand, the essential state services which are lacking and, on the other, substitute forms that have arisen to take the place of the state. I will begin by assessing what the concept of 'state' might mean to the Palestinians and the rather different meaning it has for the Shi'a of Lebanon.

For well over half a century, Palestinians have been striving for a state of their own. Its meanings are partly symbolic and partly functional. An independent state requires the possession of borders which are internationally recognized and respected, a national government and a national flag. From the functional point of view, statehood implies the broad categories of administration, coercion and welfare.

The Palestinians have long had their own flag although, throughout the period of Israeli occupation, its use was utterly forbidden. As a response, during the intifada, it became an act of defiance to display the flag. As for administrative functions: from mid 1994, there have been two Palestinian 'autonomous areas' (in the Gaza Strip and the West Bank town of Jericho), even though overall control remains in the hands of the Israelis. A PLO-run 'authority' has come into being, which is tackling some of the tasks of government by creating 'ministries' and incorporating the activities of the former NGOs. A Palestinian police force has replaced Israeli troops in parts of the former 'occupied territories'. But it is very far from being an independent state commanding external recognition and internal respect.

In the Lebanese case, the state exists already but it has been devalued as a result of its unrepresentative nature and the chaos into which it sunk between 1975 and 1990. Although, in reality, it ceased to function, it never lost its symbolic significance. Even throughout the years of upheaval, the majority of Lebanese from all religious groupings continued to place their confidence in a reconstituted state, which would promote the interests of all citizens rather than an elite few. The inter-sect system has indeed 'proved itself a remarkably hardy plant in Lebanon' (Cobban, 1985, p. 234). In recent years, the demographic balance has begun to shift and a transfer of primacy – from the Maronites to the Shi'a – is likely to take place. But this, in the opinion of one observer, is likely to benefit the democratic process in Lebanon. The Maronite ascendancy, as she suggests, 'has grown increasingly fearful in its last years, of any free expression of the will of the non-Maronite *demos*; while a Shi-ite ascendancy should have little to fear from demography. Moreover, the Shi-ites have already shown, throughout their own sect's modern renaissance, considerable use of democratic ideals, and considerable use of democratic practice. The sect's own most ancient traditions also endorsed many aspects of a generally political stance' (*ibid.*, pp. 233–4).

Ideally, the state should offer some form of protection for human rights and the rights of the community; security from external threats; a framework in which to conduct family life; a distinctive national identity; and a government which is representative of the people. For the Palestinians, a state of their own has been a longstanding dream while, for the Lebanese Shi'a, the state was flawed and in need of reform. As far as women are concerned, the absence of a state has even graver implications. In general a vulnerable group, they tend to be the first to suffer when law and order break down, and they are liable to fall victim to a variety of abuses. In the occupied territories, for example, Palestinian women prisoners are routinely subjected to sexual harassment by Israeli soldiers who are well aware of the taboos imposed by the Islamic tradition of honour and shame.

It is not surprising, therefore, that in times of adversity, tradition and religion may well take precedence as members of a community strive to make sense of what is happening to them. Their responses go beyond personal life and have an effect on the ways in which the community operates. Religion is regarded as a refuge and also a source of empowerment. Women, too, have taken advantage of religion's empowering qualities.

This raises the question of the longer-term effects of Islam, in the sense of social structures and democratic practices. The examples discussed here illustrate notable differences of direction, suggesting that the influence of Islam varies depending on the particular social situation. In the case of the Palestinians, Islam has inspired a reaction against the secular establishment while, for the Lebanese Shi'a, it has served as a rallying point for communal justice within a national framework and, thus, has tended to emphasize rather more conservative elements.

While bearing in mind the important differences between the two struggles, I will examine briefly their histories and present situations, and then draw a number of conclusions based on women's experiences, their objectives and the apparent outcomes.

Palestinian Women in the West Bank and Gaza Strip

The Palestinians, since early this century when the Ottoman Empire collapsed, formally ending the Islamic caliphate (the Ottoman Empire ended when the Turks were defeated during the First World War; its former territories were divided – in the form of League of Nations Mandates – between the victors, Britain and France), have been striving for a national entity of their own. As they watched their Arab neighbours gradually gaining independent states, they were thwarted, first by the British Mandate and then by the Zionist plan for a Jewish homeland in Palestine. In 1948, when the new state of Israel came into being, the majority of the Palestinian population was forced into exile (the state of Israel was established as a result of the war between the Jewish settlers of Palestine and the armies of the surrounding Arab countries; in the process, the majority of the indigenous Palestinian Arab population, numbering approximately 725,000, were forced to flee from their homes, and became refugees in neighbouring countries, principally Lebanon, Syria and Jordan). Of the former territory known as 'Palestine', only the West Bank and Gaza Strip remained although these too, in the six-day war of 1967, fell under Israeli control. At the end of 1987, the Palestinian uprising, known by its Arabic name as the intifada, erupted.

Throughout the entire period and until the present day, women have been active in various forms of organization, the nature of which has changed over time. In the 1920s, urban middle-class and upper-class women established charitable societies devoted to the welfare of the poor, the sick and the vulnerable. These organizations were rooted in the cultural values of a society which, although containing a sizeable Palestinian Christian minority, may be defined as Arab and Islamic. Despite their avowedly non-political stance, they could not help but be affected by the increasingly volatile political situation.

By the 1930s, the situation had deteriorated and the Palestinian population turned to mass revolt. The genuinely popular uprising of 1936–39, often referred to as the 'first intifada', mobilized the entire community, including its female members; since it utilized 'Islam' as a motivating force, their participation was regarded as legitimate.

After 1948, the Palestinians were dispersed and forms of organization changed to meet new needs. They can be broadly divided into categories of welfare and resistance, and women were active in both. After the formation of the PLO in 1964 – and of its female wing the General Union of Palestinian Women (GUPW) in 1965 – and the Israeli occupation of the West Bank and Gaza Strip in 1967, women's organizations began to undergo a process of radicalization, which may be attributed partly to increased access to education and partly to the growing urgency of the situation. Palestinians were despairing of their plight ever being resolved.

The modern 'women's movement' was forged 'out of a nationalist and grassroots activism, and nurtured by the liberating zeal of the *intifada* during its initial phase' (Usher, 1994, p. 17). It started in the latter part of the 1970s, when a number of women's committees were formed. Originally offshoots of the four principal nationalist factions (Fatah, the Popular Front for the Liberation of Palestine (PFLP), the Democratic Front for the Liberation of Palestine (DFLP), and the former Communist – now People's – Party), the committees 'sought to mobilise thousands of women from villages and camps and not just from the urban centres which had been the domain of the traditional women's charitable societies offering relief to the poor' (Ramsden and Senker, 1993, p. 61).

With the intifada, the women's committees assumed vital functions, such as the provision of popular education when schools and colleges were closed by the military authorities, the creation of a home economy so that it would no longer be necessary to rely on Israeli products, and the assumption of income-generating activities as increasing numbers of men either migrated in search of work or were killed or imprisoned by the Israelis. In addition, women were also expected to fulfil their traditional roles of preserving the Palestinian national identity and protecting their children.

There have been two outcomes for women as a result of the experiences of the intifada. The first may be described as a conservative backlash, accompanied by a growth in Islamic feeling amongst segments of the Palestinian population. This has affected women's lives in ways which have been both positive and less positive. As far as the enforcement of more modest dress and the removal of choice for women is concerned, the impact is regarded by many Palestinian women as undesirable and even oppressive. But the burgeoning Islamist movement has also exerted an empowering influence on a significant segment of the female population which had previously felt itself to be helpless and alienated. The second outcome, in contrast, has been the consolidation of a feminist agenda.

With the signing of the so-called 'Oslo accord' in September 1993 and the 'Gaza-Jericho first' agreement in May 1994 (whereby a large portion of the Gaza Strip and an enclave around the West Bank town of Jericho were handed over to a 'Palestine National Authority'), Palestinians had hoped to start moving towards democratic elections and eventually self-determination. But progress has been infuriatingly slow.

The agreement between Israel and the PLO has attracted a rapidly growing number of critics from all sections of both communities. While Palestinians accuse Israel of dragging its feet and betraying the spirit of reconciliation enshrined in the DoP, Israelis argue that, as the PLO is unable to control the extremists within its own borders, it should not be trusted to run a state. The latter part of 1994 and first half of 1995 witnessed escalating violence and fragmentation both inside the PLO-controlled zone and in Israel itself. As they are forced to endure spiralling economic hardship and stagnation on the political front, many Palestinians feel bitter, disappointed and rebellious. A rising number, particularly of young men, are being drawn to the evidently more spectacularly successful tactics of Islamist groups such as Hamas and Islamic Jihad.

As the prospect of an independent Palestinian state grows more remote, what effects are the new realities having on Palestinian women? I will review very briefly the sorts of projects undertaken by women during the intifada, the effectiveness of these projects and their ability to be sustained under changed circumstances, and the relationship between women and the Palestine National Authority (PNA).

Women's Participation in the Intifada

There are two competing schools of thought regarding the PNA. The first accuses it of failing adequately to represent women (few women have been appointed to PNA posts; there is only one female minister; and women's issues have not been high on the agenda) and, worse, of relegating them to a position of subservience. According to this scenario, women must fight back in order to gain the rights to which they are entitled as full participants in the struggle. This, of course, entails working within the existing system, however imperfect it may seem. It also involves preserving one's faith in the floundering peace process.

An alternative perspective regards the PNA as illegitimate and the current peace process as a betrayal of Palestinian national aspirations. The Oslo agreement, in the words of one critic, 'which is based on anti-democratic, arbitrary and anti-collective foundations, has the potential to empty the women's movement of much of its historical gains, particularly the recent achievements made during the *Intifada*' (Abdo, 1994, p. 12). Opposition to the accord is wide-ranging and includes both leftist and Islamist women.

During the intifada (which began in December 1987 in the Gaza Strip), women were active participants in the struggle to end the Israeli occupation and to create an independent Palestinian state. Their participation took many forms (for example, spontaneous street protests against the Israeli military presence, the formation of committees to coordinate support activities, and the setting up of production cooperatives). Women also 'discussed politics (often for the first time), and urged people who remained unconvinced to participate in the uprising' (Hiltermann, 1991, p. 50).

Production projects by women were 'part of the larger movement in the Occupied Territories to boycott Israeli goods and to develop the local Palestinian economy' (*Tanmiya*, December 1989, p. 8). Apart from offering an alternative to Israeli goods, these projects were supposed to increase 'women's economic independence, empowerment and mobilisation in society' (*ibid.*). In what has been described as 'the only clear effort at totally independent action during the uprising' (Hiltermann, 1991, pp. 51–2), the women's productive cooperatives contributed positively to the well-being of the community.

Although women's involvement in such projects failed to transform their status within the larger society, change has begun to occur and, even if resistance to this change 'is stiff, women's issues have been put on the agenda and women for the first time have begun to discuss their status in society' (Hiltermann, 1991, p. 52). In the meantime, however, the Islamist tendency in Palestinian society, as a result of a wide range of welfare services introduced by the Islamic Resistance Movement (Hamas) and Islamic Jihad, has strengthened.

The reality of Palestinian women's determination to add their concerns to the political agenda became even more apparent after the signing of the DoP. The conflict is sometimes presented as one between Hamas and the 'women's movement'. With self-rule, for example, comes the vitally important question of legislation and the impact that the 'social challenge' of the Islamists is having on the law-making process. In December 1993, the first draft of the PNA's Basic Law was presented to the women's committees. Its lack of a satisfactory commitment to the affirmation of equality between the sexes generated a fierce debate 'within the women's movement as to whether the correct posture vis-à-vis the Islamists should be one of outright rejection on the grounds of religious pluralism' or of fighting 'for a progressive interpretation of Islamic law' (Usher, 1994, p. 17).

In response, women wasted no time in preparing their own draft document of principles of women's rights. Presented to the public in August 1994, the declaration called for a parliamentary democratic system of government, in which governance 'will be based on principles of social justice, equality and no discrimination in public rights against men or women' (*Palestine Report*, 7 August 1994, p. 10). The document demanded, in specific terms, equal political, civil, economic, social and cultural rights for women, to be enshrined in legislation, but it was 'tellingly circumspect on the crucial issues of family law and personal status' (Usher, 1994, p. 17).

In the view of Eileen Kuttab, a member of the Women's Document Committee, the draft document is intended 'as a tool for struggle, to empower women on a grassroots level, to promote gender consciousness and awareness around social and political issues which in turn will mobilize women and define a framework for action' (*News From Within*, September 1994, p. 10).

However, there are a number of difficulties, both with this particular example of democratic participation and with the vision of women's rights which it embodies. To begin with, the PNA, in the absence of democratic elections and in the face of continuing Israeli and Palestinian violence, has behaved in ways which are considered profoundly undemocratic and authoritarian. The Oslo agreement, in the view of one critic, 'has ushered in a new Palestinian era in which arbitrary decisions have come to replace collective or, at least consultative processes previously practiced within the PLO structure.

It . . . bears the seeds for the growth of the dictatorship of the father figure or patriarch – as in regimes with which we have become too familiar in our Arab world' (Abdo, 1994, p. 12). This atmosphere of repression does not bode well for women.

At the same time, the document of women's rights – even if it were to be accepted by the PNA – by no means represents the views of all Palestinian women. Some are strongly opposed to this model of 'women's liberation' and consider it irrelevant to their concerns. There are two main arguments, one emanating from the Islamist strand in Palestinian political thought and the other from the on-going conflict between 'political' and 'feminist' concerns.

At a roundtable discussion, organized by the Women's Studies Center at Birzeit University (in the West Bank), on 20 March 1995, Suha Barghouti, of the General Union of Palestinian Women, commented on the 'historical prevalence of the political agenda over the feminist agenda within the women's movement'. She concluded that the slogan of 'balancing the national and feminist agendas' remained just a slogan 'and is not reflected in any of the programs of the various women's centers or committees' (*News From Within*, April 1995, p. 5).

But Amal Khreisheh, of the Women's Work Society, argued that one of the issues which should be reflected in the future plans being considered by the women's movement is the development of a feminist identity. 'What I need', she said, 'is recognition of my abilities and potential, the recognition of my role – not only recognition but also appreciation of this role . . . I think that this need should be reflected in our plans, in the form of developing a feminist consciousness through various mechanisms' (*ibid.*).

Women who identify with the Islamist parties, on the other hand, are convinced that 'Islam is the solution'. The Oslo agreement, in their opinion, is a betrayal of Palestinian national aspirations. They cannot, therefore, give their support to the PNA. Together with their male colleagues, these women have contributed to a comprehensive social welfare programme to assist the less well-off members of their society. One of the principal reasons why the Islamist movement is gaining in popularity, particularly in the Gaza Strip, is that it attempts to satisfy the basic needs of the population whilst, at the same time, mounting a determined resistance to continuing Israeli oppression. It is a movement to which many women can relate in as far as it respects religion, traditional values and the badly battered Palestinian identity.

Taking a broader perspective, it can be argued that organization-building by Palestinian women, both during the intifada and in the wake of the Oslo agreement, has been successful in the short term in the sense that it has met immediate needs (such as education, self-sufficiency, and the provision of support services for prisoners and the families of those killed by the Israeli authorities). At the end of 1994, there were 174 women's NGOs in the West Bank (including east Jerusalem) and Gaza Strip, including those registered as charitable societies. Although some of these groups have introduced gender as a key issue, others have tended to concentrate on the broader question of women's participation in the development process as a whole (*Tanmiya*, December 1994, p. 5).

However, in terms of embryonic state-building, the activities of women's organizations have, by and large, been ineffective. They have been unable to provide women with greater economic independence or to alter the basic social structures. With the coming of PNA control in Gaza and Jericho, the mechanisms of government are almost entirely in the hands of men, and women are forced to struggle even to have their concerns inserted into the national agenda. Beyond this, there is dissension among women themselves. The secular women's movement is split between those who feel that support for the PNA is the only way forward and those who oppose its arbitrary use of authority. As women's rights activist Islah Jad remarked, 'If women don't utilise the cultural space that autonomy affords to pursue their own agenda, if we focus exclusively on the narrow political question as to whether we're for or against the PNA, then in effect we are giving up the social and legal terrain to Hamas' (quoted by Usher, 1994, p. 18).

In the meantime, factionalism and ideological discord have made even the minimum consensus elusive. One would hope that as the Israelis are persuaded to make concessions and democratic elections in the PNA-controlled areas finally take place, the terms of the debate will widen and women from all strands of opinion will at last be able to make their voices heard.

Lebanese Shi'i Women

The characteristics of the Lebanese case vary significantly, and the outcome, too, promises to be somewhat different. This is largely due to history, circumstances and the nature of the struggle. Although a state has existed since Lebanon gained its formal independence from the French in 1943, it has been perceived by many as being unfair and unrepresentative. Certain groups have felt disadvantaged, especially the Shi'a, who are mainly located in the south of the country, the southern suburbs of Beirut and the Bekaa Valley, and are now believed to be the largest single sect. Their relative powerlessness was institutionalized by the Lebanese political system. The unwritten 'National Pact' of 1943 reflected the demographic realities of the time, as recorded by Lebanon's only census (carried out in 1932); it reserved the presidency for a Maronite Christian, the Prime Ministerial post for a Sunni Muslim and the position of Speaker of the Chamber of Deputies (Parliament) for a Shi'i Muslim.

During the 1960s, in response to their marginalized status, the Shi'a in southern Lebanon began to organize on their own behalf, under the leadership of the Iranian-born religious leader Imam Musa al-Sadr, who founded *Harakat al-Mahrumin* (Movement of the Deprived). The group's non-violent campaign for greater justice within the existing Lebanese system bore very little fruit and in response to a series of factors, including a continuing lack of representation at the national level, the escalating civil war, Palestinian resistance activities in the south, regular and violent cross-border incursions by the Israelis and, in 1978, the disappearance of Musa al-Sadr, the Shi'a turned to greater militancy in the shape of the Amal militia.

In 1982, after the massive Israeli invasion of Lebanon, another Shi'i militia, Hizbullah (the party of God), was formed. Taking the 1979 Iranian Revolution and the leadership of the Ayatollah Khomeini as its inspiration, Hizbullah began its existence by advocating an Islamic state in Lebanon. In an Open Letter addressed to 'the Downtrodden in Lebanon and in the World', dated February 1985, the group stated 'we do not wish to impose Islam on anybody . . . But we stress that we are convinced of Islam as a faith, system, thought, and rule and we urge all to recognize it and to resort to its law' (quoted in Norton, 1987, p. 175). Hizbullah does not possess a structure that is recognizable in the Western sense. It has not, for example, an official membership list. In its early stages, it gained strength from absorbing smaller, like-minded movements (Wright, 1988, p. 66).

From the start, Amal and Hizbullah – as a result of their opposing visions of the best way to reform the Lebanese political system – were bitter enemies and, in the latter part of the 1980s, open warfare broke out between them. Since the 1989 Taif Agreement, however, which brought an end to the civil war, they have both taken an active part in the reformed political system. After the general election in 1992, the two parties gained seats in the Lebanese parliament; both are committed to reforming the political system through peaceful means, although Hizbullah continues to fight the Israeli occupation of a broad strip of southern Lebanon, using the medium of armed struggle. It insists that the 'Islamization' of Lebanon will come in time or, in the words of its supporters, 'when people are ready'.

As a result of the very long civil war in Lebanon and the almost total social breakdown, women have had little opportunity to form their own organizations. Unlike the Palestinian example, there is no well-developed 'women's movement'. Most organizing has taken place exclusively within the confines of religious communities and in response to adverse and often desperate conditions. Before his disappearance, for example, Musa al-Sadr established a number of social institutions, such as schools and orphanages, in the south of the country. These still exist; indeed, the Imam Sadr Foundation in the southern city of Tyre, now run by the vanished Imam's sister Rabab al-Sadr, is flourishing. It should be understood that, in the absence of overall government control or national programmes, an individual's first loyalty tended to be towards his or her particular community and it was the social welfare organizations within each community which sought to take care of their own people.

As in the case of Palestinian women in the occupied territories, Lebanese Shi'i women have had no choice but to respond to the needs created by war, invasion and occupation; in the process, their identity has begun to change. Women in the south of Lebanon speak proudly of their resistance activities during the various Israeli invasions of their country. These fall mainly into the category of support: support for the male fighters by smuggling weapons and messages, support for the family and protection of their children during the absence of the men, and support of each other in times of loneliness and desperation. On the whole, women have not so much been instigators as followers, and this is in line with the Islamic concept of the appropriate role for women during times of war. The role model most often cited by the Shi'a is Zaynab, granddaughter of the Prophet Muhammad, who supported her brother Husain on the battlefield at Karbala in 680 CE.

Despite the traditional preference for working within sectarian boundaries, the war years witnessed efforts by women – in the name of reconciliation – to cross the confessional divide. These frequently took the shape of organizations aimed at alleviating the misery and physical suffering caused by the violence. For example, the Lebanese Red Cross kept going throughout the civil war and was active all across the country. Largely staffed by women volunteers, it was the only organization to cross between Muslim and Christian areas. The preponderance of female workers is explained by the fact that 'women had more free time' (interview with Mrs Nadya Saab of the Lebanese Red Cross, Beirut, 16 April 1994).

Another example is the Child and Mother Welfare Association. Situated in a mainly Muslim area of West Beirut, it has tended, on the whole, to assist the Muslim population, although other sects are not excluded. As with the Red Cross, the staff are almost all women. During the war, they explain, in the absence of a government, non-governmental organizations took over many badly needed functions, such as the distribution of food, shelter and clothing. Although the war has ended, the Association is busier than ever. It includes a home for the elderly, a hospital and a nursery school; other departments are planned (interview with some of the women on the board of the Child and Mother Welfare Association, Beirut, 21 April 1994).

Organizations with a more sectarian (in this case Shi'i) base include the Lebanese Welfare Association for the Handicapped, which was established in 1983 by Mrs Randa Berri (wife of Nabih Berri, Speaker of the Lebanese Chamber of Deputies). This very active and well-funded organization operates clinics for the handicapped in the south of the country, Beirut and the Bekaa Valley. It makes available medical, educational, social and psychological rehabilitation facilities and all its services are provided free of charge to the needy, disabled as a result of the war (interview with Mrs Randa Berri, Beirut, 11 April 1994).

These organizations have moved, with apparent ease and little choice, from wartime relief work to the provision of services to sectors of the community which are being neglected by the government. However, when speaking to the women involved with organizations of this kind, one is struck by the elitist nature of their approach. They have the appearance of classic 'do-gooders', enabled by wealthy backgrounds or the position of their husbands to devote themselves to charitable endeavours on behalf of the more distressed members of their society. Such organizations, one could argue, are in danger of relieving the recently restored national government of all sense of responsibility.

An organization that works along somewhat different – and more specifically Shi'i – lines is the Martyrs' Foundation, established by Hizbullah in 1982. Under its umbrella are hospitals, schools, nurseries, a nursing institute, a training college for teachers, orphanages and projects aimed at training women. Funding for the Foundation's work comes from private sources and there is virtually no contact with the government.

Women are able to benefit from the organization's services in numerous ways: the majority of nurses, for example, are female; women are also trained in dressmaking, hairdressing, typing, knitting, accounting and other skills. In addition, women whose husbands have been 'martyred' are assisted with the care and education of their children. This organization, with its efficient and comprehensive services, appears almost to be a substitute for the government. It disregards the supposed role of a government and its existence means that individuals tend to move within the exclusive confines of their sect, with its particular values and moral code. Rather than being part of a greater Lebanese entity, members of this community restrict themselves to a category called 'Shi'a'. This suggests that efforts at national cohesion or even the acceptance of governmental authority will be difficult.

It is entirely possible, however, that the attitudes developed by such patterns of behaviour and organization will contribute positively to the currrent process of Lebanese state-building. Women have found hitherto unimagined strength and resilience as a result of their participation in violent upheaval. They are also better educated, have access to more career choices and are gaining the confidence to voice their opinions. This too, they say, is an integral part of Islam's teachings on the role of women.

Although, with the coming of peace, national non-sectarian women's organizations are beginning to be established and a 'women's movement' is taking shape, it is difficult for many to cross the divide. They have become accustomed to operating within a religious framework. In addition, there has been an upsurge of Islamic consciousness, which has resulted in more modest dress and a generally more pious approach to life. It should be stressed that not all women are participating in the religous revival; many are avowedly secular and striving to improve the lot of all women. A great many individual women from all communities mix freely with each other and cooperate professionally, socially and politically.

Concluding Remarks

It is clear that both parallels and contrasts exist between the two case studies described above. Beginning in the early part of this century, Palestinian women have moved from social welfare organizations rooted in the country's traditional Islamic culture to secular political activism and participation in the construction of a future democratic state. They have worked in a wide variety of ways, from spontaneous demonstration to formal organization. In common with societies elsewhere, an elite has blazed the trail and attempted to forge a women's agenda based on greater equality. But this has led to disagreement as to whether national or feminist goals should take priority.

At the same time, in response to the harshness of the Israeli occupation, the lack of a satisfactory resolution to the conflict and indifference on the part of the international community, an Islamic revivalist movement has emerged. This appeals to women on two levels: it attracts many people – both men and women – because it appears to stem directly from – and be nurtured by – familiar comforting tradition; to others, the Islamist movement offers an intoxicating mix of pride and empowerment. Increasing numbers of women, therefore, are enthusiastically veiling themselves and adopting a more consciously pious lifestyle.

A significant number of Palestinian women, however, are alarmed by the Islamic trend. They are afraid that it may impinge upon their lives and remove the precariously small choices they have achieved over the years. Palestinian society remains a deeply conservative one; even supposedly 'progressive' politically active men are reluctant to openly support women's demands for greater equality and representation within the governing authority. In the West Bank and Gaza Strip, a battle is being fought among women's groups to set the agenda for the coming state.

In Lebanon – a very different society – the civil war had the effect of retarding the embryonic women's movement. In its place, sectarian and social welfare groups sprang up to alleviate the physical and psychological suffering caused by long-term violence. The Shi'i population occupy a special place in the Lebanese mosaic. In response to their traditionally powerless position in the political system and inspired by the Iranian Revolution of 1979, the Shi'a joined in the Islamic revival which was sweeping across the Middle East.

Although this trend appeared to contradict general moves towards 'modernization' (in the sense of Westernization), the modernizing project has frequently clashed with moral and communal values; it has been perceived as favouring particular groups over others, and tends to be dismissed as Western interference. As with Palestinian Islamists, large numbers of Lebanese Shi'i women – as a result of their involvement with groups such as Hizbullah and Amal – have experienced an enhanced sense of empowerment. They believe that they can influence events in their country and contribute towards the reform of the outdated political system. At the same time, as in the Palestinian case, a more 'secular' movement for women's rights in a non-sectarian state is taking shape.

In both the Lebanese and the Palestinian examples, Islam has played a profoundly important role in the quest for statehood. It has helped, in the first place, to define national identity and, secondly, to inspire greater confidence. This brand of Islam, which is politically tinged, is by no means at odds with rights and opportunities for women. On the contrary, Islam stresses that women must be educated; they may if they wish pursue careers; and they are entitled to respect and dignity within the family.

In both cases, it seems inevitable that a clash will occur between two clearly delineated 'sides': the religious and the secular. But the situation is far from clear-cut. There are bound to be battles ahead for both Lebanese Shi'i and Palestinian women in their long struggle for statehood. It may be that, for both, the use of Islam as a political weapon and an organizational framework will be a necessary but temporary phase out of which genuinely indigenous state models will emerge.

Bibliography

ABDO, NAHLA (1994) 'Beyond Hegemonic Male Discourse: Palestinian Women and the New Challenges', *News From Within*, June.

AL-AKIM, HASSAN (1993) 'Islam and Democracy: Mutually Reinforcing or Incompatible', in TAMIMI, AZZAM (Ed.) *Power-Sharing Islam?*, London, Liberty for Muslim World Publications.

AMNESTY INTERNATIONAL (1995) *Human Rights are Women's Rights*, London, Amnesty International.

COBBAN, HELENA (1985, reprinted 1987) *The Making of Modern Lebanon*, London, Hutchinson.

HILTERMANN, JOOST R. (1991) 'The Women's Movement during the Uprising', *Journal of Palestine Studies*, Vol. XX, No. 3 (Spring).

HUNTER, SHIREEN T. (Ed.) (1988) *The Politics of Islamic Revivalism: Diversity and Unity*, Bloomington and Indianapolis, Indiana University Press.

KEANE, JOHN (1993) 'Power-Sharing Islam?', in TAMIMI, AZZAM (Ed.) *Power-Sharing Islam?*, London, Liberty for Muslim World Publications.

KEDDIE, NIKKI R. (1988) 'Ideology, Society and the State in Post-Colonial Muslim Societies', in HALLIDAY, FRED and ALAVI, HAMZA (Eds) *State and Ideology in the Middle East and Pakistan*, Basingstoke, Macmillan Education.

News From Within (1994) 'The Women's Document: A Tool for Women's Empowerment and Struggle', an Interview with Eileen Kuttab, Vol. X, No. 9 (September).

News From Within (1995) 'The Future of the Palestinian Women's Movement: Continued Struggle – New Agendas', Roundtable Organized by the Women's Studies Center of Birzeit University, Vol. XI, No. 4 (April).

NORTON, AUGUSTUS RICHARD (1987) *Amal and the Shi'a: Struggle for the Soul of Lebanon*, Austin, University of Texas Press.

Palestine Report (1994) 'Principles of Women's Legal Status', 7 August.

RAMSDEN, SALLY and SENKER, CATH (Eds) (1993) *Learning the Hard Way: Palestinian Education in the West Bank, Gaza Strip and Israel* (report from the 1993 WUS Study Tour), London, World University Service (UK).

TAMIMI, AZZAM (Ed.) (1993) *Power-Sharing Islam?*, London, Liberty for Muslim World Publications.

TANMIYA (1989) 'Made by Women' December.

TANMIYA (1991) 'Women: Twice Self-Reliant' September.

TANMIYA (1994) 'Women in Development' December.

USHER, GRAHAM (1994) 'Women, Islam and the Law in Palestinian Society', *Middle East International*, 23 September.

WRIGHT, ROBIN (1988) 'Lebanon', in HUNTER, SHIREEN T. (Ed.) *The Politics of Islamic Revivalism: Diversity and Unity*, Bloomington and Indianapolis, Indiana University Press.

Chapter 5

En-Gendering the Nation-State: Women, Patriarchy and Politics in Algeria

Malika Mehdid

This review offers a case study from Algeria on the role played by gender politics – alongside other processes of struggle around class, culture, language and religion – in state formation and nation-building. Algeria has become, in view of the tragic events of the last three years, a compelling case of the relationship between women and the state in the Third World, a relationship that is necessarily negotiated and mediated by patriarchy and history. The study renders in a very summary fashion an extremely complex and intricate set of processes and power relations. It is worth noting that current theoretical work on women and the state tends to focus on the impact of the state and related issues of political and economic development on the position of women. The analytical thrust of the present chapter however lies – predominantly but not exclusively – in addressing the question of the impact of gender on the state; in other words how the nation-state is itself produced and genderized by the multiform antagonisms and conflicts informing its historical transformations.

The analysis is not structured into successive historical stages (as shown below) for chronological order but instead indicates overlapping stages in the processes of state transformations, nation-building and the concomitant construction of gender and manipulation of sexual politics as aspects of these changes.[1]

The Pre-independence Situation: Gender, Colonialism and Nationalism

Broadly speaking, the birth of the modern nation-state in Algeria is rooted in a long history of domination and control by outside forces and of indigenous resistance in sporadic or organized forms, often lacking a wide mobilization under the leadership of a particular ruler. On the other hand, tribal warfare and inter-clan conflicts allowed a territorialization of collective identity under specific banners with supreme authority granted to local patriarchs and limited accountability to monarchs or figures vested, at least after the Islamic conquest of North Africa, with the power of the Caliphate, head of the *Umma* or the Islamic Nation. In this pre-modern era, women had rigidly defined roles, mainly attached to the domestic world, although a degree of mobility was enjoyed by rural women. Their lives shared social features of sexual segregation and patriarchal organization with other societies on both sides of the Mediterranean sea. Furthermore, few changes seem to have drastically altered the status of women in the modern period although class, religion and rural or urban locations were again variables which had a significant impact upon women and differentiated between them. Historical developments too have a determining effect on the social position of women, their sense of identity and their relation to power. In the case of Algeria, a dramatic historical event in the modern period, one which had – and still has – profound effects on the development of Algerian nationhood is the country's subjection to French colonial rule from 1830 to 1962. The consequences for women and gender relations were far-reaching.

Right from its early stages, colonialism provided the context within which a modern discourse on the nation and national identity initially emerged. In the first clashes with the French armada before it even landed on the North African coast, there developed a discourse of nationhood and statehood. More particularly, it was Emir Abdlekader, an eminent leader and patriarch, who first elaborated a discourse of resistance during a bitter fight for independence he engaged in with his armies against the French invading troops for more than three decades. He led the anti-colonial struggle claiming, in nationalistic rather than provincial or sectarian terms, the territorial integrity of Algeria with its specific identity, history and cultural heritage. In such a frame of representation, Algeria, not as a nation yet but as an idea of nation to be contained within and beyond physical frontiers, was constructed as a legitimate national entity, only accountable to itself, clearly demarcated from its earlier position as a province of the Ottoman empire. Later, this discourse of nationhood found further legitimacy and coherence in subsequent movements of opposition, notably in the campaign of nationalism led in the early part of this century by another prominent patriarch, Messali El Hadj. He gathered and conceptualized the various elements of Algerian culture and history into a unified ideology of nationalism.

In spite of the divergence of programmes and political goals between various political movements throughout colonization, strong emphasis was consistently laid on the need to protect the 'Arabo-Islamic' family, a family defined in universal terms, to the exclusion of varied forms, values and frames of identity. The role assigned to females was usually a traditional one, to keep them in the realm of domesticity. This was in sharp contrast to discourses on women and the family being developed then by male reformers and nationalists in the rest of the region, especially in Iran, Turkey and Egypt. These nationalists saw the emancipation of women as necessary to the modernization of their countries. Later, with the rise of the movement of cultural resistance initiated by a number of theologians or *Ulemas* in Algeria (during the 1930s), ideas about women's progress were discussed but without the emancipatory drive of similar debates in the Middle East. Consequently, there were no sensational public gestures of unveiling the indigenous woman, events recorded by history in these other societies. The total interpenetration of the discourses between family and nation, between sexual politics and nationalism, was illustrated by the religiously based programmes of the *Ulemas* who outlined the necessity for young girls to receive moral education to enable them to raise the future members of the nation.

Consistently, throughout the colonial era, male reformist discourses or programmes of resistance overtly projected women as reproducers of the family at one level but, beyond that biologically and culturally determined role, as reproducers of the nation itself and embodiments of ideas of Nation and collective identity. Algeria, the Islamic religion, the Arabic language and the patriarchal family appeared to constitute components of national identity and the consciousness of the colonized Algerian, implicitly understood to be male. The major revolutionary movement which gathered momentum between the two world wars erupted in the final and dramatic war of liberation in November 1954; it inherited the puritan outlook of previous movements although its orientation was more secular. The active role adopted by large numbers of women from different backgrounds in the armed resistance, who often entered the war on their own initiative, was one of the most remarkable facts of the liberation struggle, noted and acclaimed internationally. However, women did not manage to undermine the rigid gender ideology already embedded in the discourses of political movements. Women's effective role, as implicitly projected by revolutionaries, was conceived of purely at the level of the symbolic, as mothers of the Nation, reproducers of its militants as well as guardians of its cultural memory and ancestral values. The painful birth of the modern nation-state in Algeria is thus rooted in a historical process, resolutely marked by a masculinist sense of popular consciousness; such a process was reinforced by the colonial impact produced by an all-embracing system of 'apartheid' and endured by the indigenous population for more than 130 years.

Imperial historical relations in Algeria were gendered as they reflected and reconstructed a traditional segregational and hierarchical model of social and sexual interactions. Within Algeria, this reading suggests that history itself becomes a typically male enterprise for the assertion of a European male desire. Western hegemony is equated with maleness, the dominated is associated with the female principle, the former having entered history through conquest and rape of the land/culture defeated, the latter having been vanquished in its forced subjection to the colonial act, chased out of history. In a symbolic formulation, the land, culture and community thus conquered have become 'feminized', that is, made to correspond to a model of femininity, resisting and yielding to a movement thrusting forward for conquest and domination.

Post-independence social and political developments that followed the move towards democratization reaffirmed the broad formulations of the present thesis about the 'en-gendering' of the Algerian nation-state by historical discourses on the family, women and identity which, in turn, mediated and

articulated ideologies of political resistance. However, if women were traditionally projected, for a long time, in a conventional patriarchal culture, as
reproducers of notions of the sacred *Umma* and of its symbolic boundaries,
their conceptual stand will shift to radically altered roles as they become
producers of the nation and of gendered meanings of resistance. Post-colonial
state-building thus becomes a process gendered in many ways and is ultimately
shaped by secular women, mostly feminists and educated women as a whole,
in shifting settings of power relations indelibly influenced by new opposition
forces, among them the women's movement which is by far the most
revolutionary.

The Post-Independence Situation

A Socialist Phase: State-Building, Populism and Patriarchy

The negotiations which took place between nationalists (mostly male) during
the last anti-colonial armed struggle (November 1954 to July 1962) laid the
fragile foundations of the future nation-state in Algeria. The tensions of those
early debates surfaced again in post-colonial power struggles and crystallized
in debates around identity, culture and ideology. The unresolved tension of
those early conflicts also led to the fractures experienced by the national scene
in the last few years.

The immediate post-independence phase, especially the Boumediene era
(1965–78) was marked by the presence of a dynamic polity which, in spite of its
internal conflicts and divisions, managed to present an all-convincing image
of strength and coherence. The state embarked on projects of development
requiring intensive urbanization and industrialization, all animated by the
revolutionary spirit of November as articulated by the regime's rhetoric. But
the gender politics of the state reflected the ambiguities of its political stand
and affected the radicalism of its conception of modernization and social
change. Soon enough, signs of a clash between the modernizing tendencies of
the state and the more conservative ideologies that characterized both the
state apparatus and social practices and discourses became apparent. These
ambiguities were yet again mediated by a discourse on the Family and the
Nation, the former requiring the control of women and the latter the control
of resources, national borders and projects of development.

Post-independence dilemmas were partly and temporarily resolved in a
manipulation of an array of ideologies such as Pan-Arabism, Arab socialism,
and Islamism which fostered a universal discourse of cultural authenticity.
Some interpretations of these various frameworks created contradictions for
their implementation: for instance, for many Islamists socialism was ubiquitous within the spirit of Islam, so no definite position has yet been adopted in
spite of the growing number of studies on the subject. However, they all
accommodate a conservative and male-determined conception of sexual poli-

tics, so it is hardly surprising to find that there seems to be less difference of opinion, especially among fundamentalist men, as to whether the Qur'anic formulations on women could actually translate into their liberation from the dominance of men.

Broadly, this initial phase of post-colonial state formation relied on two principles forged by early nationalist ideology, an implicit principle of patriarchy as social organization and an explicit principle of a 'specific' socialism as economic model, both principles claiming an authority derived from Arab-Islamic doctrine. This anchoring of the 'Revolution' as delivered by national discourses in past cultural frameworks was contradictory, creating an ambiguous interrelation between superstructure and infrastructure. Socialism was unproblematically projected as a new modernizing force for both relations of production and social relations. At the same time, a phallocratic understanding of the cultural and religious heritage survived the revolutionary upheavals of colonial and post-colonial changes. Therefore, while a new sense of national identity for both men and women was built, it required a total allegiance to the limited discourses of tradition and socialism developed by an authoritarian and populist state. The subsequent events of the country's political life over the next three decades were to be profoundly affected by successive attempts at defining citizenship and projects of society predicated on an awkward synthesis of notions of tradition and modernity, the former being derived from a supposedly harmonious and monolithically constructed cultural heritage (basically Pan-Arabism and Islam) and the latter embodied in the development projects of an apparently modern state.

The need to uphold the principles of both patriarchal control and socialist economic organization militated, in retrospect, against the development within national discourses (in their authoritative or popular forms) of heterogeneous constructions of the genders as well as against cultural and linguistic diversity. This enforced homogeneity conveyed by official rhetoric was universalized in the name of socialist egalitarian values which would resolve class inequalities as well as gender asymmetry. Therefore, a uniform but tension-ridden identity is structured within an apparently non-conflictual nation-state. Such a discursive endeavour was seen, doubtless, as essential to the construction of what the Algerian sociologist Boutheina Cheriet called a 'consensus'[2] – seen, doubtless, as necessary to the birth of a unified and strong nation-state. Consequently, voices of dissidence or claims for difference and diversity were to be swiftly suppressed or undermined as an attack against Arabo-Islamism, the sovereign nation and the family.

This initial post-colonial phase of state formation therefore articulated gender on the basis of a dualistic notion of social and material relations. This dualism relied on the combination of two organizing principles, patriarchy and socialism, within an ideology of Pan-Arabism and Islamism. As a result, social structures and gender relations were upheld and reproduced by the state which made it into a patriarchal state. However, gender divisions and sexism were not confined to social relations but equally re-enacted by a number of politically, culturally and religiously based discourses formulated within and outside the realm of the state.

However, events defeated demagogy and the hold of the state's discourse on women weakened as they were largely excluded from the exercise of political power; sexual segregation was sustained by social practice and later reinforced by legal texts (although women acquired free and equal access to education and health care). It was hoped that, by reinforcing the patriarchal structures of the family, the state would build models of alliance with men, at least those contesting its power, and consolidate itself. Women, despite some official rights (including the vote) ensuing from their militant contribution to the liberation struggle, were not seen as political actors in their own right nor as full citizens; men, especially decision-makers, were being truthful to the spirit of the Algerian saying that 'Men deal with politics, women prepare couscous'.

Broadly speaking, the official discourse on women was paternalistic and authoritarian and women, who after independence claimed their rights, were told that their emancipation was not to be prioritized over pressing issues of wider national interest such as development and strengthening of the economy. This has surely been a familiar narrative for women in many Third World countries who formulated feminist demands at crucial historical junctures. Furthermore, feminism was regarded with suspicion, as a neo-colonial import from the West, potentially corrupting and divisive for a newly independent society. In line with that viewpoint and the populist stand on national unity, women and other groups were denied the right to organize independently. Only organizations set up by the one-party state were officially acknowledged; in the case of women the National Union of Algerian Women (the UNFA) was alone allowed to speak on behalf of women and, as such, was a tool used by the government to foster loyalty in women.

Clearly, the gendering implied in the historical process of colonization needs to be constantly stressed in assessing the ambiguous formation of post-colonial identities and nation-building. At the same time, this should not be used as an excuse for passing over the ways in which the post-colonial state intensified such ambiguities. On one hand, it strengthened patriarchal control of the family and women; on the other hand, it began to undermine the authority of fathers, brothers and husbands within the family by attracting women to the outside world through education and paid work.[3] In this respect, the state, in spite of its undeclared support for the principle of male supremacy in society, 'feminized' men, allegorically replicating colonial relations and their implied sexual politics. So masculinity was reinvented as an ambiguous construction, the dubious product of a conflict between the values of the sovereign revolutionary male and the semi-colonized subject of an authoritarian and autocratic state.

The socialist regime under Boumediene best exemplified the workings and values of the 'post-colonial'[4] state as an authoritarian state. It was also a gendered state largely determined by the patriarchal basis of its power; its authoritarianism was partly defined by its undemocratic hold on power and the relationship of patronage it enjoyed with males, in other words a position imbued with patriarchal authority towards a subservient and obedient nation (on the allegorical pattern of the traditional family). It also delegated patriarchal power to men as heads of families, households and communities and stressed the roles of men as producers and women as reproducers.

However, the pressures exerted by an emergent civil society and the women's movement have been destabilizing for those boundaries implied by the relationship between the governing and the governed. Women, having come of age, demanded political rights, but their gender was persistently reconceptualized as a symbolic field where meanings are produced by men, exchanged and negotiated between them. In that sense, the local state, through its populism and interference in the social field, largely determined the persistence of a patriarchal pattern of gender relations and sex roles. But, by doing so, it provoked responses from women which were radical and far-reaching, calling into question the power of the state, the legitimacy – and nature – of its authority as well as the meaning of citizenship. In allegorical and concrete terms, a new configuration for the state in Algeria has emerged, engendering forms of political pressures that cannot be ignored any longer. The fight by Algerian women around political issues and the significance of their impact on the shaping of civil society can be viewed – especially in view of the formidable challenges women are still confronted with – as a crucially significant model of the struggle between women and the state in the Third World.

The Post-Socialist Phase: Feminism, Capitalism and Neo-Patriarchy

Shifting societal realities marked the first post-socialist government with an underlying reconceptualization of gender and power. The notion of the state as *Etat-Providence*, or as essentially a provider of health care and education and a source of employment, dissolved in the mid 1980s in the wake of an acute economic crisis brought about by mismanagement, bad planning and a substantial loss of oil revenue. There were also other factors such as the costly servicing of the national debt and the growing interference of imperialistic interests, local and global, within a state that had gradually lost its *dirigiste* mechanism. There was something of an abrogation of the old form of state as the new state removed welfare provision and sponsored internal 'marketization' of the economy. The abandonment of the socialist model and the shift to a market economy were explained in terms of a universal realignment of economic policies and a readjustment to the world economy. The repayment of the nation's burgeoning debt was therefore presented as largely dependent on the creation of positive conditions of dialogue with major financial institutions. Austerity programmes were implemented, accompanied by a social cost which soon turned out to be explosive.

This post-socialist state era was also marked by the thrust of a civil society in which feminism played a leading role. This new phase in state transformation lasted from 1978 to 1988 and was determining for subsequent societal and political developments. At the level of the state, an outstanding activity of destructuring of the social, economic, legal, political and ideological spheres took place in the name of liberalization. It thus appeared that this new model of government – less populist but no less authoritarian than the precedent – was not centred on ideas of national consensus and uniformity. In terms of social stratification, for instance, it seemed to favour, on the contrary, an approach that widened class divisions and social exclusion. The process of fragmentation which affected all spheres of social, cultural and economic activity was all-embracing and so profoundly destabilizing that it could only be understood within a context of international and regional politics which, by the early 1980s, were slowly progressing towards the end of the Cold War, a renewed phase of US intervention in the Middle East and a universal shift to the right. Nationally, a marked change of politics materialized within a framework of neo-conservative practices and apparently liberal programmes which seriously undermined the provision of health care and housing; education too suffered severe cuts and underwent a series of anti-democratic reforms. The detrimental effects were particularly felt by women whose access to these facilities became restricted. Overall, the formation of capitalism in post-colonial Algeria materialized principally during this particular phase as state capitalism with the public sector remaining predominant alongside an expanding private sector.

The advent of a capitalist state provides another stage in the development of the relation between women and the state and of the negotiation of gender. Has that negotiation radically altered under the thrust of a changing political class armed with new ideological weapons, mainly class pragmatism, petit-bourgeois conservatism and technocratic rather than bureaucratic tendencies? In a sense, these neo-politics broke away from the populist stand of the previous regime, indicating the triumphant breakthrough of right-wing groups and interests within the governmental system. Promises of social justice were abandoned not just for the obvious reasons of economic hardship, as many commentators would argue, but in view of shifting ideological values. As a result, the state's legitimacy and its already precarious authority were further eroded.

Yet again, the 'woman question' was exploited by the political class to retrieve and retain some of that lost authority and alleviate the crisis of legitimacy that threatened the basis of its power. In the eyes of the state, it became imperative, in view of the economic crisis and of the emerging institutional crisis, to offer concessions to the most 'popular' movement of social contestation, namely Islamic fundamentalism.[5] Therefore, it turned to the arena of the family to reinstitute patriarchal power and consequently some legitimacy. Through a regulation of relations inside the family and the promulgation of a Personal Status Code inspired by *Shari'a* or Islamic Law, the state stipulated, unabashedly and in unambiguous terms, the subordination and dependency of females in society and thus reclaimed, on behalf of men, a traditional patriarchal system and culture. In other words, the secret drafting in 1985 of the Family Code, already publicly rejected by women in wide demonstrations three years previously, officially reinstated the principles of male domination and the patriarchal family in an attempt to alleviate a gathering economic crisis, its ensuing social costs for men and its potentially destabilizing danger for ruling elites. In the light of these developments, especially as regards the state's move to capitalism while trying to retain communal traditional ties, it is relevant to define the local state in this post-socialist juncture as neo-patriarchal and to note the significant shifts thus experienced by both patriarchy and state in Algeria. It is useful to introduce the definition of neo-patriarchy in a post-colonial context provided by Val Moghadam:

> Neo-patriarchy is the product of the encounter between modernity and tradition in the context of dependent capitalism; it is modernised patriarchy. Whatever the outward (modern) forms of the neo-patriarchal family, society or state, their internal structures remain rooted in the patriarchal values and social relations of kinship, clan, religious and ethnic groups. A central feature of this system is dominance of the father within the household and at the level of the state.[6]

For feminist women, the legislation on the family also crystallized all the tensions of the on-going conflicts and they used it as a springboard to articulate and enter political negotiation. Feminist protest which had smouldered throughout the Boumediene era was stirred into action. The Code was seen by women as the state surrendering to the pressures exerted by emergent conservative groups, most specifically the Islamist movement. The Islamists, however, were not satisfied by what they saw as only a limited response to their demands, for they demanded the extension of *Shari'a* law to all political and legislative spheres as well as to cultural, educational and social activity; in other words they brought forward a whole programme of 'Islamification' which was aimed at installing an Islamic state. Later, by manipulating the democratization process, they would be able to implement many of their policies in the context of local government and push forward with intensive and aggressive campaigns, openly hostile to women, especially the working female whose return to the home was advocated as a solution to male unemployment.

For women, especially those already active in militant networks inside and outside universities, the drafting of the Family Code was not only a dangerous indication of the state's infiltration by, and partial alliance with, Islamic fundamentalists but also a serious betrayal of their most basic rights as enshrined in the non-segregational and egalitarian constitution (as well as the International Declaration of Human Rights, which Algeria had earlier signed). This move from the state acted as the detonator of a formidable explosion within the largely secular women's movement, leading to the mobilization of ever greater numbers of women. They all targeted their actions on the Family Code as an urgent issue: the most radical demanded its straightforward abrogation on the basic principle that women were not consulted during its drafting nor permitted to debate its provisions whilst others called for its amendment. Islamist women's groups also voiced concerns about the Family Code which they found biased in favour of men and not a fair adaptation of Qur'anic prescriptions on women and the family. Their criticism raised the useful question of interpretation or exegesis but in no way questioned the neo-patriarchal values advocated by the Personal Status Code and the related issue of female dependency as drawn by this particular document and the culture at large, including the sexual politics of the state.

Feminist associations provided one of the earliest occurrences of a civil society organizing itself. Large-scale demonstrations were held by various groups of women to protest against the Family Law; the majority of the protesters were students and professional women, housewives and women from other backgrounds. As marches were not legalized until four years later, the women's show of force on the streets (the first spontaneous event of the kind since independence) was a turning point in public life and opened the road to similar manifestations of social protest by other groups. The temerity manifested then by women has been repeated in more recent demonstrations, even though the spread of terror and violence has made such open gatherings potentially more dangerous. Following the expression used by Afsaneh Najmabadi to speak about Iranian women, the Algerian woman/feminist realized that 'to have a room of her own, [she] is now faced with subverting God and state'.[7]

That rally was deeply significant in terms of what it publicly said about women's potential for political resistance and mobilization. Female veterans from the war of liberation opened the march which started from the heart of the Casbah, the old Arab town and one of the bastions of the armed struggle against the French, at the place where Hassiba Ben Bouali, a heroine of that struggle, was killed by colonial soldiers, more than thirty years previously. The presence of the '*Moudjahidats*', survivors of that war, and the implicit reference to the memory of those who died, had a dual meaning. It imbued the protest with historical significance and placed it within a long tradition of struggle by Algerian women; it also drew a parallel between the present subordinate status of women and colonial oppression. In addition, the presence of legal feminists and women lawyers at the forefront of the march aimed at conveying a specific message about the illegality of the legislation on the family. In the wake of the rally, women's associations were formed, the most notable and radically defiant of the political and legal status quo being the Association for the Emancipation of Women, with Salima Ghazali as its president, the Independent Association for the Defence and Promotion of Women's Rights led by its president Khalida Messaoudi; a number of other feminist groups were also formed during that period with various agendas but all focused on the need to reject the new family legislation.

Boutheina Cheriet has seen the feminist movement as one of the main movements of protest which directly and forcefully challenged the power of the one-party state and helped break down the popular consensus preached and imposed by power groups over decades. The uniformity of civil life has also been questioned by religiously based movements as they rejected the legitimacy of institutional practices and traditions which tended, in their eyes, towards a Western-style secularism while claiming allegiance to Islam. Along-side these two movements of social protest, Cheriet also identifies the role played by the movement for 'Amazight', or the Berber movement, in under-mining the status quo maintained by the state around issues of identity, history, language and culture. Cheriet argues that the 'resilience of the populism of the Algerian state, built on a utopian idea of consensus, finally gave way under the pressures exerted against it by the rebellious movements'[8] and various forms and voices of popular protest. She continues:

> But all that the Boumediene era occluded was to be revealed in the 1980's, under the pressures of an increasingly complex society and the growing signs of a deep economic and institutional crisis. The process of delegitimation was initiated by three movements of which Boumediene was totally oblivious, having concentrated his efforts on neutralising Marxist as well as internal oppositions.[9]

She goes on to say:

> Almost systematically, from the beginning of the 1980's, the Berberist, Islamist and the feminist challenges came to constitute the forefront of civil protests. The first brandished the Berber character of Algeria, the second pressed its Islamic agenda, and the third cried out for the modernisation of society.[10]

Of these three, it was the feminist movement which voiced the most radical demands for progressive and modernist social, political and legislative change. As it did, the feminist protest – like other movements of contestation – to this point subsumed within academia, trade unionism and campus politics, acquired a more direct and visible activist form in the public sphere. Women's voices, across regions, classes and other boundaries, were finally being heard.

The battle over the Family Code has reflected, since it began in the mid 1960s, the ambiguities informing the practices of the one-party state. Its modern basis cannot reconcile traditionalist pressures exerted from within and outside the state apparatus. The move to adopt a *Shari'a*-inspired family legislation can be understood as yet another attempt by the political elite state to legitimize its arbitrary monopoly of power by ensuring at least some kind of ideological continuity with previous national discourses around cultural authenticity. Therefore, it would appear that if, in material terms, social justice was being undermined, at least patriarchy retained all its rights and its function as a social and ideological institution as well as the cornerstone of politics of identity. The resilient attachment to male dominance and gender hierarchy also lies in the need to nurture the cultural boundaries of identity and community.

The Democratization Phase: Internal Fractures and the Rise of Civil Society

Finally, the intensification of the social crisis on the one hand and the sharpening on the other hand of internal conflicts within the regime and multiform power struggles between right-wing and left-wing factions, between conservative and more progressive, nationalist factions led to the riots of 1988 (known since as the 'youth riots') and the beginning of the most serious socio-political crisis for the country since independence.

The event was a watershed in Algeria's modern history, opening up a short phase of democratization followed by the more recent counter-revolutionary backlash. A new pro-democratic constitution was drafted instituting notable changes such as the liberalization of the press and a multi-party system in order to redeem some of the damage resulting from that brutal divorce between state and society that the bloody street demonstrations between groups of youth and the military entailed. The situation remained volatile as the doors were now open for new conflicts between the ultra-conservatives within the government and the army, the politico-financial Mafia which has thrived under the new regime and those politicians and officials in favour of democratic reforms.

Women used the new constitution as a platform for struggle. But, while their focus on the legal inferiorization of women remained consistent, they later widened the scope of their demands to debates about the future of the nation. They used this newly acquired voice to put forward more fundamental questions about the state's ideology and the need to fight for a free, modern and republican Algeria. In contrast, the state's attitude towards women was still enmeshed in old gender images and rhetoric as its official discourse on women remained characterized by an outdated praise of their symbolic value and of their legendary past. It thus failed to address the growing difficulties women were grappling with, particularly among the urban and rural proletariat and especially in view of galloping inflation. The lack of adequate appraisal of the feminist politics of women's associations probably implied a deliberate refusal to acknowledge their true oppositional stand and was evident in the attitude of the regime towards them. It conceived of their role solely as educational, especially regarding the thorny question of birth control which it never wholeheartedly engaged with as it feared the reaction of the

religious establishment and of rural patriarchs. The role of women's associations was limited, from the viewpoint of the state, to raising awareness among
women about the use of contraceptive methods. Women's groups had themselves already raised the question of birth control as an issue of reproductive
rights and women's physical and mental health but the concern of the government over high fertility rates was rather motivated by the heavy financial cost
of a rapid population growth. Nevertheless, the official approach meant a
relegating of the work of women's groups to the private sphere. Concern over
reproduction, then, was seen to fall 'naturally' in the realm of women's organizations. However, the state soon realized that the role of associations was
definitely political, aiming at re-establishing gender relations firmly as part of
the public domain.

On Women's Day of 1989, women massively demonstrated again in the
streets to call for democratic reforms and to publicly warn against the dangers
looming ahead for the country because of the formal covert backing granted to
certain conservative platforms, mainly the Islamist fundamentalist movement
which was rapidly gaining support among the young unemployed, the student
population and some rural communities.

This era of democratization was marked by heated political disputes and
activism. During that time too, the feminist movement grew considerably,
gaining more political maturity and placing the 'women question' at the forefront of public debates. Media attention turned to feminist associations and
their leaders, although there were often implicit attempts at demonizing feminist figures. Women's groups also encountered a great deal of criticism, being
accused of falling into the tactics of opposition parties, being manipulated by
them or for condoning, in some cases, the less than progressive discourses of
some clan-based groupings. Feminist groups involved themselves in the politics of some parties in order to gain support for their cause among pro-
democratic forces and forge alliances with them, a crucial endeavour in a
political landscape so blatantly supportive of religious movements. Conversely
too, in some cases, female followers of particular political movements have
joined women's associations and, on the other hand, male democrats often
sought the support of women's groups. So, broadly speaking, women activists
were trying to negotiate the distribution of power at institutional and societal
levels, sometimes having to operate alongside – or against – male-dominated
movements of opposition. Criticism was levelled against feminist associations
for being too diverse and having disparate agendas. The critique highlighted,
if anything, the enduring legacy of three decades of monopartism and populist
uniformity when plurality of expression and diversity were institutionally condemned as divisive and conflictual. It also revealed the persistence of another
symbolic heritage, that of gender stereotyping as the individuality of women
and the diversity of their identities and voices tend to be denied in a culture
which highly values the silence of women and their invisibility in the outside
world. It was apparent, during the years leading up to the present crisis, that
the growing influence of the women's movement, now visible and vocal, en-

countered some indifference from some groups and individuals, a great deal of resistance from others and fierce opposition from the Islamist fundamentalists who simply equated – and still do equate – feminism with Western depravity and cultural alienation, if not outright blasphemy and a rebellion against God. This situation might also be taken to indicate the complexity faced by a political process of opposition trying to account for the female experience, and the difficulty faced by women in forging a unified political front in spite of a rich and diverse feminist discourse.

However, in spite of mounting criticism and attacks, the feminist movement made a tangible impact on national politics and the gender politics of the state. The male backlash stimulated feminist groupings from the major cities to organize the first national coordination of the associations. This network constituted another turning point in the history of the Algerian women's movement in that it instituted a strategic shift that enhanced the authority and legitimacy of feminist politics to operate within a patriarchal political field. Manipulation by opposition parties, criticism from the media and virulent attacks from the Islamists were seen as strategies by the political mainstream to delegitimize and depoliticize the women's movement within the spheres of political negotiation. In view of this backlash, women from various groups decided to forge a network to help unite their fragmented experiences and struggles nationwide. They created a coordination therefore strengthening women's associations independently of any political interference. The coordination constituted in itself a strong, well-organized movement of social protest.

Left-wing women's groups have radicalized their position since the focus of their struggle has been to challenge the ideological basis of the state and to call for a fundamental reformulation of civil life on the basis of a redefinition of crucial concepts of modernity and secularism. They helped draw attention to the connections between gender, class and neo-imperialism as embedded in the notion of struggle developed by some feminist groupings. Moreover, left-wing feminists worked with the trade union movement to improve the rate of female employment and education, working conditions and women's rights in the workplace as well as promote women's representation in parliament.

Overall, an outstanding influence was exerted by a number of prominent leaders of associations on the political field, positively contributing to reshaping the state configuration, en-gendering forms of struggle and opposition in a public world that has never even accounted for the mere presence of women. Nevertheless, one cannot underestimate the fact that an even greater number of women mobilized on gender issues and acting through various non-governmental organizations had visible ramifications in civil society and a tangible impact on the lives of many women. But the apparently uncritical affiliation of some female militants with the state continued to raise concern whilst the fractures, now evident in the institutional and social fabric, deepened, paving the way for anarchy and social unrest.

Malika Mehdid

A Phase of Reaction: Gender Politics, Terror and Resistance

The present phase of nation-building in Algeria has been marked by a process of destruction, in material, human and civilizational terms. It is an era defined in terms of the victory of the Far Right as a movement embracing members of the nomenclatura, parts of the opposition, Mafia interests and foreign interference. The Far Right managed to destabilize state and society, to initiate a reign of terror and instigate a systematic devastation of the country, its people, resources and history. There is now plenty of evidence to suggest that it is a phase of fascism which opened up with the cancellation of the first allegedly free general elections in post-colonial Algeria. Since January 1992, the country has lived turbulent times, marked by a gradual increase in activities of sabotage, assassinations and political violence in a culture of fear.

The earlier part of this historical drama was not as debilitating as the more recent period over the last two years. The tensions and ambiguities in state policies and state mechanisms on the one hand and the conflicts of ideology between and within the various parties and political factions have been overwhelming, finally bringing about a national crisis which has led to the collapse of the democratic process, the intervention of the army and the establishment of the state of siege. The situation deteriorated quickly in terms of security with the collapse of law and order. A quasi-civil war engulfed the country. The main parties involved in this 'war' have been government troops and armed groups claiming an 'Islamic' identity and working on behalf of the now disbanded Islamic Salvation Front (or FIS). In other words, the opposition by that party took the form of a campaign of terror with the creation of special death squads claiming to act as the armed wing of the FIS, mainly the sinister GIA (Groupe Islamique Armé).[11] The GIA, however, is not the product of the FIS alone but of the current of fascism which was part of the Algerian political fabric, dating back to the pre-independence era. The aim of the right as a whole is to prevent the peaceful development of political life towards democratic change and development. To talk of democracy and feminism in these conditions has become difficult as the matter is now about survival. Political activism for progressive causes such as women's rights was outright dangerous as this 'neo-Inquisition' resumed its course, claiming victims daily.

However, the various political groupings within the rest of the democratic opposition and the state continued their negotiating over power distribution and the future shape of the country's public life. These negotiations remain marked by faction alliance, clan solidarity and clientelism. The relation between women and the state was not so intense but rather redundant for a long time. This was to change under the influence of the women's movement which transformed many militants into political actors endowed with representativity and retaining considerable bargaining power. There is no doubt at present that no public configuration will materialize in Algeria in the future without due consideration being given to the women's movement. Official support was given to the feminist movement by president Mohammed Boudiaf, a prominent figure of the Revolution who – after the cancelled elections – was brought back from his self-imposed exile to rule the country until his assassination, six months later. Boudiaf, in contrast to past and present politicians, expressed interest in women's groups, exhorting them to fight for their rights. As a result, these groups gained, in the eyes of men at least, more weight and legitimacy. It was under Boudiaf that leaders of feminist associations were invited to join the National Transitional Council (or CNT), the highest power structure of the provisional government which replaced the dissolved General Assembly. The move constituted a landmark in the women's movement in many respects but women were divided over the issue of whether to enrol in the CNT or not. The reasons for such a split in positions towards the structure were fundamentally about the nature of the political commitment it underlined vis-à-vis the state itself, which many militants saw as deeply implicated in the violence tearing Algeria apart. And in an environment deeply traumatized by terror and increasingly dislocated in ideological and societal terms, the move to join the CNT was considered by some militants – who expressed fears of cooptation – as unwise, especially in view of the fact that it would invalidate the political independence that some militant women saw as essential to their activism. Nevertheless, other women pointed to the strategic value of a feminist positioning within such a structure, which would allow them to work for legal changes in the status of women. Some militants were strongly against the idea of joining the CNT because they saw it as divisive and undermining of the women's movement as social protest. In some respects, it certainly indicated that the movement for women's rights was being acknowledged by the state and that the transitional government wanted to involve feminists in its negotiations. Although the transitional government certainly hoped to use the women's movement to rally civil society to its fight against terrorism, it was apparent that the feminist agenda had gained new authority in the eyes of the state.

A suspension of more radical feminist activism was evident, following the turbulent post-election period. Militants adopted varied strategies of struggle: some chose to work through new frameworks of power provided by the state or the democratic opposition, others remained autonomously active within the realm of the association. Another group of feminists temporarily retreated from the public arena, defeated by the multiple discourses of exclusion and misogyny articulated by the state and the opposition, whether religious or secular and the continuation of the no less stifling legacy of thirty years of monopartism. They feel permanently trapped within various male ideologies and practices extremely hostile to female expression.

More than ever, women, especially in the poorer strata of society, suffered considerably from the combined effects of negative economic, political and social conditions and women as a whole became hostages of the crisis. Terrorist gangs soon turned to women, menacing and brutalizing hundreds of them. Crimes against women included abduction, torture, rape, gang rape and killing, crimes which were common by mid 1995.[12] The number of women murdered since the beginning of the terrorist phase was judged to be around 400, the highest number being recorded during the last twelve months. Feminists, militants, female journalists and teachers are particularly targeted, some of them forced to lead a clandestine life, having to hide from the bullets of the killers and their knives by constantly changing addresses and covering their tracks. The lack of security led some of them to seek another form of exile outside the frontiers of Algeria. However, the victimization of women did not lead to or foster their marginalization. As a whole, violence has affected women from all backgrounds but more so women in remote rural areas, small towns and the poorer city quarters of large urban centres and the capital.

The fight for secular republicanism, democracy and the repudiation of political violence as a means of solving national problems constitutes the global framework within which the resistance by female militants is articulated in this time of crisis. However, women in general are divided over the direction to be taken by state and society. Islamist women on the whole seemed to agree on the idea of a state ruled by *shari'a*. The secular women's movement has experienced fundamental splits, over ideological lines, splitting into liberal and left-wing sections, and over strategy, as some women opted for a wider engagement with the provisional government, mainly the CNT, and others favoured total autonomy from the state (although not always from alignment on some parties or movements of opposition). Common goals still, however, mobilize feminists across political lines: the legislation on the family, violence against women and birth control have so far constituted shared programmes of action. However the urgency of the challenge of fascism has rearranged the priorities of the feminist agenda: the end of the bloodshed and the return of peace are today the overriding concern and main goal of all Algerian feminists and women's groups, inside and outside the country. The specific issue of physical abuse, torture and persecution of women and young girls within the culture of terrorism remain paramount causes.

In view of the terrorism targeting female militants, some women have temporarily shifted the struggle to other fronts: this is not a demobilization in the face of mounting risks but new strategic ways of working, organizing and networking. Activities include learning to manage associations, training, attending seminars and roundtable discussions with feminists from other countries, most particularly from the rest of North Africa. The launching of the series 'Legal Texts from the Maghreb' for instance was the fruit of such activity between feminists from Algeria, Tunisia and Morocco. The hope is that these activities may enable them to influence state and society effectively through new channels of expression and struggle at home and also networks of solidarity forged elsewhere (in academic, journalistic and organizational terms and at international and local levels). Associations by Algerian women have also mushroomed abroad, especially in European countries, acting as an extension for the indigenous movement in an effort to forge an international network of solidarity with their sisters at home.

According to Salima Ghazali, there has been a consistent movement of women – and men – bearers of political projects as workers, thinkers and citizens. An active process of reflection and analysis is taking place, outside any traditional political dogma, whether dictated by the state, the democratic opposition or the 'Islamists'. She sees this move towards conceptual thought as part of a movement of 'moralization' in the Third World against the abuses of power, the clientelism and sectarianism which have so far informed the practices and values of post-colonial states.

Various issues are raised by the new local and global situation presently framing the 'women question'. For instance, in the present national context and in this time of great dangers, what does it mean for feminists to be for or against the state bearing in mind that such a state is fighting a war against terrorist groups? The question especially applies to those militants who joined the CNT and those who adopted the anti-terrorist stand of the transitional government. Is autonomy from the state an option for feminists operating inside and outside Algeria, considering the present ideologically heightened conjuncture which calls for political affiliation? And what does the notion of state imply in power terms, at a time when even part of the opposition has allied itself to the cause of the disbanded FIS and its gangs, among them a Trotskyist party led by a woman, Louisa Hanoune? Overall, the dilemma over the issue of whether to work with or without the state, to be for or against the state in the fight against terrorism, has led to significant splits in the secular women's movement.

The problematic relation between women and the state was already raised in the aftermath of the cancelled elections of 1992. Women were then criticized, mostly in Western media, for giving support to the government troops when they intervened to stop the election process. It is interesting to note that large-scale political actions undertaken by the women's movement in Algeria such as its anti-Gulf War rallies attracted no special media comment in Western capitals (in contrast, rallies organized by the Islamists against that war were publicized). Women then were invisible and their opinions about that conflict, or any major event for that matter, did not count. Suddenly, immediate world attention turned to them in that first moment when the army stepped in, with television screens projecting pictures of women apparently relieved from what was, just a few hours earlier, the imminent danger of the establishment of a religious fundamentalist state. Such a process of representation owes much to a neo-Orientalist tradition and the underlying fascination that the relation between women and Islam has long exerted on the 'West'. It is a reactivating of a stereotype that sees so-called Arab women as politically inarticulate females, not usually versed in the sophistication of ideological debates, and as pawns in the hands of male politicians. There are of course many implications to this phenomenon, especially in terms of the problematic of power between First World and Third World women.[13] But, in spite of the general perception, women, as a whole, did not condone the action by the army as it was clear that the event buried any hope for democratic change, and some women even went as far as demonstrating in the streets against the clampdown by the army. In the case of those who did not voice protest against it, a number of factors explain their position, the most relevant being the illegal and anti-constitutional formation of the party in question, the FIS, which should not have been allowed to run for elections in the first place but did because it was effectively lobbied and backed up by the ultra-conservatives and the neo-fascists. The republican orientation of the Algerian army as an institution with the duty to protect the country against internal or external aggression was also invoked. The army in Algeria in that sense did not act differently from European armies which rallied against the Nazi and fascist forces during the 1930s and 1940s. In Algeria, the army played the role of safeguard against the establishment of a totalitarian regime. The fact that women would have been the first casualties of such a regime and those with most to lose finally convinced many women that the intervention of the troops to halt the election process was not a tragedy as great as that of the FIS in power. The implications of such a position in regard to the questions both of democracy and of feminism remain, however, problematic, and certainly no understanding of the issues at hand can be achieved without a relocation of the problematic of women and state within the historical, geo-political framework of Algeria. Broadly, the question of working with or without the state (or 'for' or 'against' it) has divided women; at the same time, the issue is too complex and cannot accommodate a simple answer to the question as to whether a feminist position could accommodate an alliance – even a temporary one – with the state. What being 'with the state' means in the particular context of Algeria might, in some respects at least, be defined in terms of agency or the articulation of a form of coalition and common public resistance to the threats of genocide, anarchy and neo-imperialism created by the terrorist movement. At the same time, the campaigning by some women's groups in terms of consciousness-raising regarding national problems of terror and violence, which is carried out inside and outside the country, might converge with, and usefully serve, the anti-terrorist work led by governmental groups in the realm of the military as well as that of diplomacy.

Some militant women such as Salima Ghazali saw the official invitation extended to women to enrol in the CNT as an attempt by the state to neutralize the most radical women and to 'intrumentalize' the issue of women as the masses of women did not experience, as a result, better conditions in terms of employment, housing and education or in terms of images of women in society. According to her, the state thus managed to instrumentalize part of feminist discourse. Ghazali's position has recently developed into a fierce criticism levelled against those women and women's groups whose anti-terrorist campaigning is oblivious to the violence of the state and its own abuses of human rights and implication in the causes of the crisis, a position she develops in her editorial articles for the newspaper *La Nation*. However, her criticism again polarizes the issue into 'for' or 'against' the state as she lumps together within the same category liberal women who may have spoken and acted on behalf of the regime with pragmatic interests in mind and militant women such as the lawyer Leila Aslawi (whose husband was murdered by the death gangs because of the activism of his wife) and Khalida Messaoudi, one of the most radical feminists of the women's movement; both women are staunch advocates of democratic change. Ghazali and women like her could, however, be accused of giving equal status to those murdering civilians and those defending them and wrongly equating the atrocities of terrorism committed by the GIA with an unspecified and more conceptually broad notion of political violence. In fact, this debate becomes not only indicative of the genderizing effect that the 'women's question' and its complexities eventually have on the political process but formative in terms of the impact it therefore has upon on any attempt at national reconciliation and on shaping pro-democratic struggle and discourse.

The Way Forward: Un-Gendering the State?

The key feature of Algerian civil and public life in the last few years has been the issue of violence, originating from armed Islamist groups and the military actions against them by the state. This polarization of the power struggle as apparently between two forces has led to the deaths of thousands of citizens, among them an increasing number of women. This dirty, undeclared war is being fought on several fronts with the civilian population engaging in its own multiform resistance, especially in rural areas where the defence of some villages against terrorist attacks has taken the form of militias.

This situation raises fundamental questions about violence, its relation to history, state transformations, and patriarchy as well as the gendered nature of both political behaviour and ideological struggle. The situation has led to a questioning of current notions of the post-colonial state as a monolithic bloc of centralized power, control and fear and of state-building as a harmonious process which should at some historical stage of its evolution be naturally propelled forward by development and democratization. The Algerian case shows that internal and external pressures contribute to state formation in a significant manner and that even a strong state, forged in a long anti-colonial struggle and imbued with revolutionary ideas articulated by a centralized governmentality, can fall into dangerous fragmentation and division, allowing the hijacking of the revolution which first produced it. The nation-state becomes the site of conflict and confusion but also of resistance, simultaneously constructed and destructured by all the ruptures and tensions which have so far shaped its historical trajectory. Today, the ideological trends which have torn apart the social and political fabric are materialized into legitimate – and not so legitimate – parties, associations and movements of opposition, in relation to a state shaken in its very foundations by the tide of neo-fascism.

It will be valuable here to explore the issue of the 'genderizing' of political culture through the problem of terrorist violence against women. The discussion will provide further evidence to my argument that violence against women in Algeria, whether domestic or political, in other words whether expressed in the private or public realm, is a manifestation of a phallocentric order. This order is epitomized by the terrorist bands. For them, women have constituted a group to be targeted specifically and the question must be raised as why this is so, especially if one bears in mind that this systematic victimization of women in a state of war is rather unique. Although violence against women in situations of conflict are common, the mass rape of women in Bosnia being one of the most tragic examples, the experience of physical abuse, murder and torture of women in Algeria remains a deliberate and rather terrifying case of a genocide motivated by gendered considerations which have become historicized and politicized. The reasons appear to be of both a conceptual and ideological order. I will briefly review some in what follows.

First, it has become evident that women are targeted primarily as women, and then as intellectuals, workers, feminists and as wives, sisters or mothers to men enrolled in the security forces. The violence against them becomes in this sense an expression of a deep hatred – and phobia – of women. The campaign of assassinations of women and young girls and their abduction by men of the GIA translates into a dramatic transfer in the private and the public spheres of what must be read as systemic violence (symbolic as well as physical) against women. It is a coercive and brutal way of removing women from the public world and teaching them where 'their place' should be. It expresses, in other words, patriarchal aggression, typical of a society that nurtured machismo, the fear of women, male pride and hostility to a great extent. It is the result of a sustained cultural and political process, both historical and contemporary, that tended to emasculate men and marginalize women. Females have also been, during the post-socialist era, the object of systemic demonization in the Islamist fundamentalist discourse.

In addition, the violence against women who do not wear a *hijab* can be associated with the hatred of modernity. There is hardly a need to stress that the fundamentalist-fascist movement is led by extremist men whose hatred of modernity – among other things – will necessarily translate into a rejection of, and attempts to destroy, democracy, freedom and indeed women, as manifestations of modernity. One of the most obvious signifiers of modernity in North Africa is the educated or working female. If such a female is not a *mutahajiba*, she becomes, in the eyes of traditionalist Islamist males, a strong signifier of modernity and Westernism. Such a woman undoubtedly represents a project of society, one which is based on individual freedoms, independence and equality and oriented towards secularism. The emancipation of women, starting with their unconditional rights to education and work – and the image of the emancipated female – inevitably imply the progress of society and constitute the condition for democratic change within a world that respects pluralism and difference. On the other hand, in a traditionally patriarchal society, gender functions as a marker of individual and collective identity; aggressions against women, regardless of their identities and age, thus become charged with messages of death and war against that society which has invested in femininity cultural meanings and historical continuity.

At a more psychoanalytical level, these neo-fascists are also males who have cultivated, to dangerous levels, frustrations of a sexual, material, political, intellectual and spiritual order; frustrations requiring a displacement for feelings of impotence and failure. It is more appropriate, in view of the ideological basis of such a movement and the witch-hunting it instigated against women, secular intellectuals, artists and various other groups of people, to refer to it as a neo-Inquisition. The forces of this neo-Inquisition have also recognized the significance of women in the resistance against them. This courageous resistance, to which many parliamentary, feminist and other groups around the world have paid tribute (alongside men from the democratic opposition inside the country), has taken the form of public rallies to speak out against the killings as well as an everyday, more general, expression as women leave their houses daily to go to work, to school, shopping and so forth. This is a daily form of resistance. Many militant women have also remained active in non-governmental organizations and various associations.

Second, the impact of the feminist movement on the democratization process and the secularization of the state have been paramount, as I have shown. As a whole, the women's movement has been significant in the emergence of civil society through the impact it has had on the development of a culture of opposition. Nevertheless, it had to take into account and reflect in its discourse a social reality still largely determined by references to Islam. On the other hand, the impact of women on the forces of democratization has gradually led to the formation of an effective republican and largely secularist front to counteract the fascist movement and the state. The women's movement has proved to be a force endowed with a great potential for mobilization and resistance. Women have effectively fostered cultural awareness within the diaspora of movements on the right (religious and cultural conservatives) as well as on the left. Nevertheless, the various stages of social transformations were also marked by diverse appropriations of resistance and cultural oppositions. Some might reject the radical anti-terrorist stand of some activists and other women; however, their courage and that of the masses of women will undeniably determine the outcome of the present power struggle.

Again, political processes appear as deeply imbued with the gender values constructed by specific social relations. Nation-building reads as a gendered process, part of a political culture which has so far constituted the privileged field of recurrent phallocentric discourses and practices. These have regenerated the perennial nature of sexual politics and patriarchal designs and as such invested them with ideological interest, the definition and construction of gender thus becoming an institutional concern, one which is intimately bound up with state transformations.

Ultimately, gender politics is what crystallizes out from the ubiquity of feminism or feminist-inspired practices, ideas and resistances in the democratization process. From being the embodiment of ideas of Nation and collective identity in pre-independence culture, women were effectively able to transcend the limitations of that role and, so to speak, give birth to new boundaries and more egalitarian visions for all.

Understanding the gender politics of the state and of political culture in Algeria should shed some light on the complexities of the 'women question', on the process of nation-building, and on the intimate relation between the two. The promulgation of the Family Code has indicated in a telling manner the gendering process underlying the state and made visible the gender negotiations informing its institutional practices as well as the embeddedness of notions of the female body and sexuality in its culture. The underlying concern of legislation on the family is the control of female sexuality and the safeguarding of patriarchy. Through its endorsement, the state has inscribed itself into the sphere of tradition and religion as well as implicated itself in the production of a negative and quasi-reactionary pattern of social change. Conversely, for feminists, gender has become a political category and the focus of an ideological struggle with the neo-patriarchal gendered state. Now, gender politics needs to be the focus of analysis in order to explain the specifics of development and resistance in the Algerian context.

One way forward for state and society lies in reversing the trend towards polarization, notably regarding the genders. What is needed therefore is perhaps a process of un-gendering which, in the context of a phallocratic nation-state, would imply a demasculinization that might resolve the conflict born of the reinvention of the traditional patriarchal family through legislation. Gender would no longer be the site of communication and negotiation between men for the strategic re-enforcement of identity states. Since the women's movement has constituted one of the most important movements for social contestation, the 'women question' must be addressed in an institutional framework as an issue of human rights and a prerequisite for democracy. The patriarchal subject of history must be replaced by a humanized and deconstructed subject and history itself must undergo a process – among other things – of catharsis. Ultimately, an exercise in the undermining of phallocentrism will require an exploration of the layers of the psyche through language and fragment the polysemy of terms such as *fitna*[14] which equates female beauty and power of seduction with the notion of anarchy and chaos or split the root *umm* which attaches the meaning of motherhood to that of nationhood, respectively conveyed by the terms *umm* (mother) and *umma* (nation). While feminists have been blamed for the collapse of society, at least in terms of morality, feminism as a practice has already deconstructed the dichotomy of Mother and Nation as it has powerfully subverted the symbolic revolutionary parable of the woman as Mother or reproducer of the Nation, replacing it with a narrative of struggle, that of women as initiators of new political discourses and statehood. This was achieved through a decentring of the discriminatory Phallus from its historical, quasi-sacred and universalizing location as the Signifier of national culture.

As a final word, gender is still engendered into all neo-political discourses, including that of the reactionary right, as the Great Repressed. Its distillation in the reactionary current era is a ubiquitous 'gender politics' since all the projects are engendered by gender concerns (even those of the right). So the repression against women will continue but will not succeed because it maintains the centrality of gender and since gender politics remains at the heart of all political discourse now, dominant and oppositional. The work at un-gendering in the context of Algeria, that is, de-phallicizing political and social processes, has only just begun.

Notes

1 I am very grateful to Salima Ghazali, an Algerian feminist activist, for discussing with me the issue of women and politics during the summer of 1993.

2 Boutheina Cheriet, 'The Resilience of Algerian Populism' *Middle East Report*, Vol. 22, No. 1 (Jan–Feb 1992).

3 This argument is debated by Fatima Mernissi in her book *Beyond the Veil: Male-Female Dynamics in Islamic Societies* (El Saqi, 1989).

4 The expression 'post-colonial' is used here conceptually, as a way of defining a particular form of state rather than a chronological stage of state development; that is, from colonial to post-colonial. In other instances in this chapter, the term 'post-colonial' stands literally for 'post-independence'.

5 Expressions such as 'Islamic fundamentalism' and 'Islamism' are used here as broad and loose concepts and should not be taken at face value. These terms usually refer to specific social or political movements which claim to adopt the Islamic doctrine as their main framework and programme. There are as many definitions of these terms as there are 'Islamist' movements. Islam too is understood here as a general and unspecified concept which needs to be contextualized by the specific situation and history of each country and community.

6 Val Moghadam: 'Neo-Patriarchy in the Middle East', in *The Gulf War and the New World Order*, Bresheeth, H. and Yuval, N. (Eds), London, Zed Press (1991).

7 'Hazards of Modernity and Morality: Women, State and Ideology in Contemporary Iran', in *Women, Islam and the State*, ed. by Deniz Kandiyoti (Macmillan, 1991), p. 70.

8 Cheriet, p. 14.

9 *Ibid.*

10 *Ibid.*

11 The formation of the GIA is not well known yet; it seems however that it is not simply composed of Islamists who engaged in a form of Jihad (holy war), but of a number of individuals and groups with varied interests,

including mercenaries who are working for local and/or outside forces and interests.

12 The rapists also resort to a form of rape which they legitimize by calling it *Zawaj Al Mut'a* or 'marriage of pleasure', a form of wedlock practised in shi'a culture. It allows matrimony between a man and a woman for any length of time agreed between them with straightforward divorce at the end of it. It goes without saying that the women captured by the GIA have no say in this 'union' and because of the rotation of 'wives' among the men in question, it becomes gang rape.

13 This issue is discussed in more detail in the following forthcoming article: Mehdid, M. 'Feminism, State and the Post-Colonial Condition: the Algerian Experience', paper to be given at the forthcoming Democracy and Gender Conference, University of warwick, 1996.

14 These associations carried by the term *fitna* have been noted by a number of scholars in their work.

Chapter 6

Democratization, Feminism and the State in Chile: The Establishment of SERNAM

Georgina Waylen

With the return to competitive electoral politics in a number of Latin American countries, the viability of 'state feminism' has come under scrutiny as one mechanism with which to achieve change. So far most of the analyses of 'state feminism' have taken place in the context of the developed world (Stetson and Mazur, 1995). This chapter explores one attempt to engage with the state to effect some change in the position of women in a less developed country.[1] It will be done through an examination of SERNAM (Servicio Nacional de la Mujer), the Chilean women's bureau, established during the consolidation of competitive electoral politics by the in-coming civilian government. As such it provides a interesting case study of state feminism in the context of democratization. Because it is impossible to analyse the nature and efficacy of an institution like SERNAM in isolation from the wider context, this case study also highlights the nature of the relationship between different women's movements, the state and political parties in one political conjuncture. When examining this type of example, a number of questions must be considered. What possibilities exist for women's movements in their relationships with political parties and state? How much space and manoeuvrability can exist within the state for women's movements to achieve their aims? Or do they simply get coopted, lose autonomy and have to submit to the agendas of others (see Waylen, 1993)? What happens to other movements which stay outside the state? The exploration of these issues can only be historically and conjuncturally specific.

The assumption that the nature of the state is not fixed provides the starting point. Indeed, the state has no necessary relationship to gender relations, but this is evolving, dialectic and dynamic. 'The state' can rarely if ever be seen as a homogeneous category. It is not a unitary structure but a differentiated set of institutions, agencies and discourses, the product of a particular historical and political conjuncture. It is far better to see the state as a site of struggle, not lying outside of society and social processes, but, on the one hand, having a degree of autonomy from these which varies under particular circumstances, and, on the other, being permeated by them. Gender (and racial and class) inequalities are therefore buried within the state, but through part of the same dynamic process, gender relations are also partly constituted through the state (Pringle and Watson, 1992). The state therefore partly reflects and partly helps to create particular forms of gender relations and gender inequality. State practices construct and legitimate gender divisions. Gendered identities are in part constructed by the law and public discourses which emanate from the state (Showstack-Sassoon, 1987).

Because the relationship between the state and gender relations is not fixed and immutable, battles can be fought out in the arena of the state. Consequently, while the state has for the most part acted to reinforce female subordination, the space can exist within the state to act to change gender relations (Alvarez, 1989; Charlton, Everett and Staudt, 1989). At different times and within different regimes, opportunity spaces can be used to alter the existing pattern of gender relations. Women's relationship to the state, particularly its welfare element, can also be seen as a site of contestation which provides the context for mobilization, and the welfare state can function as a locus of resistance. The actions of the state can also become a focus for political activity by groups outside the state, for example poor women campaigning for an extension of services. Alvarez (1990) has argued that the extension of the remit of the state into the realm of the private has the effect of politicizing the private, for example through issues such as abortion, rape and domestic violence. This politicization then gives women's movements a handle to campaign around and influence the political agenda. Shifting the boundary between the public and the private then becomes an important point of influence (Alvarez, 1990).

Different groups of women therefore interact with the state in different ways, and can have some influence over the way in which the state acts. Feminist analyses therefore have advanced from looking at the way the state *treats* women unequally in relation to men, to examining the ways in which particular states act to construct gendered state subjects, and the public/private divide in different contexts. As part of the process of engagement with the state, interests and identities can also be constructed. It is therefore important to analyse under what conditions and with what strategies women's movements can influence the state and policy agendas. Debate has centred around whether women's movements should attempt to work with the state and political parties. Australian 'femocrats' argue that the state is a potential agent of empowerment and feminist strategies should involve winning gains from it (Watson, 1990).

Some Chilean feminists have shared this view and attempted to influence the state directly in the course of the transition to democracy. An important characteristic of this transition was the role played by heterogenous women's movements, particularly in its early stages. But it has also seen the reconstitution of a strong and traditional party system and the subsequent demobilization of popular movements including women's movements. The transition has been narrowly defined to focus on the political to the exclusion of the social and economic, as the civilian governments have maintained the liberal economic policies of the military government and had a narrow economic focus on social questions such as poverty alleviation. During the initial opening, concerted campaigns were undertaken by some feminists and women party activists to influence the political process. The resulting centre/left government, dominated by the catholic-influenced Christian Democrats, was committed in its programme to establishment of the women's bureau SERNAM, but with an unclear brief. The complex and contradictory fate of SERNAM can therefore only be understood as part of this wider process of democratization.

In order to explore how these processes unfolded in the transition and consolidation of competitive electoral politics it is useful to divide the transition into three phases as events which occurred in the two periods prior to the civilian government taking power – 1983 to the end of 1986 and 1987 to the elections – had important implications for the return to competitive electoral politics in the post-1990 period.

1983–86: The Breakdown of Authoritarianism and Period of Social Mobilization

In 1983 a mass opposition movement emerged in Chile, moving away from the pattern of sporadic and isolated protests which had been occurring since the military coup of 1973, and marking the beginning of the widespread reconstitution of civil society. The mass mobilizations were seen by many as providing the key both to overthrowing Pinochet and his authoritarian regime, and to the creation of a new type of more open and democratic politics. Also running alongside the mass mobilizations was the re-emergence of the political parties whose activities became increasingly central in the opposition movement (Petras and Leiva, 1988; Garreton, 1989).

During this period of mass opposition to the dictatorship, diverse women's movements had a high visibility. The human rights organizations, the Agrupaciones, comprising mainly women, highlighted disappearances and other abuses perpetrated by the military government; popular movements, active around social and economic issues, grew rapidly in response to the severe economic crisis faced by Chile; and feminist movements, including 'popular feminist' groups, campaigning around gender inequality, (re)emerged onto the public scene (Arteaga, 1988; Valdes and Weinstein, 1989; Kirkwood, 1990; Valenzuela, 1991; Waylen, 1992). Feminists played a visible role in the opposition, participating in the mass mobilizations and days of protest and organizing demonstrations for International Women's Day.

Once political parties began to reconstitute, all social movements (including feminist ones) were under pressure to decide on a strategy: whether it was to be autonomy from or integration into the unfolding political process (Valenzuela, 1990). Some feminists decided on integration as the best way of pursuing a feminist agenda and moved into the political parties. They tended to be middle-class professional women, and they were active in the more moderate parties of the centre and renovated left. The Christian Democrats were pressed by a group of professional women working in conjunction with the women's department of the party, who produced a set of proposals for inclusion in the party's *proyecto alternativo* in 1984. Women's sections were set up in some of these political parties: for example, in 1986 the Federacion de Mujeres Socialistas (FMS) was established in one faction of the socialist party to help increase the influence of feminism in national politics.

The political opposition formed into two groups in 1983, the moderate Alianza Democratica (AD) which increasingly favoured a strategy of *negociacion* (negotiation) and the left-wing Movimiento Democratico Popular (MDP) which advocated *ruptura* – the violent overthrow of the military dictatorship. Women's organizations tried to remain united in the face of a divided political opposition through broad umbrella movements such as Mujeres por la Vida, which was formed in 1983 and attracted over 10,000 women to its first meeting. It was active under the slogan 'Democracia en el Pais y en la Casa' (democracy in the country and in the home) underlining the feminist demand that democracy would have to be rethought if it really was to include women. Despite the efforts to prevent it, party factionalism did have an impact on women's organizations: for example, as the umbrella organization MEMCH 83 became more associated with the radical strategy of mobilization associated with the MDP, many of the feminist and more centrist women's groups left it (Molina, 1989).

The umbrella organization Mujeres por la Vida also played a role in the Asemblea de la Civilidad, a broad and moderate opposition front opposing the dictatorship formed in 1986. A women's petition was included in the Demanda de Chile, a document submitted to the military government in 1986 and (the feminist and socialist) Maria Antioneta Saa sat in assembly as the women's representative. However, in a trend which was to recur, it was the middle-class women's organizations which became more integrated into national politics and some popular women's organizations felt Mujeres por la Vida did not represent them in the assembly (Angelo, 1990).

1987–89: The Transition Begins and Political Parties Regain Hegemony

In the period from 1987 to 1989, two events set the tone for the transition to competitive electoral politics and had important implications for the nature of the civilian government which could take power in Chile. First, as the military regime began to allow a limited political opening, the political parties gained control over the unfolding process to the detriment of the social movements. Second, the centre and centre/left decided that a change of government would not be achieved solely through the process of social mobilization and moved towards a strategy of reaching agreement with the military government through a negotiated transition of pacts made within the political elite. The centre and centre/left parties became the dominant force and negotiation the dominant strategy within the transition. The left and other organizations, such as human rights groups and popular organizations, not adhering to the strategy of *negociacion* but to *ruptura*, became increasingly marginalized in this middle-class transition of negotiated pacts. In 1988 a plebiscite was held in which people voted yes or no to Pinochet continuing as President. As a result of his resounding defeat, competitive elections were held in 1989.

Women's organizations were also affected by these dynamics. The questions of what role they should play in relation to wider political developments became even more pressing. These developments, in combination with the experience of the Asemblea reinforced the belief of some feminists that more than ever it was necessary to enter political process, while others decided to remain outside (Molina, 1990). Much of the feminist movement reorientated itself and debated: the ways in which women should 'do politics' (*hacer polttica*); the alliances they should make; and the aims they should have. Some organizations such as La Morada remained sceptical about the benefits that a formally democratic government would bring women in terms of any real shift in the balance of power between the sexes (Molina, 1989). Meanwhile others argued that the experience of the Pliego and the Assembly demonstrated several things: the shortcomings and deficiencies of women's politics; the difficulty of articulating women's demands in formal politics; and the lack of receptivity of political parties and social organizations to women's demands. The conclusion drawn by many was that while the pressing task was to enter the political process, there was a need to preserve autonomy at the same time.

Many feminists made increased efforts to enter politics during this period and appeared to make significant headway within the political parties of the centre and centre/left. The emergence of a feminist agenda was most noticeable in the Christian Democrats (DC), the newly formed Humanist Party, the Partido por la Democracia (PPD), the new umbrella party of the renovated left, and the Socialists. It was these parties which formed the Concertación, the centre-left coalition which contested the 1989 elections and was in many ways a continuation of the moderate alliance tentatively established after 1983. Women had the greatest visibility and presence within renovated socialism. The FMS continued its work within the socialist party, and, after its formation, in the PPD, putting forward proposals for inclusion in the opposition's programme. However, Molina has argued that the proposals of the Christian Democrat women were some of the most fully elaborated of all the opposition, but some of these (for example, around reproductive rights and divorce) conflicted with the basic moral and religious ideas which inspire Christian Democracy.

Old tensions which had existed between the *feministas* (feminists) and the *poltticas* (female activists within political parties) were reduced as many *poltticas* became more sympathetic to the aims of feminists. Indeed Serrano

(1990) has argued that, during this period, tensions were transformed into a debate about the styles and options which were established as alternatives. Many women activists began to value an autonomous women's axis whose existence could help them in their activities in political parties (Angelo, 1990). However, while several parties were prepared to make general statements about women's equality they were not prepared to seriously restructure power to allow women greater access to decision-making processes within them, often segregating them in separate organizations. The FMS had little actual power to change the actions of party organizations. The PPD adopted a quota system for women, but ignored it on occasions, for example in its political council and in the selection of candidates (Saa, 1990).

The perception of women's continued lack of influence in the run-up to the 1988 plebiscite and selection of very few women candidates (around 5 per cent of the total) for subsequent elections provided the major impetus for the creation of the autonomous Concertación de Mujeres por la Democracia in 1988. It was formed by women from a wide range of parties in the Concertación (the coalition contesting the elections) together with independent feminists (including academics and activists, many of whom were middle-class professionals). The Concertación de Mujeres can be seen as growing both out of a tradition of attempts to create a united women's movement to influence the political agenda and out of the attempts of feminists to influence the centre and centre/left political parties. However, as had been the case with some of the earlier attempts to create a united movement, some women active in the popular organizations again felt that the Concertación de Mujeres did not represent their interests (Angelo, 1990).

The Concertación de Mujeres had a threefold aim: first, to raise women's issues on the national political scene; second, to work in presidential and parliamentary campaigns on behalf of the Concertación; and third, to formulate a programme on women for future democratic government. The eleven commissions of the women's Concertación produced a document which included a proposal for a ministry for women, and for changes in education, law, employment, health, and the family. These proposals were presented to the Concertación as demands and most of them were incorporated into its electoral programme (Montecino and Rosetti, 1990). The visibility of women's movements during all phases of the transition in combination with the activities of feminists within centre/left parties had meant that those political parties felt that they could not ignore the demands of the Concertación de Mujeres.

'Women's issues' had been firmly placed on the political agenda in the following form: the Concertación was now committed to 'fully enforce women's rights considering the new role of women in society, overcoming any form of discrimination'. However this on its own was not acceptable to all in the coalition and the statement that the 'government will enforce the measures required to adequately protect the family' was added, leaving the proposal with what were perhaps contradictory aims from the start.

The goals were to be enforced through:

1 legal changes: improving women's legal position;
2 social participation: the incorporation of women into the political system and labour market;
3 the creation of a national machinery at state level which would propose policy and oversee its implementation by other ministries.

It was therefore anticipated that these goals would be implemented through policies specifically aimed at women, but that these would not be ghettoized away from mainstream development policy but integrated into the work of all relevant government departments.

These proposals came out of the strategy of direct engagement of parts of the Chilean feminist movement with the political process and it is highly unlikely that, without this pressure, the Concertación would have adopted these ideas. According to Valenzuela (an academic, feminist activist and later part of SERNAM), members of the Concertación de Mujeres assumed that the government (and by implication the state) was a gender-neutral tool which could be used in gender-based ways, that is, that engaging with the state would be a relatively straightforward process to bring about an expansion of rights and democratic procedures through which women would also be incorporated as full citizens (Valenzuela, 1992). There was also an assumption that relationships with women's organizations outside the state would be relatively unproblematic. Neither of these two assumptions has been borne out in practice.

1990 to the Present Day: The Consolidation of Competitive Electoral Politics[2]

The centre-left Concertación was elected convincingly in the elections of 1989 and took office in 1990. Clearly some space did then exist within the state to introduce gender-based policies but the government's programme on women has only been partially implemented. In order to explore why this has occurred, it is useful to consider which parts of the programme have been initiated and to what effect and thereby understand why there have been complex and contradictory outcomes both within and outside of the state.

The major way in which the Concertación programme on women discussed above has been implemented has been through the establishment in 1990 of SERNAM, the Servicio Nacional de la Mujer, which was modelled on similar bodies in Spain and Brazil. After pressure from the feminist movement, SERNAM was created through a law rather than a presidential decree so that it is less vulnerable to abolition. As a result of right-wing opposition the bill was toned down: the functions of SERNAM were reduced, its capability to execute programmes was removed, its personnel reduced, and while its director was in the cabinet, SERNAM was placed under the auspices of the Ministry of Planning. SERNAM's personnel, many of whom were involved in drawing up the Concertación de Mujeres' original proposals, are activists drawn mainly from NGOs or academics. But while they are not civil servants with experience of government, many are members of the Chilean political class with connections to Concertación politicians. In the first four years of its existence, SERNAM's president and vice-president were partners of the leaders of the Christian Democrats and the Socialists (Macaulay, 1995).

SERNAM's budget has been small. According to some sources it was initially established with US $2m plus US $1.5m from outside. Almost three-quarters of the initial budget for 1990–91 was allocated to pay for the fifty-nine staff and the remaining quarter for goods and services (Mensaje Presidencial on Bill to create SERNAM, 1990). Outside funding came primarily from foreign governments (Sweden, Norway, Denmark, Holland and Spain) and NGOs and other international organizations such as the EU, IBRD, FAO and UNICEF. Foreign funding could potentially have given it greater autonomy from government, but much of it has been short-term and some is now being replaced by state funding. SERNAM initially benefited from the shift of foreign funding from the grass-roots NGOs, which had received resources directly during the dictatorship, to the new civilian government.

The role and functions of SERNAM were unclear at its establishment as it was not made into a full ministry. While its institutional location in the ministry of planning means that it should be at the heart of planning and policy-making, it has no concrete mechanisms to influence government decisions and as we will see is therefore dependent on other methods such as negotiation and personal contacts (Goetz, 1994). However, four priorities were determined:

1 the establishment of a Programme for Women heads of Household;
2 the establishment of a Network of Information Centres in Women's Rights;
3 the establishment of a Violence against Women Programme;
4 the introduction of Legal reforms.

What SERNAM Has Done

SERNAM has carried out multiple roles, although its limited functions, particularly its weakness in overseeing other departments and in making policy, has resulted in a concentration on public awareness building, implementing pilot projects and pushing for legal changes (Goetz, 1994).

SERNAM has experienced its greatest problems in its role within the state. Its brief within the government to coordinate with other ministries, particularly those concerned with social policy, has been problematic. There is no formal machinery with which it can oversee the work of other government departments, and contact points are neither high-ranking officials nor often interested in gender issues. SERNAM also provides training to civil servants to increase gender awareness but this too has been problematic. Because of the voluntary attendance, only those already committed to gender awareness, with few top-level officials among them, have taken part. But again because of its small budget and lack of staff it has been largely ineffective. As a result of its lack of power within the state, progress often depends more on the existence of already committed individuals with influence within ministries than on the actions of SERNAM. Results can therefore depend on the existence of feminist 'gatekeepers' or sympathizers at all levels: for example, Jorge Arrate (then leader of the socialist party and partner of the ex-vice-president of SERNAM) provided a high-level commitment to working with SERNAM in the Ministry of Labour. While some of SERNAM's contacts have been good because many SERNAM officials are members of the political class, it also leaves SERNAM vulnerable because commitment to the organization is because of personal or factional reasons rather than programmatic ones (Macaulay, 1995).

SERNAM has been more effective in some of its other briefs. As part of its role in information gathering and dissemination, it has commissioned research from outside academics. Its communications brief was financed by foreign aid and UNICEF until 1993, and much of its publicity has been relatively successful but because of underfunding has been limited. A network of Information Centres for Women's Rights (CIDEMs) has also been established to provide women with information on their rights (Matear, 1993). The centres were also meant to maintain links with women's movements outside the state and to promote women's organizations. They were initially funded by the EU but that money has now been withdrawn. But despite the potential autonomy offered by foreign finance, CIDEMs have been constrained in their activities, concentrating more on social benefits and poverty rather than gender issues.

As SERNAM cannot set up programmes on its own account, it has concentrated on establishing pilot projects for others to continue. The majority of the programmes have focused on income generation in some form or other. Many of these have been seen as part of a move away from the broad emphasis on empowerment of programmes of many grass-roots NGOs to a much more narrowly defined 'market empowerment' which fits in with socio-economic policies of government, that is, an emphasis on poverty reduction through increasing individual access to the market, for example by training women for the labour market (Schild, 1994). Among the programmes have been employment training for women in both traditional and non-traditional jobs. Its female heads of household programme has caused controversy from opponents for destroying the family and SERNAM has had to couch its support for it in terms of the better results for social policies which can be obtained by increasing the income-generating capacity of the needy. Other programmes have included a microenterprise support programme and childcare for temporary agricultural workers (Matear, 1993).

The domestic violence against women programme is an exception to this pattern. Its establishment was a result of campaigning by feminists and the commitment by feminists in SERNAM to it. Initially no funds were allocated but the programme secured international funding in late 1992. It has initiated research to discover the extent of the problem and organized training programmes for the police and civil servants. SERNAM has also campaigned for legal reforms. It has worked for more rights for women in the labour market to be incorporated into labour law, particularly for service sector workers such as domestic servants. It has agitated for changes in the civil code: working on changes to legislation on marriage and on the legitimacy of children. In the field of criminal law SERNAM oversaw the domestic violence bill which finally became law in 1994, three and half years after first being presented and after much opposition.

Some space has therefore existed for SERNAM to achieve some of its goals, but this has been limited. Some of the obstacles have been practical, for example the limited budget, inexperienced personnel and lack of power within the government. The effectiveness of many of its projects is dependent on other ministries beyond SERNAM's control, and with decentralization will be dependent on the municipalities over which central government has little influence. However it is also necessary to understand the wider political context in order to comprehend the outcomes. SERNAM has faced opposition from a variety of sources within the state and the political superstructure. First, it has come from the right-wing political parties such as RN and UDI. Before its establishment, the right-wing opposition mobilized against SERNAM. Despite the claim that its goals were to implement the UN convention which had been ratified by military government and to protect the family, it was seen as a threat to social order and the family on the part of feminists and socialists. Second, the Church has opposed some of its proposals and in part this reflects the transformation of the Chilean Catholic Church from playing an oppositional role under military rule to a more conservative one (Schild, 1992). From 1988 onwards the Church began retrenching its social and educational programmes to concentrate more on spiritual concerns. In addition the Catholic Church as an institution is opposed to divorce and reproductive rights and has 'traditional' views on the position of women. Its relationship with the Christian Democrats, the majority partner in the Concertación, means that it has some indirect influence over SERNAM: for example, SERNAM's deputy director was removed after a row with a senior church figure. SERNAM has also faced opposition from within the Concertación, particularly from the right of the Christian Democrats, which highlights the contradictions which exist within the coalition.

This has meant that the greatest space to achieve change has existed on those issues which are considered least controversial. These centre around social and economic measures such as women's employment training which are seen as part of poverty alleviation and income generation. Huge tensions have appeared around issues such as divorce and reproductive rights, particularly abortion. Those more gender-specific measures which threaten to change the nature of gender relations directly are more difficult to get accepted.

Indeed gender issues are, according to Valenzuela (1992), the most significant point of disagreement within the coalition, as there is general agreement on most other aspects of social and economic policy. However, despite these difficulties, some important legal changes have been made.

There have also been divisions within SERNAM itself, which reflect divisions between the parties, especially between the Christian Democrat orientated members who tend to have more conservative views particularly about the family, and the Socialist women who tend to have a more 'feminist' agenda (Matear, 1993). This lack of agreement, both on analysis and on what action should be taken about certain issues, has meant that SERNAM has not been able to come up with a position on abortion and has avoided the issue instead. Personnel are often appointed along party lines to make sure of a balance between the political parties in the Concertación rather than because of links to women's movements, feminist beliefs or technical training or ability. The new director is a friend of President Frei's wife, headed the commission on the family, and is seen as more conservative.

SERNAM has also had an ambivalent relationship with women's movements outside the state. The criteria for the selection of personnel have contributed to a sense of alienation from SERNAM felt by some women's groups. Many women's organizations (some of which are often seen as radical feminist) have been wary because SERNAM is regarded as an arm of the state (*La Boletina*, n.d.). Popular women's movements, relegated by many of SERNAM's programmes to the role of consumers, in particular are confused as to what SERNAM does and do not feel represented by it. There has also been some disillusionment with what is considered to be SERNAM's lack of a radical approach. The nature of the projects now being funded has shifted towards projects focused around narrow market-oriented economic aims: MOMUPO (Movimiento de Mujeres Populares) has criticized social policies which treat poor women as isolated individuals without allowing for the creation of collective spaces. It is claimed that SERNAM's policies can also have a differential impact on different groups of women: for example, it is claimed that changes to laws on property between men and women affect poor women negatively because property will be split and as a result poor women could lose the roof over their heads which is the most significant thing they have.

There is a general consensus that women's movements, particularly popular women's movements, along with many other social movements, have lost momentum since the return to competitive electoral politics. Schild (1994) (contrary to what she sees as the analysis of some feminists within SERNAM) attributes this in part to the existence of SERNAM. Women's movements in this view have been beheaded by the creation of SERNAM and the subsequent migration of feminists into the state. They have also lost potential resources because funds which used to go directly to NGOs are now channelled through the state and organizations then have to bid for them. This procedure has led to accusations that SERNAM has a clientelistic relationship with NGOs, comfortably coexisting with them and providing 'jobs for the girls'

(Schild, 1994). Under these conditions resources are also more likely to go to middle-class organizations proficient at form-filling and knowing their way around the system rather than to popular organizations, and as a result some autonomous women's organizations have lost out. SERNAM is therefore caught in a potentially contradictory position as, according to Valenzuela (1992), SERNAM loses potential power through any reduction in the strength of the autonomous women's movements outside the state as its existence is due in part to their strength and the pressure that they brought to bear on the political parties which now form the government. But, at the same time, SERNAM's existence could be part of the very conditions which are undermining those movements.

Conclusions

These complex and contradictory outcomes must be seen as part of the whole process of democratization and reflect many trends seen in the Chilean transition more generally. They are in part a result of a narrow middle-class transition characterized by negotiated pacts and without a radical agenda for change. Those social movements remaining outside of the unfolding political process have been increasingly marginalized. However, some space for change did exist in this political conjuncture. The nature of the state was potentially more fluid at this moment of transformation than at other times, but this space was limited by the nature of the transition.

Clearly the state has become an arena for gender struggles. SERNAM's role within the state has been difficult. While the lack of consensus over SERNAM's role and its lack of finance has impeded its activities, other factors have played a key role. It is not an autonomous body but part of the government and the state. SERNAM is closely tied to the political parties which form the government and is split along those lines. But at the same time it lacks the necessary power to influence policy-making, and in its dealings with other ministries it has faced some resistance. It is unclear what implications for its position the reduction of foreign funding and its replacement by state funding will have.

The state has not, therefore, proved to be the neutral tool some feminists had thought it was. It has been possible to achieve certain outcomes but not others. SERNAM has faced overt opposition for measures which threaten to alter gender relations. Those changes associated with some notion of strategic gender issues/empowerment are more difficult to achieve while more narrowly focused economic measures centred on poverty alleviation are far easier. However, SERNAM has been relatively successful in politicizing issues hitherto confined to the private sphere, such as domestic violence and teenage pregnancy, as well as abuse in the public sphere such as sexual harassment at work, thereby helping to challenge the public/private boundary. There has been little if no success in increasing the number of women in the political processes and in positions of power in government which was one of SERNAM's original aims.

The relationship with movements outside the state is complex. While SERNAM was never established as a body to represent women's movements, some organizations do feel that SERNAM does not represent them. But SERNAM has a differential relationship with different groups of women. Most of its personnel are professional women while the organizations feeling most marginalized by it are made up of poor women. It is also unclear how far it would be possible for SERNAM to represent the interests of different women's movements within the state. Its equal opportunities plan was drawn up without widespread consultation with groups outside SERNAM. While SERNAM has acted perhaps to add to the decline in women's movements, it needs autonomous movements backing it outside the state to give it greater power within the state. Feminist movements have lost some leverage within the government because in the process of transition women's movements have become less active and the government can afford to reduce its commitment to a feminist-inspired programme because the agenda was originally determined from outside by women's movements and brought into the political parties by feminist activists. No easy generalizations about SERNAM are therefore possible. Engagement with the state has proved to be a complex and difficult process giving rise to some opportunity spaces as well as unforeseen obstacles.

Notes

1 An earlier version of this chapter has appeared as 'Women's Movements, the State and Democratization in Chile', in *IDS Bulletin*, Vol. 26, No. 3, 1995.
2 I am grateful to Anne Marie Goetz, Veronica Schild and particularly Ann Matear for supplying much of the information in this section.

Bibliography

ALVAREZ, S. (1989) 'Politicising Gender and Engendering Democracy', in STEPAN, A. (Ed.), *Democratising Brazil: Problems of Transition and Consolidation*, Oxford, Oxford University Press.

ALVAREZ, S. (1990) *Engendering Democracy in Brazil: Women's Movements in Transition Politics*, Princeton, Princeton University Press.

ANGELO, G. (1990) *Nuevos Espacios y Nuevas Practtcas de Mujeres en una Situación de Crisis: Hacia el Surgiemiento y Consolidación de un Movimiento de Mujeres. El Caso de Chile*, Santiago, Cuadernos de la Morada.

Georgina Waylen

ARTEAGA, A. (1988) 'Polttizacion de lo Privado y Subversión del Cotidiano', in CEM *Mundo de Mujer: Continuidad y Cambio*, Santiago, Centro de Estudios de la Mujer.

LA BOLETINA, (n.d.) (magazine of MEMCH 83), No. 1, Nueva Epoca.

CHARLTON, S., EVERETT, J. and STAUDT, K. (Eds.) (1989) *Women, State and Development*, New York, SUNY Press.

GARRETON, A. M. (1989) 'Popular Mobilization and the Military Regime in Chile: The Complexities of the Invisible Transition', in ECKSTEIN, S. (Ed.) *Power and Popular Protest*, Berkeley, University of Cailfornia Press.

GOETZ, A. M. (1994) *The Politics of Integrating Gender to State Development Processes*, Geneva UNRISD Discussion Paper.

KIRKWOOD, J. (1990) *Ser Politica en Chile. Los Nudos de la Sabiduria Feminista*, Santiago, Editorial Cuarto Propio.

MACAULAY, F. (1995) 'Gender Relations and the Democratization of Local Politics in the Transition to Democracy in Brazil and Chile', paper presented to the PSA Annual Conference, York.

MATEAR, A. (1993) 'SERNAM: Women and the Process of Democratic Transition in Chile 1990–93', paper presented to Society of Latin American Studies Conference, Manchester.

MOLINA, N. (1989) 'Propuestas Politicas y Orientaciones de Cambio en la Situación de la Mujer', in GARRETON, M. A. (Ed.) *Propuestas Politicas y Demandas Sociales*, Vol. 3, Santiago, FLACSO.

MOLINA, N. (1990) 'El Estado y las Mujeres: Una Relación Dificil', in ISIS *Transiciones: Mujeres en los Procesos Democraticos*, Santiago, ISIS Internacional.

MONTECINO, S. and ROSSETTI, J. (Eds.) (1990) *Tramaspara un Nuevo Destino: Propuestas de la Concertación de Mujeres por la Democracia*, Santiago.

PETRAS, J. and LEIVA, F. (1988) 'Chile: The Authoritarian Transition to Electoral Politics', *Latin American Perspectives*, Vol. 15, No. 3, pp. 97–114.

PRINGLE, R. and WATSON, S. (1992) '"Women's Interests" and the Post-Structuralist State', in BARRETT, M. and PHILLIPS, A. (Eds.) *Destabilising Theory: Contemporary Feminist Debates*, Cambridge, Polity.

SAA, M. A. (1990) Interview with Maria Anonietta Saa, *Crttica Social*, May.

SCHILD, V. (1992) 'Struggling for Citizenship in Chile: A "Resurrection" of Civil Society?', paper for Latin American Studies Association Congress.

SCHILD, V. (1994) '"Becoming Subjects of Rights": Citizenship, Political Learning and Identity Formation among Latin American Women', paper for XVIth IPSA Congress, Berlin.

SERRANO, C. (1990) 'Chile Entre la Autonomia y la Integración', in ISIS *Transiciones: Mujeres en los Procesos Democraticos*, Santiago, ISIS Internacional.

SHOWSTACK-SASSOON, A. (Ed.) (1987) *Women and the State*, London, Hutchinson.

STETSON, D. M. and MAZUR, A. (Eds.) (1995) *Comparative State Feminism*, London, Sage.

VALDES, T. and WEINSTEIN, M. (1989) *Organizaciones de Pobladoras y Construción Democratica en Chile. Notas para un Debate. Documento de Trabajo*, Santiago, FLACSO.

VALENZUELA, M. E. (1990) 'Mujeres y Polttica: Logros y Tensiones en el Proceso de Redemocratización', *Proposiciones*, 18, pp. 210–32.

VALENZUELA, M. E. (1991) 'The Evolving Roles of Women under Military Rule', in DRAKE, P. and JAKSIC, I. (Eds.) *The Struggle for Democracy in Chile 1982–92*, Nebraska, University of Nebraska Press.

VALENZUELA, M. E. (1992) 'Women and Democratization in Chile', paper presented to Conference on Women and the Transition to Democracy in Latin America and Eastern Europe, Berkeley.

WATSON, S. (Ed.) (1990) *Playing the State*, London, Verso.

WAYLEN, G. (1992) 'Rethinking Women's Political Participation and Protest: Chile 1970–90', *Political Studies*, Vol. 40, No. 2, pp. 299–314.

WAYLEN, G. (1993) 'Women's Movements in Latin America', *Third World Quarterly*, Vol. 14, No. 3, pp. 573–88.

Chapter 7

Dis/Organizing Gender: Women Development Agents in State and NGO Poverty-Reduction Programmes in Bangladesh

Anne Marie Goetz

Contemporary concerns with institutional capacity-building in the public services of Third World states are most often animated by preoccupations with efficiency, and rarely with institutional capacity for gender-sensitivity, or enhanced responsiveness and accountability to women. This chapter is concerned with the issue of gender-sensitivity of state bureaucracies in the development process. It approaches this from the perspective of the experiences and attitudes of lower-level women bureaucrats in a government poverty-reduction programme in Bangladesh, and contrasts their work with that of their counterparts in the non-governmental sector, to control for significant differences in institutional environments and organizational forms. The comparison with the NGO sector is also important given its popularly assumed 'comparative advantage' in implementing gender and development (GAD) projects. The chapter finds that from the perspective of women's experiences as development agents, neither the 'comparative advantage' of NGOs in GAD work, nor, on the other hand, the resistance of state bureaucracies to gender equity, can be assumed. The employment of increasing numbers of women development agents has the potential to transform the quality and nature of development service delivery to women, but gendered organizational structures in both institutional arenas limit their impact on development practice. However, certain features of state employment enable women state agents to develop 'oppositional' perspectives on their work, and this can point to productive institutional changes in women's interests.

Bangladesh has adopted a range of measures to promote women's welfare, including legal reforms, institutional innovations, such as the establishment of the first Women's Affairs Ministry in the Asia-Pacific region in 1978, and the elaboration of a wide range of national development programmes targeting resources to women. Feminist critics have questioned the quality of these commitments, given the government's simultaneous drift over the last twenty years towards an Islamicization of the state (Kabeer, 1989; Goetz, 1995a), pointing out that most development programmes targeting women have remained underfunded, and marginal to national development planning (with the exception of family planning programmes). Also, the design of these programmes and the nature of the resources reaching women have tended to contribute to a 'feminizing' or 'gendering' of their participation in development by reinforcing conservative gender role assumptions as to their proper place as secondary contributors to family survival (Feldman and McCarthy, 1984; Feldman *et al.*, 1983). Bangladesh also has one of the most dynamic non-governmental development sectors in the world, with over 12,000 NGOs varying in size from village-level associations to large development organizations with quasi-corporate structures. These NGOs have pioneered alternative approaches to addressing women's needs in development, some of which have become models for gender and development work elsewhere in the world.

Frustrated with the resistance of state bureaucracies to gender-equity concerns, many aid donors have shifted to working through the non-governmental sector, in Bangladesh as elsewhere. Buvinic's examination of the 'psychology of donor support' shows that donors feel 'these organizations [are] more receptive than government agencies to the problems of poor women' (1989, p. 1046). The 'comparative advantage' of NGOs over state institutions, at least for community-level development work, is said to inhere in their closer relationship to their beneficiaries and their flexible, non-bureaucratic structures (Fowler, 1988, p. 8). Another advantage is held to be their investment in committed staff, unlike government institutions in which generalist bureaucrats may be rotated across different agencies and programmes, and be less committed to their clientele than to the bureaucracy itself (Montgomery, 1988). These propositions regarding the 'comparative advantage' of NGOs have largely not been tested with regard to gender issues, although some recent evaluations have deeply challenged the assumption that the equity-focused strategies of NGOs can stretch beyond class issues to embrace gender power conflicts (Vivian and Maseko, 1994; White, 1991). In spite of growing evidence that NGOs can be as resistant to feminist concerns as state bureaucracies, the folklore of NGO gender sensitivity and orientation to egalitarianism is part of the broader neo-liberal enthusiasm for private sector social provisioning and a derogation of the public sector's capacity to promote social change and human development.[1]

This chapter does not set out to compare NGO and state GAD programme outputs with a view to testing these assumptions. Instead, it explores the experiences of women staff on either side of the state/NGO institutional divide to explore the development of institutional spaces, or 'room for maneouvre' (Schaffer, 1984) for leadership in women's interests. Gender and development programmes are about improving the responsiveness and accountability of development organizations to poor women's needs and interests, and the concept of 'women's leadership' is used here to express this qualitative change in development management. This differs from the conventional understanding of leadership as a quality of charismatic guidance and management exercised by an individual. 'Women's leadership' involves institutionalizing women's presence in decision-making processes in such a way as to enhance women's participation and above all, their capacity to validate their interpretations of women's needs and interests. Ideally, this capacity can be shown by men as well as women, and implies a process which should occur not just within the organization, but among beneficiaries also. The concept of 'women's leadership' draws on Molyneux's distinction between practical and strategic interest articulation in development processes (Molyneux, 1985). In the following discussion, the focus is not on individual and visible women leaders, but rather on the pursuit of women's interests at the development micro-level, as expressed through the experience of women development agents, the nature of their interactions with their female clientele, and the degree to which they are able to develop and act upon 'oppositional' perspectives which may challenge those of their male colleagues. The focus is also on how different organizational systems affect and are affected by the development of women's leadership at the field level.

The Organizational Configuration in Rural Development in Bangladesh: The State, NGOs, and the Role of Field Workers

The particular focus of this chapter is on rural development agencies, both state and non-governmental, because they are central arenas for competition over access to development resources in a largely agrarian economy where poverty has disrupted traditional survival systems – as is the case in Bangladesh, with its problems of landlessness and a relatively stagnant rural employment situation (Sanyal, 1991). More importantly, they are the focus here because, in dealing with the needs of rural producers, they are central arenas in which gendered inequalities can be mirrored, reproduced, or, alternatively, challenged, depending on the ways they interpret women's productive and reproductive needs in development. As a result, these agencies are part of the institutions determining the distribution of resources and social values between women and men, contributing to the social construction or organization of gender difference.

This chapter draws on research conducted in Bangladesh in 1993 on the experiences and perspectives of staff, women and men, in two large rural credit and employment generating programmes, one a state-run organization, the other a prominent NGO.[2] The government Rural Poor Programme is the government's largest credit-based rural development programme targeting landless people. It is divided into several foreign-funded components, and the programme with the smallest foreign Technical Assistance component (the Rural Development 12 (RD-12) programme, funded by the Canadian International Development Agency (CIDA)) was chosen for study on the grounds that this made it more representative of state management practices. At the time of this study it had 350,000 members, 59 per cent women (by early 1995 women had shot up to 70 per cent of the membership). At the field level, 44 per cent of its staff were women. The NGO, the Bangladesh Rural Advancement Committee (BRAC), is the world's largest indigenous NGO, with over a million members, and is widely respected as a model for NGO development work in the country and elsewhere. The research focused on its credit and rural development component, the Rural Development Programme (RDP) (other programmes include its Non-Formal Education Programme, and the Women's Health Development Programme), which, at the time of this study, offered a credit-based rural development package to well over 700,000 members, over 70 per cent of them women (by late 1994, 85 per cent of BRAC credit was targeted to women). In contrast to the government organization, 15 per cent of its regular programme staff at the field level were women, and less than 10 per cent of its quasi-voluntary staff at the village level, the Programme Assistants, were women.[3] These two organizations were chosen as being broadly representative of state and non-governmental approaches to poverty-reduction programmes with a strong focus on targeting women. Though twice the size of the government organization, and better resourced, the NGO is broadly comparable to the government operation in that both were delivering a similar development package and using similar methods.

These credit programmes involve, in principle, an active *disorganization* of discriminatory structures of gender difference, to the degree that they assign women management authority over cash resources which are intended to shift upwards their rate of market engagement to enable them to take lead roles in household and community survival. In Bangladesh, institutional innovations pioneered by the Grameen Bank and BRAC are justly famous for adapting credit delivery systems to accommodate the gender-specific constraints of poor rural women in accessing credit. Innovations include the substitution of social collateral, in the form of peer group guarantees, for physical collateral; bringing banking to the village; changes in the timing of group meetings and the places they are held; and the development of appropriate training and technology. These innovations have been adapted by the government's RPP, and other government poverty-reduction programmes (Montgomery *et al.*, 1994), in response to persistent criticisms as to the gender and class biases in many government programmes (Feldman and McCarthy, 1984). These changes have unquestionably eased poor women's access to loans in Bangladesh, as attested by the enormous increase in women's membership of these programmes since the mid 1980s (Goetz and Sen Gupta, 1996). Women in Bangladesh have proven themselves capable borrowers and are famed for their high repayment rates on these programmes.

Channelling important cash resources to poor women, at the bottom of the social hierarchy in Bangladesh, has never been unproblematic, and it arouses significant social resistance. Many studies of both NGO and government poverty-reduction programmes detail problems of elite capture of resources, or active subversion in terms of destruction of programme efforts (Kramsjo and Wood, 1992; van Schendel, 1987; Wood, 1985); and any programme which targets non-traditional resources to women is bound to face these problems to an even more intense degree. One form of social resistance is the phenomenon noted by some observers of the diversion of control over women's credit to their male relatives (Goetz and Sen Gupta, 1996; Ackerly,

1995; Rahman, 1986; Montgomery *et al.*, 1994), a diversion which reflects in part market constraints on women's capacity to use loans profitably, but also cultural prejudices as to the propriety of women's responsibility for investing cash resources for the household.[4]

This cultural resistance is not restricted to the community level, and exists, inevitably, within development agencies themselves. State bureaucracies, with their status-oriented, hierarchical and elitist cultures, are commonly assumed to be resistant to equity-oriented development programmes, in contrast to NGOs which pride themselves on their egalitarian ideologies. However, analysts of the fate of gender policy in a range of state and non-governmental settings the world over have pointed to common forms of resistance in male-dominated organizational settings. At an individual level, gender policy can provoke personal hostility in reaction to what is seen as cultural interference, especially when GAD policies are seen as an external imposition. At an organizational level, it disrupts accustomed patterns of resource distribution, and the ideologies and practices that develop around this (Staudt, 1990; Goetz, 1992; Yudelman, 1990). When significant numbers of women staff are recruited to help implement women-targeted programmes, something which is necessary given that Bangladesh's purdah context makes men's access to women's worlds problematic, hostility or resistance can be exacerbated. A new cadre of women staff can disrupt accustomed patterns of organizing work, given their different capabilities, interests, and constraints, their greater needs for security, and their different distribution of obligations between work and home. Because very often neither the targeting of resources to greater numbers of women beneficiaries, nor the addition of new women staff, is preceded by gender training or other efforts to institutionalize changed objectives and orientations in the organization, justifications for reorienting programme efforts to favour women may not be clear. Without occasion to develop commitment to new programme orientations, they may not be seen as legitimate.

It is at the level of programme implementation in the field that resistance, mis-comprehension, or lack of commitment to gender policy goals can result in processes of 'feminizing' interpretations of women's needs and interests in development. However progressive and transformative the commitment to gender policy may be at the top level of organizations, one of the most critical arenas for the realization of the spirit of that commitment is at the interface between development workers and the organization's clientele. The everyday work practices and attitudes of field workers is the key to engineering the 'fit' between policy and local reality. The ways these *de facto* policy-makers exercise their personal discretion in identifying people deemed deserving of organizational membership, in controlling the levels of inputs and information they deliver, and in interacting with beneficiaries, will affect the beneficiaries' views of their own identities and capacities. This is particularly important when dealing with women beneficiaries, because of the complex socio-psychological dimensions of the transition from internalized gender-linked feelings of inferiority to personal and collective emancipation. For women's empowerment, then, it becomes critical to invest in a positive deployment of field-worker 'discretion' in women's interests – in the development of women's leadership at the level of policy implementation.

A potential source of this leadership is the women staff of rural development agencies. In Bangladesh there are now well over 100,000 women working in rural development, and though the majority remain in largely sex-stereotyped development sectors such as family planning, child welfare, home economics and handicrafts, a growing number are staffing credit-delivery organizations, especially at the field level. The very presence of women development agents in the largely male-dominated world of rural credit programmes, doing the male-identified work of handling money, is in itself a leadership resource. In Bangladesh, rural development work is a strongly masculinized arena. Field work requires high mobility, interactions with strangers, and work demands outside of normal office hours; these impose special problems for women. To the extent that the mobility and activities of women development agents in rural areas break strict rules about appropriate patterns of female deportment, these women personify a social revolution, and their work establishes them as social pioneers. By challenging part of the process of the social construction of gender, they are making a 'gender disorganizing' impact. The next sections explore how far women staff are able to carry this 'gender disorganizing' effect into their work.

Dis/Organizing Gender

Common ways in which societal class and gender power relations 'leak' into women-targeted special credit programmes include: tendencies for women from outside of the poverty target group to join credit groups and dominate them (Rozario, 1992; Khan and Stewart, 1992); tendencies for women's loan investment patterns to remain corralled within traditional, low-profit, sex-typed activities, promoting little significant change in levels of market engagement (Mayoux, 1995); and the tendency for financial and managerial control over some loan-funded activities to be taken by men. This research found that these class- and gender-biased programme implementation patterns existed in both the state and NGO programme (with problems of mis-targeting, and of male appropriation of loans slightly higher in the state organization; see also Goetz and Sen Gupta, 1996). There were no significant differences, in terms of these problems, between the performance of women or men field-worker-managed groups in either programme. This suggests that these problems are caused by gendered features in programme design, and by the particular class and gender interests which compose the rural development equation in Bangladesh, both in the community and the bureaucracy.

Where women and men field staff in both programmes differed in relation to these patterns of 'reorganizing' gender in programme implementation, was in the opinions and attitudes they expressed about them, particularly problems related to gender relations. For example, in a survey of staff members of both BRAC and RPP, there was a marked difference between the views of men in both organizations and those of their female colleagues on the question of the main constraint to working effectively with poor women. Although both men and women mentioned a range of constraints such as a lack of education, socio-cultural factors, male attitudes, overpopulation, lack of solidarity and awareness, economic problems, constraints on the mobility and effectiveness of staff themselves, and problems with programme design such as rigid lending procedures, the biggest category of 'constraint' identified by about 30 per cent of the men in both organizations was poor women's lack of education (often expressed as their 'ignorance'). The responses of women staff in both organizations were more evenly distributed across other constraints, but very few identified poor women's 'ignorance' as a problem, and the biggest category of constraint they identified was problems in their own personal effectiveness as development workers (22 per cent of BRAC and 35 per cent of RPP women staff mentioned this). This reflects practical problems in women's work, which will be discussed later, but it also suggests an attitudinal difference. Women staff are highly conscious of their own limitations, many of which are imposed by the difficulties of managing their role contradictions as working women in a culture hostile to women's freedom and mobility. Their male colleagues, however, were more prepared to identify the shortcomings of their beneficiaries as the main problem, effectively putting the blame on poor rural women for problems in efficient programme implementation.

Two statements from NGO field workers illustrate this contrast in relation to a problem field workers faced in mobilizing women to attend training courses at the NGO local Area Office. According to the male field worker, women rejected learning opportunities out of fear and 'dependence':

> We are trying to conscientize women through training and motivation, but without much effect – they're still dependent on men. They don't want to go for training or any learning opportunities. They're afraid of it. (85)[5]

Women staff were more prone to refer to processes of 'oppression', implying an active process of constraint or prevention:

> When there is any residential training husbands don't want to let wives go. Even to get loans women have to come to BRAC offices. Husbands want to come and take loans instead. . . . Women's husbands are the biggest obstacle. Husbands think that if their wives come to groups they'll learn more and won't obey husbands, and all the domestic work won't get done. (36)

Women staff were much more likely than men to mention gender-related problems faced by poor rural women, and it was they who first pointed out to the interviewers that poor rural women face difficulties in retaining control over the use of their loans. This issue was integrated to the interview process to investigate staff opinions on the matter. When asked, the majority of women and men staff in both organizations acknowledged that the practice of women sometimes transferring loan control to their male relatives existed. However, women staff felt this to be more problematic a practice than men, with over 60 per cent of women in both organizations concerned about the problem. Although 50 per cent of the men in BRAC, and 40 per cent of the men in the RPP, acknowledged the problem, they tended to express somewhat more resigned and fatalistic views about it, saying that it was hard to change patterns of gender relations in the household. Women staff were more interested in making suggestions as to how to cope with this problem by 'conscientizing' the male relatives of women borrowers, investing in closer supervision for higher-profit investment activities for women, or moving away from credit altogether to developing small rural industries which could employ women. Women's greater concern over the issue appeared to indicate a difference of opinion with male colleagues as to the productive capabilities of poor rural women, and as to their rights to control financial assets. The following example from a woman government field worker illustrates this:

> One woman who had neither children nor a husband was doing domestic labour, and became a samity member and applied for a loan. I supported her loan proposal for a small trade business but the office did not approve it. The office said she has no husband or son so how will she run the business? I think she could have – that's why I proposed her! (58)

This contrasts with the opinion of a male NGO field worker:

> Our objective is to develop the family so if the husband earns the money what is the problem? What is the constraint? The man is also spending the money for the family. Even if men spend extra money on cigarettes, etc., women will be developed. (81)

Few other than the higher-ranking or Head Office-based staff members of either organization had received gender training at the time of this research. The lack of gender training could account for a lack of clarity amongst field workers in terms of understanding the purpose of channelling credit to women, with the distinction between women's financial empowerment and a general improvement in household welfare not highlighted in field operations. Nevertheless, women staff showed a different level of appreciation of gender issues in their work from men, and were particularly sensitive to issues of women's rights to control development resources.

The mechanics of gendered space management and the rules governing access to and conduct around women in a purdah society account for some of these differences in perspective and receptivity to women's needs. Women field staff have much greater access to women's worlds than do male staff. They can enter their houses and make direct contact, rather than negotiating with women's male guardians first. Rural women members of these programmes often said that they could not raise with male staff issues such as family planning, inheritance and custody rights, dowry, divorce and desertion, sexual assault and molestation, and domestic violence. These are all issues whose resolution is important for processes of empowerment, and, at a more practical level, they determine whether a woman is able to invest her loan and its profits independently, and are therefore rightly part of any credit programme targeting women.

Male staff's relationships with village women were necessarily constrained by gendered behavioural norms. Though many had a very positive and brotherly relationship with programme members, the fact that their sex endows them with greater social status than women introduced problems of distance and deference which distorted processes of mutual exchange. Men were also often constrained by social convention to contact women's male guardians first for permission to interact with women. This male-channelled process of mediating the relationship between a development organization and its female clientele reinforces traditional gendered understandings of people's rights, identities, and authority in the public arena; women participate in development on male sufferance, not their own initiative.[6] At the level of programme implementation, it has the inevitable effect of linking women's development resources to men's community and personal interests.

The separation of women's and men's worlds has some interesting implications for problems of class bias and corruption – problems observed in this study primarily in relation to the government organization. Where differences between women and men government staff occur around the problem of corruption or elite capture is where occasions for these processes require contact with powerful men, whether within the bureaucracy or in the community. No less immune than their male colleagues to pressures to promote local power interests for personal gain, women staff are nevertheless deeply constrained by the gender norms which forbid contact with non-family males. This taboo on mixing with non-kin males works most strongly within the bureaucracy itself, where the imperative of maintaining sexual propriety constrains women from getting too closely involved with male colleagues in corrupt practices. In the very few cases where corruption was discussed during interviews, women government staff made a direct connection between sexual harassment and corruption, citing cases where incitement to risk their professional integrity (by fudging accounts, for instance) was accompanied either by the threat of sexual harassment, or by the woman's fear that collusion would create suspicions amongst colleagues of sexual impropriety. Women resist by creating a safe and separate sphere of operation for themselves, but the negative consequence of this is that they also reinforce their exclusion from

significant decision-making processes both within the local development bureaucracy and at the level of local community management.

It would be a mistake to assume on this evidence that women staff are
necessarily less prone to corrupt practices than men staff. It may simply be that
they have fewer opportunities and skills in this area. Nevertheless, while
gender relations remain the same in the bureaucracy and in the community,
women staff may be engaging less in such practices, and in consequence,
possibly disrupting or interrupting some resource-diversion processes.

The evidence presented above of the greater local-level sensitivity of
women development agents in both organizations to their beneficiaries' needs
and experiences in development is a resource which should be built upon for
the promotion of GAD goals. It cannot, of course, be assumed that the
differences between male and female staff in this area are the expression of
some natural solidarity or sisterhood between women lower-level bureaucrats
and their beneficiaries. Women development agents, whether working for the
state or NGOs, are largely middle-class. Indeed, in terms of urban backgrounds and educational achievements, they sometimes have a more elite
formal status than their male counterparts, as it is difficult to recruit suffi-
ciently educated women from more conservative rural backgrounds. As a
result, they may identify more strongly with dominant class interests, and with
the interests of their organization, than with their impoverished clientele. But
to the degree that there is an incipient expression of alternative perspectives
on rural women's problems and on the purpose of targeting resources to them,
how far are women able to articulate their perspectives in opposition to their
male colleagues? How far do they carry individualized perceptions into an
analysis of gendered constraints – in society, on their own lives, and on the way
their organizations function?

Perspectives on Gender Issues and Women's Interests

Put simply, what we are looking for here is a critical perspective on gender
relations, a feminist perspective. However, the term 'feminism' is a contentious one to use in this context. In the West alone, it is not self-evident that it
describes all forms of revolt against discriminatory cultural scripts for gender
relations. Elsewhere, and certainly in Bangladesh, its use can be rejected as a
cultural invasion. In this context, therefore, no effort was made to establish
any 'index' of feminist awareness; rather, the interest was in identifying
whether women staff expressed perspectives on themselves and their organizations which demonstrated criticism of gender discrimination.

The critical change needed for effective implementation of gender and
development policy is a capacity to be receptive to the needs and interests of
poor women, which requires an awareness of problems of gender and class
inequality, and of one's own position in gender and class hierarchies. To
investigate whether field staff were familiar with thinking about gender as a

constituent, rather than contingent, factor affecting people's social prospects, they were asked a deliberately leading question about whether there were similarities between women staff and women beneficiaries – in other words, whether they shared common sociological characteristics. There was a clear difference in responses of women and men in both organizations. The majority of male respondents argued that no conditions or circumstances were shared between women staff and beneficiaries because of differences in class and education levels. Women, on the other hand, were able to project from their own experiences of gender discrimination and so 'recognize' the gender-based oppressions of poor women, in spite of the class differences between them, as a typical statement shows:

> Of course there are similarities between us and poor women. Even though we have education and jobs, still, how many among us can exercise authority and give decisions? In the same way, how can the rural women give decisions? (25: NGO field worker, woman)

In spite of the greater class- and status-conscious culture of the civil service, slightly more of the government women staff (71 per cent) identified gender-based similarities than the NGO women staff (63 per cent). Disaggregated by staff category, this difference was most significant at the lowest level of NGO staff, the Programme Assistants, who were deeply reluctant to acknowledge points of commonality with their beneficiaries. The majority of respondents in this category insisted on class differences between themselves and beneficiaries, even though most of them have village backgrounds, and are often from economically insecure families. Their concern to distance themselves from beneficiaries reflects a struggle to assert status against their very low position in the organization. Also, staff in this category receive less training than other field staff, are less integrated to the organization and less exposed to new ideas, and have fewer opportunities to reflect on social development issues. Their aversion to identifying themselves with beneficiaries warns against easy assumptions as to any natural solidarity between women within a particular class category on the basis of shared gender characteristics.

Staff were asked whether they were aware of the 'gender and development' concern in development, and whether they could explain what it was about. Given that none of the interviewees had had training in gender and development, responses indicated whether they had picked up an understanding of the issue indirectly, either through other training in social development issues, or through exposure to current development discourses. More women than men in both organizations explained 'gender and development' either as a project of changing gender relations, or as the more liberal-feminist project of enabling women to compete with men. NGO staff had much more exposure to the issue, with 75 per cent of women Programme Organizers (and 40 per cent of their male counterparts) able to offer a definition of the term. In the government organization, 30 per cent of women Field Organizers, but none of the men, were conversant in gender and development ideas. The contrast between male staff across the two organizations is possibly indicative of different levels of commitment to social change issues, and also possibly attests to the greater exposure of BRAC staff to current development discourses in an organization which is very popular with donors, in contrast to the more closed culture of the government service. What is striking in this context is that so many women government staff were able to pick up information on gender and development concerns, in spite of the absence of discussions of gender relations in their training or policy work.

The picture which begins to emerge is of a more gender-aware culture in the NGO, and of a polarization in the government service between an almost gender-obtuse culture amongst male field staff and their women colleagues' interest in the issue. Turning to issues of gender within the organizational context, government women staff appeared more willing to identify gender-related problems in the workplace than NGO women staff. On a range of different measures, such as personal perceptions of influence on decision-making, women's perceptions of whether their male colleagues had respect for them, or whether their male subordinates showed appropriate deference, the government women staff emerged as far more critical of their male colleagues, particularly with regard to problems of sexual harassment. NGO women staff, in contrast, were defensive of their organization and of their male colleagues. Differences in willingness to engage in criticism of the organization reflect in part differences in security of tenure and therefore the freedom to risk oppositional attitudes, with lack of job security in the NGO imposing a greater degree of control over the content of personal statements to outsiders in the context of this research. The problem of job security will be discussed shortly. Differences in critical views on gender-related problems at work also reflect a real difference between the two organizations in expressions of contempt for women, and occurences of sexual harassment. As will be discussed shortly, the NGO insists on respectful behaviour between staff, and punishes sexual harassment and amorous advances by men with transfers or dismissals. In the state organization, in contrast, sexual harassment is barely acknowledged, at a formal level, to be an offence, and the expression of derogatory views about women's work is more overt. Women respond with strategies for self-protection, but also a sharper condemnation of male behaviour, and sharper awareness of problems of gender relations in the organization.

It seems obvious that where a working environment is more sharply masculinized, resentment, unease, and criticism from women might be more overt. But is the NGO any less male-dominated or male-oriented than the state organization? That NGO women staff were much less willing to criticize their organization or their male colleagues reflects a much stronger culture of conformity in image management and discourse control, and may disguise the extent of gender-related problems. Observation of NGO women staff showed that they shared problems with their government counterparts in terms of coping with gender-related tensions at work, particularly in gaining respect from colleagues. But all staff members of the NGO are highly constrained to put on a progressive social face in public and tend to refrain from voicing their resentments to outsiders. As one male NGO Programme Organizer said, concerning his relations with women subordinates, the Programme Assistants (PAs): 'Now I regret saying in the group discussion that all women are weak. I have to call the women PAs *apni* and *appa*[7] in front of other people for the sake of the programme's image' (76). Interviews with the men revealed resentments beneath the veneer of image management:

> We are equivalent in qualifications to the women but women are working less than the men, can't do what we do, can't tackle crises on the spot. Yet they are getting the same salary. Men are good for public functions, for *anything*, representative work, making quick decisions, any kind of problem. In meetings women don't contribute to problem-solving. It's their nature to keep quiet. (101: NGO field worker, man.)

Differences in the expression of criticism may also be due to the sheer lack of opportunity for networking between women and group reflection on these issues in the NGO. As noted earlier, the NGO has few women staff, representing 6 per cent of Programme Organizers (the first step on the professional ladder of BRAC staff), and 8 per cent of the field-level supervisors, the Area Managers. In contrast the government organization has reached a situation of near-parity in the sex ratio at the level of Field Organizers (45 per cent women), and 27 per cent of the important township-level managers – the Thana Rural Development Officers – are women.[8] In terms of concentrations of staff in individual offices, just 15 per cent of BRAC women staff (in the sample) work in field offices with seven or more women colleagues, and it is not uncommon to find just two or three women field workers in offices with twenty to thirty men.[9] In the government organization, there is something close to a 'critical mass' of women in most field offices, with the majority, 77 per cent, in offices with seven or more women colleagues (out of a total of about fifteen programme staff). This means that women staff are less isolated and exposed, and possibly more able to build on mutual support. It must be noted, however, that the RPP is very unusual in this respect compared to other state bureaucracies in Bangladesh, where women are in a much more distinct minority. The presence of enough other women to counter isolation and marginalization in the field offices of the state organization seemed to afford women the chance for sharing perspectives and developing mutual support systems. Having a woman superior, for example, appeared to help in fighting off male intrusions on women's privacy, as is suggested by this observation from a woman Field Organizer:

> Most of us are scared of the [male second-in-command]. He has a loud voice and he always wants to know personal things about us.

Once I needed leave for a personal affair. He asked for details but [my female boss] reprimanded him and said it wasn't his business. (58)

Nowhere was the difference in women's willingness to voice resentment or criticism more evident than in the nature of group discussions held with male and female staff in field offices. These were much more animated in the state organization, where women defended their views (and men were also more rough and dismissive), compared with the NGO where women were usually outnumbered five to one, and there was little disagreement between women and men in discussions of social problems.

While there was a clear difference in women's expression of gendered critiques of male behaviours and of the organization itself between the NGO and the state organization, it is important not to romanticize government women staff's perceptions as a coherent politicized analysis of gender problems in the development bureaucracy. Nevertheless, differences in expressions of overt criticism prompt questions about reasons for these differences, and about factors which impede or encourage the development of an incipient oppositional consciousness. The differential density in the presence of women in the organizations is not the only cause of differences in degrees and quality of women's 'voice'. It itself is a symptom of organizational management strategies and cultures which operate in sometimes contradictory ways when it comes to supporting women's leadership.

Disciplining Difference: Gender in the Bureaucracy

Feminist analysts of organizations have demonstrated that gendered features of organizational structures, practices, and cultures will favour the capacity of certain groups within the organization to flourish, both in terms of their management efficiency and their capacity to pursue their interests in decision-making (Acker, 1990; Hearn *et al.*, 1989; Goetz, 1992, 1995b). Typical gendered organizational constraints on women include the way the management of organizational time and space can favour male capabilities, since they rarely accommodate women's responsibilities in the private sphere, or cultural obstacles to their mobility and security in rural areas (particularly relevant in Bangladesh). Organizational cultures which favour male expressions of authority and even sexuality can undermine women's influence on decision-making, by limiting their capacity to generate respect, or to develop power and patronage networks. These gendered organizational features produce barriers to women's leadership in two respects: at the level of their competence or efficiency strictly in terms of management expectations, and at the level of their capacity to articulate and defend alternative perspectives on women's interests in development.

Both the organizations studied recognized that women staff had different needs from male staff and had adopted creative measures to enhance their effectiveness as development agents. Both, for instance, had strong equal opportunities recruitment policies, occasionally even suspending the recruitment of men in order to boost female staff numbers. Both had provision for maternity leave, special extended leave facilities for women to cope with family obligations, and facilities for staff to hire-purchase vehicles (bicycles and motorcycles) to enhance their mobility, and both were beginning to introduce gender and development training. The NGO had also created an internal women's advisory committee to review women staff's concerns. Both organizations help women to cope with the socio-cultural constraints they face by giving strong top-level backing for women's presence in the organization (in the case of RPP-RD-12, this is also underwritten by the donor organization's strong stance on this issue). The RPP-RD-12 also compensates for women's lack of socialization for management roles through the provision of special management training.

Where the NGO (and many others like it in Bangladesh) differed strikingly from the state institution in its reaction to the sociological change in its workforce represented by women staff was in its much more self-conscious and explicit approach to coping with gender difference. Thus the social pioneering role of women staff was highlighted through a range of organizational conventions such as informal dress codes and behavioural rules requiring women staff to work and behave like their male colleagues. They ride bicycles and motorbikes, they are expected to work at night if necessary, and they live away from home and family in office quarters. For safety on vehicles and freedom of movement they wear the female equivalent of trousers (the shalwar kamiz), which, in rural areas, is usually abandoned by married women or adolescents over 16 for the sari, associated with adult womanhood. An explicit amendment to the organizational culture, the 'Community Living' rules for interpersonal behaviour in BRAC offices, reiterates a commitment to egalitarian principles and tolerance and implicitly enjoins men to show respect for female staff. Measures such as the provision of field accommodation and eating facilities for field staff (except the Programme Assistants) are designed to minimize the demands of the domestic sphere on women's time, and the preferential hiring of single women and men highlights the concern to free staff time from domestic concerns. Measures such as the provision of adequate sanitary facilities for women in field offices and several days' optional 'desk leave' from field work to cope with menstruation responded to some of the pressures of coping with the physical demands of field work imposed by women's biological difference.

None of these kinds of cultural measures were taken in the government organization, where gender *difference* was not highlighted as an issue to be addressed through measures targeting sex-typed workplace behaviour or deportment. The formal hierarchical management culture of the civil service is dominant, somewhat at odds with the egalitarian social and economic development goals it promotes through its credit programme. The admission of women staff to this working environment is not accompanied by the kind of self-scrutiny which occurs in the NGO, resulting in higher overt levels of hostility to women staff.

The effect of these measures on the nature of women's presence in the organization, their management efficiency, and their leadership capacities is somewhat counter-intuitive. Despite the NGO's progressive measures, it has a poor record of retaining women staff in the field, with a drop-out rate of over 60 per cent, and, as seen above, low numbers of women staff overall compared to men, compared to a situation of near-parity in the staff sex ratio in the government organization. Reasons for this contrasting staff retention rate do not all have to do with management practices. One of the main explanations is that government employment is of much higher status than NGO employment. Even though salaries are lower in government employment, job security is perceived to be higher, longer-term benefits such as pensions are better, and certainly the social prestige attached to working in the civil service is higher, making employment more acceptable to women's families.[10]

Other explanations, however, have to do with the impact of the two management systems on women's capacity to cope with the pressures of managing their conflicting roles, as well as challenges to their gender identities. In government service, women are better able to accommodate traditional features of Bangladeshi womanhood with their work lives than in NGO service. The restriction of working hours from 10 to 5 in government service left women time for domestic responsibilities, unlike the NGO, which operates essentially a 24-hour, 7-day-a-week 'on-call' response system. Since staff live at the office in the NGO, it is impossible to escape the call to work. It is also next to impossible to have a family, and although Area Managers are given larger living quarters in the office to accommodate a family, few women could persuade husbands to join them.[11] In the government organization, no pressure was put on women staff to ride the vehicles available to them through the programme, and none did. In contrast, bicycle riding for at least a year before graduation to a motorbike is obligatory for all of the NGO's field staff. This represents a powerful assault on social expectations, and accounts in part for the very high drop-out rate of new recruits, and the reluctance of young women's guardians to permit them to work for the NGO.

While these factors promote women's retention in the government organization, they do not necessarily promote their management effectiveness or leadership capacities. In allowing women to maintain their obligations in the private sphere, and their traditional gender identities in public, they minimize women bureaucrats' challenge to gender ideologies. In not expressing as radical a social message in their public identities, they can counter opposition from home, while at work, their presence in the bureaucracy does not challenge masculinist management practices. The fact that women can use management practices to admit of the maximum possible time at home means that they do not take part in the male world of after-hours decision-making, limiting their potential impact on the organization. This also means that their male colleagues develop lower expectations of their work performance, resulting in resentment, and patronizing behaviour wherein women staff can be passed over for important assignments. Finally, because they walk or take rickshaws to reach credit groups, which is time-consuming, their performance rate can be lower than male colleagues.

In contrast, the NGO's management strategy requires change in gender role expectations both at home and at work. By favouring single women at recruitment, by requiring them to live in field premises, by providing accommodation and eating facilities, the NGO gives women the opportunity to resist conventional patterns of domestic obligation, while releasing time for more work. These policies are a direct challenge to a range of ties and tyrannies in the private sphere which are part of the gendered construction of asymmetries of power and significance. But this also means that women are obliged to become 'sociological males' (Kanter, 1977) at work if they wish to retain their employment in an organization which prides itself on its intense work culture. They have to minimize the significance of connections to the home, to family, to children; they have to demonstrate a capacity to devote all their time to the organization. The result is a striking difference in the personal lives of women field staff in the two organizations, with 75 per cent of NGO women field workers single compared to 39 per cent of government women field workers. At the area office management level, 60 per cent of women managers in the NGO are single, compared to 10 per cent of the government women managers.[12]

In a culture where marriage is universal, postponement of marriage beyond the age of 30 imposes enormous social and psychological costs on women. This, along with the tensions of gender identity management, contributes to the high drop-out rate. The committed and hardworking women who remain have proven themselves the equals of their male colleagues, but the condition of survival is emulation of male behaviour. Many BRAC women staff, for instance, shun the special measures available to them such as extra leave facilities or menstruation desk leave out of an aversion to attracting attention for their difference or for an implicit disability (Rao and Kelleher, 1995, p. 72). Gender difference, rather than being accommodated by the organization, is denied by women themselves, in response to performance expectations. This may counter male resistance to their organizational presence, and certainly means that they are efficient development workers, but does it make them effective leaders in women's interests?

One indication of the ambivalence they may feel about their demanding social role is the way they manage their appearance and deportment in rural areas. Few women in either organization respect purdah, which is of itself a strong statement. However, the intensified social criticism faced by BRAC women staff because of their obligatory form of social presentation appears, in many cases, to provoke compensatory forms of behaviour, where they demonstrate their social propriety and femininity by other means. Many wear a long white cotton jacket over their clothing when in the field; ostensibly this is for dust protection, but it also acts as a symbolic gesture towards purdah. One BRAC woman field worker described an incident where she was accused by a village man of lacking morals because she was not respecting purdah and was travelling freely. She returned on her motorcycle, and with her helmet, jacket, and gloves on, pointed out to him that she was more covered up than his wife, who 'wasn't wearing a blouse . . . and [was] having a bath in the open pond without any clothes, and so are the men' (63). While this represents a creative form of resistance, her argument still worked within the framework of purdah values. These efforts to underplay the radical social message they embody are understandable, but may also demonstrate reluctance to identify with the social project they are expected to promote in a hostile environment.

Opportunities for Women's Leadership in the Bureaucracy

Both institutional arenas constrain women's opportunities to develop and act upon oppositional perspectives. What is notable, however, is the greater willingness of the women state bureaucrats in the sample to take a gendered perspective on the problems they experience in their work. It must be stressed, of course, that this is an observation of an incipient phenomenon. Women's gendered perspectives were expressed privately, in the interview context, and bar the group discussions in field offices, these views by and large do not receive a public airing. Nevertheless, some structural features of bureaucratic organization which support these women's apparently greater propensity to develop oppositional views can point to some positive features of state employment from the perspective of engendering women's leadership.

Certain dimensions of the bureaucratic form, such as predictability, clear specification of rules and procedures, and, in the case of state employment, relative job security, are resources for women in that they provide spaces to defend their employment rights and to manage their private lives; they are also avenues for reasonably safe redress against unreasonable treatment. Their security of job tenure allows them to carve a space in which they can manage domestic pressures and also cope comfortably with cultural conflicts around their gender identity management. Bureaucratic procedure sometimes serves them well in struggling against the caprice of local injustices from management. Many of the women staff interviewed had successfully sought redress for problems such as unfair punishment transfers, mis-treatment by superiors, pressure to engage in corrupt practices, non-compliant subordinates, and exclusion from decision-making, by going straight to the Dhaka headquarters to argue their case. There was a strong perception of the fairness of top-level decision-making, where local problems could be made public rather than hidden in the obscurity of the field. In this context, many women staff expressed anxiety about plans to decentralize RPP management and decision-making authority to the district level, where they would come under the control of the local government bureaucracy, and lose the security of top-level support.

The civil service framework for the work of women development agents has some advantages in terms of the social acceptability of targeting development resources to women. Women in government offices can make the bureaucracy a less threatening arena for rural and poor women. In villages, women bureaucrats can draw on their status as government employees to ease their acceptance in ways not available to NGO women staff. The way government women staff manage their presence in villages, their measured pace in moving through the countryside, and their more traditional dress, mean they can spend more time on social interaction with villagers and less time combating resistance.

The possibility that this may ease the social acceptability of efforts to bring development resources to women was suggested, indirectly, in the violent backlash reactions against NGOs in Bangladesh in 1994. In isolated incidents around the country, NGO projects were attacked, with BRAC non-formal schools (in which girls are a majority), and women field workers, singled out for attack. There were no incidents, however, of attacks on RPP operations or personnel. This backlash has been widely attributed to the hostility of fundamentalist Islamic groups towards efforts to change women's status, fuelled by the national witch-hunt against the writer Taslima Nasreen. Others explain it as an unconnected series of local reactions – particularly from local elites – against the proliferation and power of NGOs, their interventions with the village poor, and the foreign interests they are assumed to represent (Ziauddin, 1994). The absence of attacks on the RPP reflect the fact that, as a government organization, it is seen to be more legitimate. Also, of course, the fact that, like other government programmes, it tends to work through, rather than against, local elites, means it is more acceptable to the power brokers behind the attacks. RPP women staff offered another explanation. They suggested that they have greater acceptance in village communities than NGOs because they walk to their work, taking time to interact with villagers, and are not transferred frequently, and thus become a more familiar part of the village environment, and are more trusted. Undeniably they also have a stronger claim on state authority, which in a situation of instability no doubt also made them more secure.

There are many negative aspects to the bureaucratic dynamic. Women find space and occasion to develop resentments because they are marginalized and patronized by male colleagues. Their relatively greater job security gives them some opportunity to express their views, but concern to get one of the very rare promotions can pit them against each other. Their oppositional perspectives relate primarily to their own conditions of employment, and there is little opportunity or incentive to prompt a transition from personal to collective opposition, given the competition between women for scarce positions, the absence of an internal organizational space for women to network, and the absence of top-level women patrons (the very few women at the Head Office are very isolated). At a minimum, however, they have been able to manipulate different aspects of the bureaucratic form to their advantage.

In contrast, a common feature of management cultures in many NGOs, often held to be their great advantage, is flexible and adaptable procedures, informal and rapid decision-making processes, and staff who serve on the basis of commitment, rather than corporate ambition. BRAC is somewhere between the two types of management culture, rapidly expanding out of its small voluntaristic origins into a development corporation, with growing pains from contradictory organizational incentives (Rao and Kelleher, 1995). New recruits, for example, these days less animated by ideology than career concerns, are rarely given written job descriptions, and may be dismissed for what are seen as minor offences, with little perceived uniformity of control over the actions of their field superiors in this respect, and no clear avenue of appeal. Staff complain that frequent and substantial policy changes are pressed on field offices without prior consultation, and instant adoption of policy changes, as well as uniform high performance, is expected. While such practices may have been successful and necessary for flexibility when the organization was a fraction of its current size, they create tensions in a large and complex organization.

Where dismissal occurs frequently, high performance and demonstration of commitment to the organization's interests is critical. In a context of rapid expansion with a stress on high performance, particularly in managing credit, these interests militate against the long, slow work of seeking sustainable solutions to social problems such as women's subordination – in effect, working against women's interests in development. Performance standards based on rapid loan recovery are to some extent masculinized, as they deny the value of the slower institution-building work that women may do more effectively with their rural groups. Finally, high work intensity means that opportunities are scarce for discussions of personal and professional problems. This adds up, for women staff, to pressure to identify with male interests both in the development process and within the organization, as there are neither opportunities nor incentives to develop leadership in women's interests. Indeed, this can be penalized if it means spending more time in the village, or more time working through problems and concerns with women colleagues, especially if this is seen as a possible drain on the efficiency of the organization.

Conclusion

That women government staff appear to take a gendered critical perspective on their work and their organization appears to be a function of two dynamics, not always positive. On the one hand, certain features of bureaucratic process and frameworks allow women to carve a space for themselves within the bureaucracy, and to feel some security in expressing their views at the field level. On the other hand, the sharp cultural polarization of male and female worlds in the bureaucracy may galvanize a clearer awareness of gendered patterns of discrimination. Foucault has argued that an openly visible coercive law and practice may inflame a dissenting consciousness much more effectively than what he calls 'normalizing power', which exacts recognition through a positive, inclusive use of power (Foucault, 1979). Put more directly, it is easier to recognize a wolf when it is not wearing sheep's clothing. Women bureaucrats experience sharper gender tensions in the workplace because these are not denied, as they are in the NGO, through a culture of conformity to a masculine standard of performance and behaviour.

The discussion in this chapter of contrasting approaches to managing women's organizational presence does not produce clear conclusions about preferable approaches, bar the observation that security of job tenure and established and transparent patterns of seeking redress for grievances are important resources for stabilizing women's organizational presence. Whilst the government organization has provided the minimum conditions for retaining women staff, the NGO context, in contrast, allows for important experimentation. The importance of BRAC's work in pioneering an alternative pattern of gender identity management for women in the Bangladesh context cannot be underestimated. For instance, BRAC has been much more open than the government organization to self-scrutiny, through its Women's Advisory Committee, mentioned earlier, and the extensive internal gender training programme it has recently initiated. It must be stressed that the women who stay the course in BRAC are much more visible within the organizational hierarchy than women in the government organization, whose critical perspectives were, after all, voiced privately, in the interview context. The location of BRAC, and the NGO community in general, on the cutting edge of development innovations, and its relative freedom from many of the negative constraints associated with bureaucratic organization, makes it a critical arena for challenging the many gendered social and organizational constraints on women's leadership capacities.

Nevertheless, the observation of ways in which women can use the formality of bureaucratic procedure and the status of government employment to their advantage points to the potential of working through the state in women's interests. This is of course contingent on top-level support for the retention of women staff, and on women finding means of building up from their individual experiences to develop a leadership resource in the bureaucracy for women. This depends upon a broader political process, on building connections between women's organizations and women bureaucrats, and developing a coherent women's constituency in civil society. But institutional changes to consolidate women's presence and confidence within the bureaucracy can help. In the end, the state remains a key institution for pursuing sustainable society-wide changes, and the only institution which is broadly accountable to society. While NGOs have an important role in demonstrating directions for change, the project of pursuing equity concerns through the bureaucracy remains critical.

Notes

1 This is part of new 'governance' concerns in development, where state failures and fiscal crises have promoted pressures to retract the state from social sector provisioning, shrink its functions generally, and galvanize 'civil society' both to expand its watchdog functions over state activity and to take over social provisioning functions which the state does not perform efficiently. The clearest statement of this position comes from World Bank 'governance' documents, such as World Bank 1994. For critiques, see Williams and Young, 1994; Jeffries, 1993; Goetz and O'Brien, 1995; Vivian, 1994.

2 This research was funded by the UK Economic and Social Research Council, and I was assisted in the field work and data analysis by Rina Sen Gupta, my research collaborator, with Rina Roy and Cathy Green working as research assistants. I am deeply grateful to BRAC and RPP-RD-12 for giving permission for this research.

3 Just after this study was completed the staff in this cadre were incorporated as regular staff members.

4 The local attacks on NGO operations in 1994 were seen by some observers as a form of resistance or backlash politics by Islamic groups against the prominence of women-focused development interventions in rural Bangladesh, an issue which will be debated later in this chapter.

5 Numbers in brackets are references to the long interview data.

6 Women are of course not passive in this process and may manipulate it to their own ends, trading off direct control over a development resource like credit for the right to take part in group activities and have access to travel or new training opportunities, for example.

7 *Apni* is the formal form of 'you', and *appa* means 'sister', a respectful form of address.

8 The thana is an administrative unit between the village and District levels.

9 The NGO does have a unit designed to give women space to express their views: the Women's Advisory Committee, which holds meetings with women staff in field locations. This, however, is seen as strongly linked to management concerns, and some of the mid-level women staff interviewed argued that it has not yet proven a forum for critical discussion of the organization or the behaviour of male colleagues.

10 In fact, Field Organizers in the RPP were not part of the civil service proper; only staff at the supervisory level and upwards were. Nevertheless, these lower-ranking staff benefited from association with the civil service, and the prospect of being promoted into it.

11 Since the time of this study, BRAC has changed its residential

requirements and married staff are now permitted to live outside of office quarters. It has also taken steps to reduce work intensity at field offices by suggesting regular scheduled hours for work. These latter measures still sit somewhat uneasily with its current drive for rapid expansion, which imposes high performance pressures on staff.

12 The marital situation of men in the NGO is similar, with 63 per cent of the Programme Organizers and 50 per cent of the Area Managers single. In the government organization, 31 per cent of the male Field Organizers and 3 per cent of the Thana Rural Development Officers are single. This represents less of a social stigma for men than for women, however.

Bibliography

ACKER, JOAN (1990) 'Hierarchies, Jobs, Bodies: A Theory of Gendered Organisations', *Gender and Society*, Vol. 2, No. 4, pp. 139–58.

ACKERLY, BROOKE (1995) 'Testing the Tools of Development: Credit Programmes, Loan Involvement, and Women's Empowerment', *IDS Bulletin*, Vol. 25, No. 3, July, Sussex.

BUVINIC, MAYRA (1986) 'Projects for Women in the Third World: Explaining Their Misbehaviour', *World Development*, Vol. 14, No. 5, pp. 653–64.

BUVINIC, MAYRA (1989) 'Investing in Poor Women: The Psychology of Donor Support', *World Development*, Vol. 17, No. 7, pp. 1045–57.

FELDMAN, SHELLY and McCARTHY, FLORENCE (1984) *Rural Women and Development in Bangladesh: Selected Issues*, Oslo, NORAD.

FELDMAN, SHELLY, AHKTER, FARIDA and BANU, FAZILA LILY (1983) 'Population Planning and Rural Women's Cooperatives in IRDP Women's Programme: Some Critical Issues', in HUQ, J. *et al.* (Eds) *Women in Bangladesh: Some Socio-Economic Issues, Vol. 1, Women for Women*, Dhaka.

FOUCAULT, MICHEL (1979) *History of Sexuality*, London, Allen Lane.

FOWLER, ALAN (1988) 'Non-Governmental Organisations in Africa: Achieving Comparative Advantage in Relief and Micro-development', IDS Discussion Paper 249, Sussex.

GOETZ, ANNE MARIE (1992) 'Gender and Administration', *IDS Bulletin*, Vol. 23, No. 4, October, Sussex.

GOETZ, ANNE MARIE (1995a) 'The Politics of Integrating Gender to State Development Processes: Trends, Opportunities, and Constraints in Bangladesh, Chile, Jamaica, Mali, Morocco, and Uganda', Occasional Paper No. 2, United Nations Research Institute for Social Development, Geneva.

GOETZ, ANNE MARIE (1995b) 'Institutionalising Women's Interests and Gender-Sensitive Accountability in Development', *IDS Bulletin*, Vol. 26, No. 3, Sussex.

GOETZ, ANNE MARIE and O'BRIEN, DAVID (1995) 'Governing for the Common

Wealth? The World Bank's Approach to Poverty and Governance', *IDS Bulletin*, Vol. 26, No. 2, April, Sussex.

GOETZ, ANNE MARIE and SEN GUPTA, RINA (1996) 'Who Takes the Credit? Gender, Power, and Control over Loan Use in Rural Credit Programmes in Bangladesh', *World Development*, Vol. 27, No. 1, January.

HEARN, J., SHEPPARD, D., TANCRED-SHERIFF, P. and BURRELL, G. (Eds) (1989) *The Sexuality of Organisation*, London, Sage.

JEFFRIES, RICHARD (1993) 'The State, Structural Adjustment, and Good Government in Africa', *Journal of Commonwealth and Comparative Politics*, Vol. 31, No. 1, pp. 20–35.

KABEER, NAILA (1989) 'The Quest for National Identity: Women, Islam and the State in Bangladesh', IDS Discussion Paper 268, Sussex.

KANTER, ROSABETH MOSS (1977) *Men and Women of the Corporation*, New York, Basic Books.

KHAN, N. and STEWART, E. (1992) 'Institution Building and Development in Three Women's Village Organisations: Participation, Ownership, Autonomy', mimeo, Research and Evaluation Division, BRAC, Dhaka.

KIRLELS, EDDA, with AKHTER, SHAHEEN (1990) 'Role and Situation of Women Development Workers in Non-Governmental Development Organisations in Bangladesh', mimeo.

KRAMSJO, BOSSE and WOOD, GEOFFREY (1992) *Breaking the Chains: Collective Action for Social Justice among the Rural Poor in Bangladesh*, London, Intermediate Technology Publications.

MAYOUX, LINDA (1995) 'From Vicious to Virtuous Circles? Gender and Micro-Enterprise Development', UNRISD Occassional Paper 3, Geneva.

MOLYNEUX, M. (1985) 'Mobilisation Without Emancipation? Women's Interests, the State and Revolution in Nicaragua', *Feminist Studies* , Vol. 11, No. 2.

MONTGOMERY, J. (1988) *Bureaucrats and People*, Baltimore, John Hopkins University Press.

MONTGOMERY, RICHARD, BHATTACHARYA, DEBAPRIYA and HULME, DAVID (1994) 'Credit for the Poor in Bangladesh: The BRAC Rural Development Programme and the Government Thana Resource Development and Employment Programme', mimeo, Swansea.

RAHMAN, R. I. (1986) *Impact of the Grameen Bank on the Situation of Poor Rural Women*, Dhaka, Bangladesh Institute of Development Studies.

RAO, ARUNA and KELLEHER, DAVID (1995) 'Engendering Organisational Change: The BRAC Case', *IDS Bulletin*, Vol. 26, No. 3, July, Sussex.

ROZARIO, SANTI (1992) *Purity and Communal Boundaries: Women and Social Change in a Bangladeshi Village*, London, Zed.

SANYAL, B. (1991) 'Antagonistic Cooperation: A Case Study of Non-Governmental Organisations, Government and Donor's Relationships in Income-Generating Projects in Bangladesh', *World Development*, Vol. 19, No. 10.

SCHAFFER, BERNARD (1984) 'Towards Responsibility: Public Policy in Concept and Practice', in CLAY, E. J. and SCHAFFER, B. B. (Eds) *Room for Maneouvre: An Exploration of Public Policy Planning in Agricultural and Rural Development*, London, Heinemann.

STAUDT, KATHLEEN (1990) 'Gender Politics in Bureaucracy: Theoretical Issues in Comparative Perspective', in STAUDT, K. (Ed.) *Women, International Development, and Politics: The Bureaucratic Mire*, Philadelphia, Temple University Press.

VAN SCHENDEL, WILLEM (1987) ' "Ghorar Dim" – Rural Development in Bangladesh', *Journal of Social Studies*, 39, Dhaka.

VIVIAN, JESSICA (1994) *Social Safety Nets and Adjustment in Developing Countries*, UNRISD Occasional Paper 1 for Social Development, Geneva.

VIVIAN, JESSICA and MASEKO, GLADYS (1994) 'NGOs, Participation, and Rural Development: Testing the Assumptions with Evidence from Zimbabwe', UNRISD Discussion Paper 49, Geneva.

WHITE, SARAH (1991) *Evaluating the Impact of NGOs in Rural Poverty Alleviation: Bangladesh Country Study*, London, ODI.

WILLIAMS, DAVID and YOUNG, TOM (1994) 'Governance, the World Bank and Liberal Theory', *Political Studies*, XLII, pp. 84–100.

WOOD, GEOFFREY (1985) 'Targets Strike Back – Rural Works Claimants in Bangladesh', in WOOD, G. (Ed.) *Labelling in Development Policy*, London, Sage.

WOOD, GEOFFREY (1988) 'Plunder without Danger: Avoiding Responsibility in Rural Works Administrations in Bangladesh', *IDS Bulletin*, Vol. 19, No. 4, Sussex.

WOOD, GEOFFREY (1994) 'Sirs and Sahibs: Government and Technical Assistance Relations in Rural Development Projects', in WOOD, G. *Bangladesh: Whose Ideas, Whose Interests?*, London, Intermediate Technology Publications.

WORLD BANK (1989) *Bangladesh: Public Expenditure Review*, Asia Country Department, Washington, D.C.

WORLD BANK (1994) *Governance: The World Bank's Experience*, Operations Policy Department, Washington, D.C.

YASMIN, TAHERA (1993) 'Women, Work, and NGOs: Looking at Reality', mimeo, Oxfam, Dhaka.

YUDELMAN, S. (1990) 'The Inter-American Foundation and Gender Issues: A Feminist View', in STAUDT, K. (Ed.) *Women, International Development, and Politics: The Bureaucratic Mire*, Philadelphia, Temple University Press.

ZIAUDDIN, ALI AHMED (1994) 'NGOs Are Under Attack! Why?', *Daily Star*, Dhaka, September 14.

Chapter 8

Working from Within: Women and the State in the Development of the Courtyard Economy in Rural China

Tamara Jacka

Introduction

Following the death of Mao Zedong in 1976, the newly-appointed leaders of the PRC set in motion a series of reforms aimed at promoting rapid market-driven economic growth and modernization. These reforms have included decollectivization, the promotion of private business, the development of a labour market and pricing deregulation. They have had profound consequences for both society and the state,[1] and have been the subject of a flood of Western scholarship, including numerous works on the impact of the reforms on women's status, welfare and role in society (Croll, 1983; Davin, 1988).

These works have been important in drawing our attention to the fact that 'the benefits to women of many of the new policies introduced into China in the past five years cannot be assumed' (Croll, 1983, p. 128) and that in a number of ways the bonds of women's subordination have been tightened through recent reform policies (Davin, 1988, p. 136). However, in common both with the majority of other analyses of social change in contemporary China and with much of the feminist literature on gender relations in other developing countries, these works are limited by an inadequate theorization of state-society relations. In the majority, the state is portrayed as a discrete and homogenous entity that formulates policies to serve its own interests, which are distinct from, and largely inimical to, the interests of ordinary women. Changes in society are then seen as a direct result of the state's implementation of its policies. In this top-down approach there is little consideration of the role of gender relations in shaping the interests of both the state and women, or of the impact of gender relations on the formulation and implementation of state ideology and policies. Women (and men) tend to be portrayed as the passive objects, or recipients, of state policy. Their own desires, choices and actions, whether they be to instigate change, implement state policy, mould it for their own purposes, or resist it, are hidden.

In the 1990s there is a need, I argue, for a shift in focus in the analysis of social change in China, so that the issues raised here are placed at the centre of attention. The beginnings of such a shift are already visible. Writers such as Vivienne Shue (1988), Jean Oi (1989) and Daniel Kelliher (1992), for example, have challenged prevailing assumptions about state power in China. They have argued that whilst the state in China is comparatively very 'strong' and society very 'weak', this does not mean that the state is the sole agent of change whilst society is merely the object of that change (Kelliher, 1992, pp. 20–39). Partly in response to the large amount of evidence suggesting that in the reform period, far from controlling and being the sole agent of change, the Chinese state has itself been having trouble in keeping up with the pace of change, these writers have shifted the focus of attention away from state policies toward reform as a process, involving complex interactions and conflicts between various elements in state and society.

These new works on state-society interactions, however, largely ignore gender relations. Indeed in recent works on gender relations in contemporary China, questions about the nature of state power and of the relationship between state and society are rarely addressed directly. In the late 1980s and early 1990s, however, a few writers have adopted approaches to gender relations which address women's agency and give an idea of the complexity of state/gender interactions. For example, in her study of gender and power in rural north China, Ellen Judd moves away from a focus on the effects of state policies on women to discuss the 'alternative strategies pursued by both local rural leaders and by rural women themselves in response to current policies and opportunities' (Judd, 1990, p. 24). Elsewhere, she argues that 'there is no differentiating feature of Chinese life that is more profound, continuing, and asymmetrical than gender. . . . The reconfiguration of state power in process in rural China draws force and legitimacy from its immanence in the politics and power of gender' (Judd, 1994, p. 257).

In this chapter my aim is to contribute to the discussion of interactions between state and gender through an analysis of women's work in domestic sidelines, or, as they later became known, the courtyard economy. Promotion of this aspect of the rural Chinese economy has been a key facet of reform policies in rural China in recent years. The chapter is divided into four sections. In the first section I examine the Chinese state's approach to domestic sidelines and the courtyard economy, focusing, in particular, on the reasons why the state has gone from suppressing this sector of the rural economy between the 1950s and 1970s, to encouraging its expansion in the 1980s and 1990s. In the second and third sections of the chapter I look at the actions that women themselves have taken to expand the courtyard economy, and discuss the merits that they see in this type of work. The final section undertakes a critical assessment of the development of the courtyard economy as part of a strategy for improving rural women's position in society.

The State's Approach to Domestic Sidelines and the Courtyard

In the collectivization drive undertaken by the Chinese state in rural areas in the 1950s, communes took over ownership of almost all means of production and employed peasants to work in production teams in return for a share of the total output of the team. They did, however, also allow peasants to use time outside commune work hours and the labour of household members not engaged in commune work to undertake 'domestic sidelines' (jiating fuye), such as hunting and fishing, the cultivation of vegetables, small-scale animal husbandry and the home production of handicrafts, for their own consumption and profit.

Domestic sidelines are generally regarded in rural China as women's work, even though certain activities, particularly hunting and fishing, are undertaken by men, and others, such as vegetable growing, commonly involve the work of men and children as well as women (P. Huang, 1990, p. 203). Handicrafts, sewing, and the day-to-day care of domestic livestock are usually undertaken by women, especially older women, in conjuction with domestic tasks.

As a consequence of the association with domestic work and the fact that they are considered women's work, domestic sidelines have, until recently, suffered a kind of invisibility. Despite their importance for the food intake of the family and also for the cash income they bring in, domestic sidelines have tended to be omitted in peasants' accounts of their productive activities, and women's work in this area has often not been recognized, by themselves or others, as a contribution to the family economy.

Such work was also regarded with suspicion by the Communist Party under Mao Zedong both because it was productive and because it could potentially detract from or threaten the commune economy. Consequently, while domestic sidelines were generally recognized by the state as an important source of supplementary foodstuffs and cash income, at times, most notably during the Great Leap Forward (1958–60) and the years following the Cultural Revolution (1969–76), they were suppressed.

In 1978, however, the right of commune members to engage in domestic sidelines and to sell their produce in free markets was reaffirmed (CCP, 1978, p. 13), and in subsequent years domestic sidelines were promoted as a means of diversifying the rural economy. Concurrently, a process of decollectivization was intitiated, in which various forms of a 'production responsibility system' were introduced as a means of improving incentives for peasant production by linking the remuneration of work more closely with performance. Initially this was done within the commune framework but by 1983 this had largely broken down. Most areas had adopted a responsibility system in which households took over production management and simply paid taxes to the production team. This devolution of economic management meant that peasant households could now make their own choices about what areas of production to engage in according to their particular abilities and the interplay of local prices and supply and demand. In many cases their choice was to reduce time and labour in crop planting and to expand their domestic sideline activities.

Domestic sidelines took on a new role in the rural economy in the 1980s and 1990s, and perceptions of them changed, with rural officials now recognizing their potential for boosting local economic growth (P. Huang, 1990, p. 218). Since about 1984, the term 'domestic sidelines' itself has increasingly been displaced in the media by the term 'the courtyard economy' (xiao wuan jingji or tingyuan jingji). The two terms do not refer to exactly the same activities; the latter term is used in reference to activities undertaken in the home or courtyard but does not usually include hunting, fishing or gathering (Zhang, 1987, p. 65; Qi, 1993, p. 24). The significance of the change of name is twofold. Firstly, the new term stresses the physical location of certain activities in the home or courtyard. Secondly, it removes the sense that such activities are less important than collectively organized activities. By recognizing them as part of the economy the state has accorded these activities a greater value than was previously the case. Encouragement of the courtyard economy has come from all levels of the state. In the national media, the successes of women working in the courtyard economy are lauded and at the local level state officials provide a range of incentives to encourage women in this sector.

Encouragement has come, in particular, from the All-China Women's Federation. This is a 'mass organization', affiliated with the Communist Party, with representation at all levels of government, from the national congress down to the village. It has the dual task of mobilizing women around Party policy and protecting women's interests. Currently the Women's Federation is the only significant organization in China whose focus is to undertake practical work to improve the situation of women, although in recent years a number of women's research groups and studies centres have also been established.[2]

Many people, both inside and outside China, regard the Women's Federation as merely a mouthpiece for the Communist Party and dismiss it as either more concerned with pursuing the Party's interests than with fighting for women's interests, or as unable to fight effectively for the latter (see, for example, Hooper, 1985, p. 109; *ZGFN*, Nov. 1980, pp. 2–3, quoted in Honig and Hershatter, 1988, p. 318). There is considerable truth in these views. The policy of the Women's Federation is indeed determined largely by the Communist Party, and it is constrained in its work with women, both because of this and because it has little of either resources or power. However, part of my aim in this chapter is to challenge one of the assumptions that I think underpins the negative attitude toward the Women's Federation; that is that there is always a dichotomy between what the state wants and what women want, that the state is always 'bad' for women, and that only those outside of, and opposed to, the state can further the cause of women's liberation.

Since the mid 1980s the key aim of the Women's Federation in rural areas has been to alleviate poverty and improve the involvement of women in the commodity economy (ACWF, 1986, pp. 2–5). Central to the achievement of this aim has been the provision of short-term training courses for women in the courtyard economy (Huang Qizao, 1989, p. 2). The Women's Federation also provides legal advice to women working in the courtyard economy and makes links with other bodies to help women obtain bank loans and to assist them with the supply of raw materials, feed for livestock and other inputs, and with the marketing of their produce (e.g *RMRB*, 27 January 1985).

Aside from a concern to improve women's position in the economy, the enthusiasm for domestic sidelines and the courtyard economy shown by the Women's Federation and other state bodies is part of a general enthusiasm for commercialization and industrialization in the rural economy. In this respect, the courtyard economy is seen as belonging to the same category as more specialized, larger-scale and more capitalized forms of rural industry. Part of the importance of the courtyard economy for the state is that it is seen as being transitional to, and acting as a springboard for, developing these other forms of production. Indeed many specialized households began by engaging in agriculture and sidelines and then, finding the sidelines to be more profitable, made these their main form of production.

However, the courtyard economy is not only important to the state as a transitional stage on the way towards more capitalized development. It is also valued, in its own right, as a set of subsidiary occupations existing between primary agriculture and industry, that requires little capital investment and can make use of 'surplus' or 'auxiliary' labour, time and resources, to produce goods at very low cost.

Two examples may help to illustrate the role which the state sees domestic sidelines and the courtyard economy as playing. In an article published in 1986 the head of the Rural Policy Research Office of the Central Committee Secretariat stressed the importance of small-scale, family-based animal husbandry, crop planting, handicrafts, sewing and services as sources of employment for surplus labour. He stressed, in particular, the importance of such work for the numerous women who are 'clever and dextrous', yet underemployed (*ZGFNB*, 18 August 1986). Another article published in 1988 claimed that in Pingyuan County, Shandong, 100,000 women participated in the courtyard economy. It said that

> in rural commodity production the county government found that because of women's physiological, psychological and biological characteristics, their abilities were not being given full play. In order that this group might also contribute to commodity production, the county government called on women to develop the courtyard economy, this being particularly suited to their special characteristics. (*NMRB*, 17 May 1988).[3]

That it is recommended as an area of work particularly suited to women is, I would argue, an integral aspect of the state's encouragement of the courtyard economy. This is partly related to the problem of surplus – predominantly female – agricultural labour. Improved productivity, stimulated by the introduction of the production responsibility system, has released a large amount of labour from agriculture. However, in the early stages of reform, and even today in remote inland areas, there are not enough alternative forms of employment for this labour (see, for example, *FNGZ*, September 1984, p. 24) as markets, services and transport are all relatively underdeveloped. Despite massive industrialization of the Chinese countryside, many such areas still have few local industries and those that exist often employ workers on only a part-time, temporary basis. In addition, peasants in these areas lack the capital and the skills necessary for work outside agriculture. All this makes it difficult for peasants in less developed areas to find non-agricultural employment, either in their home county or elsewhere. Nevertheless, many peasant families have found it advantageous to withdraw surplus workers from full-time agriculture (rather than letting them be underemployed in the fields as would have happened under the commune system) so that they can do the family's domestic work.

In such circumstances, women have been the first to be withdrawn from agricultural work. This illustrates a longstanding identification of women primarily as domestic workers and only secondarily as workers 'outside' in agriculture. Thus the courtyard economy has been encouraged by the state, in part, as a way of relieving unemployment and discontent amongst women who have lost their jobs in agriculture.

More recently, and in particular in more developed areas, new patterns of employment have emerged and the courtyard economy has served a slightly different purpose. With the establishment of local industries and the removal of restrictions on labour movement, opportunities for rural non-agricultural employment have greatly expanded, providing numerous peasants with the chance to get out of farming, which has a lower status, is considered more arduous and is generally less profitable than employment in industry. However, most peasant households continue to feel the need to hold onto their land as a basic form of security and to provide grain for consumption and tax. In any case, competition for non-agricultural employment remains high. In this, women, especially older, married women, are disadvantaged, both by lower educational levels and by discrimination. In rural industries, for example, fewer women than men are employed, in part because the recruitment policies of some industries, especially heavy industries, discriminate against them.[4] Some rural industries also do not employ women after they have married or had a child. Furthermore, women have fewer chances for promotion than men in township enterprises and their wages tend to be lower. As a consequence of these factors, in many households men work in industry, whilst women, especially older ones, are left with the responsibility for agriculture.

In areas where a large shift of labour into non-agricultural occupations has occurred, the courtyard economy has served to boost the incomes of women 'left behind' in agriculture and domestic work. This has, in turn, both helped to keep agricultural production going and relieved pressure on the state and collective sector to provide non-agricultural employment.

From the state's point of view there are further advantages of the courtyard economy which relate to its particular relationship to other parts of the economy, to its 'subsidiary' nature, and to its location, both physically and conceptually in a domestic sphere.

In some cases the 'subsidiary' aspect of the courtyard economy means that women are relatively more keen to undertake the production of specialist commodities that other business people and enterprises avoid because of the high risks involved. Production in the courtyard economy can prove very lucrative in the short term, but in general, no one line of production in this sector is highly profitable for very long. When the relatively high returns to be gained from the production of a novel item attract other producers, demand declines and prices are pressed downwards. Then, as Philip Huang explains,

> When prices drop below what peasants will tolerate for spare time work, they simply stop producing the item until the market recovers. . . . The shocks are cushioned by the fact that the production is only a sideline, so that the household can move out of the activity without devastating consequences to its fundamental livelihood. (1990, pp. 217–18).

Another advantage of the courtyard economy is that it makes full use of the family's existing material resources, including building space, water and electricity (where it is available), sewing machines and other tools. In addition, the existence of women working in the courtyard economy, whilst simultaneously minding children and doing domestic work, obviates the need for larger-scale collective enterprises to provide childcare facilities, and reduces the domestic workload of workers in those larger enterprises. The fact that most families retain at least one woman on the land, combining crop growing with work in the courtyard economy, also means that families produce most of their own food, and consequently, factory employers do not have to pay their peasant workers wages sufficient to cover the total cost of reproducing their labour (Potter and Potter, 1991, p. 331).

Finally, by subcontracting tasks to women working at home, both local and international capitalists have taken direct advantage of the old link between unproductive domestic work and domestic sidelines, and the belief that what women earn in the courtyard economy is merely a secondary addition to the primary income of the family enabling them to keep workers' incomes down, and hence to maximize profit (Nee and Su, 1990, p. 9). Anecdotal evidence suggests that a large proportion of women's work in home-based sewing, weaving and handicraft production is tied in with the rest of the economy in this way.

The discussion so far suggests two important points about the reform process and the interaction between gender relations and the state. First of all, the impact that reform policies have had on patterns of employment and production has been shaped in crucial ways by gender divisions of labour. Secondly, the state makes use of, and itself shapes, gender divisions and gender ideologies. This is apparent in the way in which the courtyard economy has been promoted as particularly suited to women. However, this is just one element of a state-sponsored shift in gender ideologies which is, I would argue, an integral feature of the state's new strategy for development and of its attempts to legitimate its rule. Thus, whereas during the Cultural Revolution (1966–76) it was claimed that 'what men can do, women can do too', this slogan is now repudiated, and in education and the media it is stressed that physiologically and psychologically 'women and men are different', and each have their special characteristics and abilities (Honig and Hershatter, 1988, pp. 13–40). This change in gender ideology relates in part to the current leadership's perception that divisions of labour in general improve efficiency and enable contrasting demands, especially between modernization and employment generation, to be met more readily. It is also central to the current regime's repudiation of the Cultural Revolution and what it deems to be that period's excessive radicalism and egalitarianism (Young, 1989, pp. 261–3). Finally, a strong emphasis on women's roles as mothers and domestic workers, and, by extension, as the guardians of social order and morality, has been a central element in the state's attempts to combat post-Cultural Revolution cynicism and discontent amongst young people, to curb what are seen as the undesirable consequences of the 'open door policy' and the promotion of a market economy – that is, excessive materialism, selfishness, and 'spiritual pollution' – and to promote values and standards of behaviour conducive to social stability and modernization.[5]

The way in which a particular gender ideology has been promoted in the development of the Chinese courtyard economy can be likened to the 'housewifization' of women working in household handicraft production in India and other developing countries. Maria Mies' study of the lace makers of Narsapur clearly illustrates the role that 'housewifization' plays. In Narsapur, Andhra Pradesh, India, poor rural Christian and Hindu women produce lace doilies at home. These are then sold through an extensive network of male agents, traders and exporters. Lace production contributes about 90 per cent of the state's handicraft export earnings and has become very profitable for the male traders. But the women who make the lace earn appallingly low wages, and in spite of a 6-to-8-hour day at lace work, on top of 7 hours of other productive work and domestic work, they are not considered 'workers' but rather 'housewives'. The women originally took up lace making as a spare-time activity in order to supplement their husbands' insufficient incomes. As Mies says, 'As they are defined as housewives, this production does not upset the patriarchal reproduction relations within the family and it prevents the women at the same time from demanding a just wage' (Mies, 1982, p. 172).

She goes on to argue that

> This housewifisation, based on older forms of sexual segregation . . .
> is the necessary precondition for the extraction of super profits from
> the lace workers. The domestication of women and the propagation
> of the ideology that women are basically housewives is not merely a

means to keep their wages below the subsistence level but also to keep women totally atomised and disorganised as workers. (Mies, 1982, p. 176)

The degree of exploitation of the Narsapur lace makers is worse than anything yet occurring in China. However, the structures which underpin such exploitation as occurs in rural India are also in place in rural China, and it is possible that in the future women working in the Chinese courtyard economy will be exploited in the same way and to the same extent as in India. On the other hand, if rural development in China continues to expand the range of employment opportunities available to rural women, this will increase their power to demand higher incomes in the courtyard economy as well as in other sectors. Another important factor in determining the degree of exploitation of women in the courtyard economy will be the extent to which the women are able to work together to defend their interests, and the extent to which their interests are supported by the state and local government. In this regard, as I will argue shortly, the role of the Women's Federation will be very important.

Women's Interests in the Courtyard Economy

In the previous section I focused on the state's interests in promoting women's work in the courtyard economy as a way of maximizing the use of a flexible and cheap source of labour. Yet the expansion of the courtyard economy cannot be understood solely as the top-down manipulation or exploitation of passive women. We must also take into consideration the fact that households and women, themselves, see important benefits to working in this sector. Moreover, it is usually peasant women who take the initiative to develop production in the courtyard economy, with local officials providing support and encouragement only after they have judged that such production will be viable in the longer term.

Some reports suggest, in fact, that especially in the late 1970s and early 1980s, when private entrepreneurial activities were still viewed with suspicion by many officials, permission to expand production in the courtyard economy came only after considerable pressure was applied on local leaders by women who had lost their jobs in agriculture and had no alternative employment (see, for example, *ZGFN*, March 1979, p. 5). Other reports show the courtyard economy being developed largely through the initiative of one particularly enterprising woman, who then employs, or passes on her skills to, other women in the village (see, for example, *ZGFNB*, 20 June 1986; *ZGFN*, October 1985, p. 46).

In the majority of rural families, one or more women are engaged in the courtyard economy, at least to the extent of raising one or two pigs and a few chickens. As I have suggested, women sometimes seek more substantial work in the courtyard economy as a result of underemployment or unemployment in agriculture and the lack of alternative forms of work. In other cases, women, especially older women, choose to work in the courtyard economy as a way of supplementing their income from agriculture. The limitations on opportunities for female employment in industry discussed above are often a factor in their decision to work in these sectors.

Sometimes, however, women choose to work in the courtyard economy in preference to employment in industry. For example, in Zengbu in the early 1980s young rural women were eager to work in the factories being established as joint ventures with Hong Kong capitalists. However, where well-paying work in the courtyard economy was available it was deemed preferable to working in a factory. In Pondside, for example, the young women chose to work at home, making bamboo sticks used in the production of fireworks, rather than work in local factories (Potter and Potter, 1991, p. 321).

One of the benefits of the courtyard economy most commonly cited by rural women is its income-earning potential. The range of incomes that can be earned from the courtyard economy is enormous – from very little to more than half the family income in the case of specialized households. Surveys suggest, however, that the average per capita net income earned in domestic sidelines or the courtyard economy amounts to roughly one-third of the average rural income (*ZGNMB*, 22 May 1983; *NMRB*, 17 July 1986). As Delia Davin points out, 'much sideline production is monotonous, isolated, under-capitalized and, even by Chinese standards, poorly remunerated. Only exceptionally are large amounts of money made' (Davin, 1988, p. 140).

A minority of women working in the courtyard economy have, however, earned incomes much higher than the local average, usually by engaging in a new and novel line of production, and/or by specializing in one line of production and developing it into a specialized household or private enterprise (for examples, see Qi, 1993). It is in part examples of such high incomes, given much publicity in the press, that attract women to the courtyard economy.

Discussions with peasant women, and reports in the media, suggest, however, that two other equally important factors drawing women to the courtyard economy are firstly, the work's flexibility – the fact that it can be done at any time and can easily be fitted in with women's domestic work – and secondly, the autonomy and control over their own time and labour that women obtain. This is contrasted favourably with employment in the fields under the commune system, when women's labour was managed by production team officials, and with employment today in rural industries, where few women attain management positions and female employees have little freedom or control over the production process. As the women in Pondside said, 'we like the freedom of working at home at our own speed; if we work for ourselves we don't have to add shifts or work all night' (Potter and Potter, 1991, p. 321).

Positive statements such as this should not, however, blind us to the ways in which women's power and autonomy in the family are constrained, and may indeed have become more so as a result of a return to family farming. By shifting the management of labour allocation and income distribution from the production team back to the family, the introduction of the production responsibility system has once more strengthened the authority of the male head of the family – an authority that is underpinned by women's relative insecurity in the family due to a patrilocal marriage system.[6]

In addition, in some cases women's work in the courtyard economy has itself further reinforced men's authority. This is partly because of the strong associations between domestic sidelines and domestic work, which tends to render the former invisible. Thus where, as in the past, women's work in the courtyard economy consisted of raising a small number of domestic live stock, the strong associations between such work and domestic work, combined with the relatively low cash income from such work, may render its contribution to the family economy invisible, consequently maintaining the lower status of the women who do such work. However, with the newer and more lucrative sidelines, high income and public prestige is likely to translate into greater authority for women in the family.

Pointing to a more concrete problem, Delia Davin has suggested that under the commune system the majority of women worked in the fields with women and men from other families, but under the new system women working in the courtyard economy have fewer opportunities to communicate with people outside their family, and hence are more vulnerable to the dictates of parents, husbands and in-laws (Davin, 1988, p. 138).

This is particularly true of women whose work in the courtyard economy is solely for family consumption. An important part of the reform programme has been, however, to encourage commercialization of production in the courtyard economy. This has increased women's interaction with people outside the family, for example when they take produce to market. In some cases women's work in the courtyard economy involves them negotiating loans and arranging business deals, as well as marketing. However, much of the work that women undertake in activities such as weaving and handicraft production is subcontracted; here they are not involved in the business side of the work and thus have little interaction with people outside the family. Furthermore, even where work in the courtyard economy is not subcontracted in this way, it is more common for women not to be involved in business transactions with non-family members. As in pre-1949 China, such activities are considered to belong to the male 'outside' sphere, and are commonly undertaken by the woman's husband, even though he may not be involved in the production itself.

In this chapter so far I have shown that the expansion of the courtyard economy has resulted from both the state and peasant women pursuing their interests in that sector. Both sets of interests have, in turn, been shaped by particular gender divisions of labour and by a development strategy in which those divisions are promoted. I have demonstrated that for women, work in the courtyard economy is seen to offer the potential for generating substantial incomes and for providing them with a degree of autonomy and flexibility not possible in larger-scale industry. I have argued, however, that just as there is the potential for the courtyard economy to bring important benefits to women, there is also the possibility that they will be severely constrained and exploited. Both the potentially negative and positive aspects of the courtyard economy relate to its domestic and subsidiary nature. Thus, while the fact that the work is undertaken by women at home gives women more flexibility than employment in industry, it also leaves women vulnerable to the demands of husbands and other relatives and to exploitation by capitalists, both Chinese and foreign.

In the final section of this chapter, I will examine the activities of the Women's Federation in encouraging women in the courtyard economy and will ask whether, or to what extent, the Federation is helping women to maximize the benefits to be gained in this sector and to minimize the potential for exploitation.

First, however, I wish to discuss the position of the small number of women entrepreneurs who have developed their activities in the courtyard economy into 'specialized households'. It appears that these women have been able to develop the potential of the courtyard economy to the full, and consequently are amongst those to have benefited most from rural reform.

Woman Running Specialized Households

Specialized households (zhuanyehu) are high-earning rural households which derive most of their income from just one area of either agricultural or non-agricultural production or services. A 1988 study estimated that there were approximately 4 million specialized households (Summary of World Broadcasts, 5 October 1988).

According to an investigation carried out by the Women's Federation in fourteen regions across China, specialized households run by women (funu wei zhu de zhuanyehu) comprise 35 to 40 per cent of all specialized households and in some developed regions the figure is as high as 55 per cent (*RMRB*, 31 October 1986). In comparison with the tiny proportion of collective and state-run industries with women in management positions this figure is high. This may be because, firstly, specialized households are family-based and usually employ no more than a few non-family members, if any. A woman running a specialized household is, therefore, more acceptable in terms of the view that women's work should be confined to the domestic sphere. Secondly, the majority of specialized households have evolved from domestic sideline production, which, as we have seen, is dominated by women. The fact that there are not more women running specialized households suggests, however, that once a woman's activities in the courtyard economy reach a certain scale and become more profitable than other productive activities available to the family, their management is often taken over by the male head of the family.

In an investigation of 403 specialized households run by women conducted in Huairou County, Beijing, in 1988 it was found that 65 per cent of the women earned incomes higher than their husbands and in 80 per cent of the households the women managed all financial matters (interview with head of Huairou County Women's Federation, September 1989). Other examples cited in the media show women running specialized households in control of most aspects of the production process, including contracting with other bodies, taking out loans and being responsible for investments and the sale of produce. In addition, some women running specialized households achieve positions of considerable status in their village by employing other people, by teaching others their skills or by helping them to set up their own businesses, and by joining the Party or receiving 'labour model' status (Jilinsheng Fulian Xuanjiaobu, 1984, pp. 14–15; *ZGPN*, May 1986, p. 12; *NMRB*, 12 June 1986).

It might be supposed then, that women running specialized households have a high degree of authority in their own family, and that they are also breaking down existing gender divisions of labour or, to put it another way, that they are successfully using their work in the 'domestic' courtyard economy as a launching pad from which to enter the male preserve of business and public prestige.

There are a number of caveats to be made to these propositions. In the first place, there are considerable variations in meaning attached to the term 'running a specialized household' and in the powers and responsibilities a woman in this position has. Thus, some of the women I have interviewed do seem to be in control of their line of production. Others, although they do most of the work and have the necessary technical skills, share responsibility with their husbands. In keeping with traditional gender divisions of labour, it is the latter who arrange loans and sign contracts, seek business, and generally represent the family to the outside world.

It must also be recognized that the people who run specialized households are a privileged minority among peasants. Such people are commonly set apart from others by a number of characteristics. Their families tend, first of all, to be larger and to contain more able-bodied labourers than the average, allowing for the greater and more efficient deployment of family labour, and reducing the need to hire outside workers (Zhao, 1988, pp. 67–8). In addition, many of the people who run specialized households are able to do so because they have contacts with officials who give them preferential treatment in terms of securing credit and arranging contracts, for example, or because they themselves are officials (Conroy, 1984, p. 23).

People running specialized households also tend to have above-average levels of education (Jilinsheng Fulian Xuanjiaobu, 1984, p. 14; Zhao, 1988, p. 73). Lack of education is likely to limit any increase in the number of women running specialized households, both in terms of absolute numbers and as a proportion of the total. Approximately 70 per cent of all illiterates are women, and drop-out rates amongst girls in rural primary and secondary schools are high (Rai, 1992).

Development of the Courtyard Economy as a Strategy for Improving the Position of Rural Women

In light of the somewhat ambivalent picture drawn here of women's work in the courtyard economy and as managers of specialized households, what are we to make of the Women's Federation's efforts to support and encourage women in these areas, and the centrality of such efforts to the Federation's work with rural women?

In an article published in 1984, one county Women's Federation in Shanxi province explained that it became involved in promoting the courtyard economy because of the large number of women surplus to the needs of agriculture who had no alternative means of employment, and also because it observed how some women had become wealthy by working in the courtyard economy. It cited the following advantages to work in this sector: first, the work is flexible, and can be accommodated with women's domestic work responsibilities. Second, it arouses women's enthusiasm for studying science and technology and trains a large number of women managers. Third, it provides women with an income and hence raises their economic status and helps to protect their legal rights; and finally, it advances the development of the commodity economy (Shanxisheng Huairenxian Fulian, 1984, pp. 24–5).

In Shanxi, this article implies, the courtyard economy was encouraged by the Women's Federation in a context in which large numbers of women were unemployed or underemployed and had no income. In this context, I would argue, support for women in developing the courtyard economy is indeed an initially expedient way of providing women with an income and hence of improving their status and self-respect.

Yet women are being encouraged to develop the courtyard economy – not just in the poorer, less developed parts of rural China where there are few alternatives for employment, but also in the most economically developed regions. It must be asked whether such work enhances women's opportunities for income generation, personal development and status improvement, in a way that is comparable with work in other areas of the economy, or whether it leads to marginalization and exploitation of women in a 'dead-end' part of the economy. In considering this question it is worth reflecting both on Maria Mies' discussion of 'housewifization' and on Ester Boserup's statement that

> some developing countries . . . have programmes for training women in crafts and home industries. Where women live in seclusion, to teach them a craft which they can do at home may be the only possible first step towards bringing them into the labour market. . . . But the effect of offering this kind of training to women who do not live in seclusion may be to drag them into low-productivity jobs rather than to help them to find more productive and remunerative employment (Boserup, 1970, p. 221).

It has been a common dream of the peasantry through the ages to get off the land and off the farm, and now in the 1980s and 1990s, with rapid industrialization and the development of a market economy, that dream is being fulfilled by more and more rural inhabitants. From this viewpoint, those who work on the land and on the farm are the unlucky ones. By focusing their efforts on training women in farm work, whether it be in the courtyard or in the fields, and by reinforcing notions that such work is women's work, the Women's Federation could be said to be colluding in a perpetuation of women's lower status.

On the other hand, in China, as we have seen, the courtyard economy is a dynamic and growing aspect of the rural economy, which provides the potential, at least, for earning high incomes and improving one's authority and status in the family and in the wider society. Furthermore, echoing claims made by peasant women themselves, Women's Federation officials point out that the most attractive alternative to work in the courtyard economy generally available to rural women, that is employment in larger scale rural industry, offers them less autonomy and scope for self-development than the courtyard economy, and that management of such industries is overwhelmingly male (Judd, 1990, p. 37).

Finally, in rural China, as elsewhere, gender divisions of labour are constructed and maintained through a formidable web of institutions, power relations, social acts and beliefs. Given this, and given its own limited resources and power, the Women's Federation perhaps feels that the most worthwhile strategy is not to continually challenge existing gender divisions of labour, but rather to concentrate on making those divisions work as far as possible to the benefit of women.

In light of these factors, I would suggest that in China, support for women in the courtyard economy is a viable strategy for enhancing women's social and economic position. I would nevertheless argue that such support cannot be effective without including certain elements.

First of all, in view of the fact that the market for goods from the courtyard economy is constantly in flux and no one line of production in this sector seems to be highly profitable for very long, what is most required in terms of training for the courtyard economy is basic literacy and numeracy, a grounding in generally applicable technical skills, and some knowledge of accounting and of the workings of the market. These are also the types of skills that will enable women either to move out of the courtyard economy if it ceases to be a viable form of production or to move onto something bigger and better.

Second, in order to avoid exploitation and to help women retain control over their labour and the products of their labour, some training in accounting, legal matters and management skills is also required. As I have suggested, there is a further need for women working in this sector to be organized to defend their interests, and for support from the state to protect them against excessive exploitation, for example by subcontractors.

Looking, then, at the efforts of the Women's Federation to support women in the courtyard economy, I would argue that, in terms of training, there needs to be a shift away from the current emphasis on short-term classes in specialized technical skills, and more effort directed at improving basic education and developing skills in accounting and management.

The prevention of exploitation is not a major focus of the Women's Federation's current work in the courtyard economy. Nevertheless, it does play a useful role in liaising with other bodies, for example, local government, banks and contractors, on women's behalf. It also encourages solidarity amongst women in the courtyard economy by organizing meetings for women in this sector to exchange their experiences and by urging successful women entrepreneurs to pass on their skills and lend support to other women starting up ventures in the courtyard economy (Shanxisheng Huairenxian Fulian, 1984, pp. 25–6). Finally, although it has few resources, and its reputation amongst women is poor, the Women's Federation has shown in recent years that it can act as an important lobby group to defend women against the worst forms of exploitation, discrimination and abuse.[7]

Conclusion

In this chapter I have explored the various pressures, constraints, alternatives and opportunities which lead both the state and rural women to support the expansion of the courtyard economy. In the process, I have suggested a model somewhat different from that most commonly employed in recent Western studies of women in China. Instead of viewing change in women's lives in terms of the impact of state policies, I have argued that such change results from the actions of both women and the state, pursuing interests that sometimes conflict and sometimes coincide.

These interests have been shaped in crucial ways by gender divisions of labour and gender ideologies. Thus, from the state's point of view, gender divisions of labour between domestic and public, or outside, spheres mean that women in the courtyard economy can be exploited as a cheap and flexible labour force. At the same time, these divisions of labour mean that for some women the courtyard economy is the only form of employment available, while for others it is preferable to employment in industry where they have little autonomy and little chance of being involved in management.

Western analyses of Third World women's involvement in production similar to the courtyard economy commonly focus on the state's exploitation of women in such work. I have argued in this chapter, however, that to examine the development of the courtyard economy in China solely from this angle is problematic because it removes women's interests and women's agency from the picture and because it denies the possibility for action from within, or with, the state to further women's interests. I have shown, firstly, that many Chinese women see benefits in working in the courtyard economy and, secondly, that while the state plays a supportive role, in most cases development of this sector occurs as a result of initiatives taken by individual peasant women themselves. Finally, I have argued that support given to women in the courtyard economy by state agents, in particular the Women's Federation, can mitigate exploitation in this area of work, and help women to improve their economic and social status.

Notes

1 In this chapter I employ the Weberian concept of the state to refer to administrative bureaucratic and coercive apparatuses. The main components of the state in China are the Communist Party, the government and the People's Liberation Army.
2 For an account of the emergence of these organizations see Wan Shanping, 1988.
3 The article does not explain the features of the courtyard economy that make it 'particularly suited to [women's] special characteristics'. The usual meaning attributed to this phrase, however, is that the work is not as physically demanding as other work, and/or that it is related in some way to women's roles as mothers and domestic workers.
4 On the other hand, however, the workforce in many light industries is comprised mainly of young women.
5 For further discussion of recent changes in gender ideology see Honig and Hershatter, 1988, and Jacka, 1993.
6 Under this system, just-married women leave their natal family to join their husband's family which is often in a different village.
7 An important example is the Federation's campaign against calls for women to 'return to the kitchen' to relieve employment pressures in state-run industries. See Jacka, 1990.

Abbreviations

ACWF	All-China Women's Federation
CCP	Chinese Communist Party
FNGZ	*Funu Gongzuo* (*Woman-Work*)
NMRB	*Nongmin Ribao* (*Peasants' Daily*)
PRC	People's Republic of China
RMRB	*Renmin Ribao* (*People's Daily*)
ZGFN	*Zhongquo Funu* (*Chinese Women*)
ZGFNB	*Zhongguo Funu Bao* (*Chinese Women's Daily*)
ZGNMB	*Zhongguo Nonmin Bao* (*Chinese Peasants' Daily*)

Bibliography

ACWF (1986) 'Xin shiqi nongcun funu gongzuo de xin renwu' ('New Tasks for Rural Woman-Work in the New Era'), *FNGZ*, August, pp. 2–5.

BOSERUP, ESTER (1970) *Woman's Role in Economic Development*, New York, St Martin's Press.

CCP (1978) 'Communiqué of the Third Plenary Session of the 11th Central Committee of the Communist Party of China', *Peking Review*, No. 52, 29 December, pp. 6–16.

CONROY, RICHARD (1984) 'Laissez-Faire Socialism? Prosperous Peasants and China's Current Rural Development Strategy', *The Australian Journal of Chinese Affairs*, No. 12, pp. 1–34.

CROLL, ELISABETH (1983) *Chinese Women Since Mao*, London, Zed Books.

DAVIN, DELIA (1988) 'The Implications of Contract Agriculture for the Employment and Status of Chinese Peasant Women', in FEUCHTWANG, STEPHAN, HUSSAIN, ATHAR and PAIRAULT, THIERRY (Eds) *Transforming China's Economy in the Eighties: Vol. 1, The Rural Sector, Welfare and Employment*, Boulder, Westview Press, and London, Zed Press, pp. 137–44.

FNGZ, September 1984, p. 24.

HONIG, EMILY and HERSHATTER, GAIL (1988) *Personal Voices: Chinese Women in the 1980s*, Stanford, California, Stanford University Press.

HOOPER, BEVERLY (1985) *Youth in China*, Australia, Penguin.

HUANG, PHILIP (1990) *The Peasant Family and Rural Development in the Yangzi Delta, 1350–1988*, Stanford, California, Stanford University Press.

HUANG QIZAO (1989) 'Zai di si qi pinkun diqu xianii fulian zhuren peixun ban shang de zongjie jianghua' ('Concluding Speech at the Fourth Training Class for Heads of County Level Women's Federations of Poor Areas'), *FNGZ*, November, pp. 2–5.

JACKA, TAMARA (1990) 'Back to the Wok: Women and Employment in Chinese Industry in the 1980s', *The Australian Journal of Chinese Affairs*, No. 24, pp. 1–24.

JACKA, TAMARA (1993) *The Impact of Reform on Women's Work and Gender Divisions of Labour in Rural China, 1978–1993*, unpublished doctoral dissertation.

JILINSHENG FULIAN XUANJIAOBU (Propaganda and Education Department of the Jilin Provincial Women's Federation) (1984) 'Tigao funu kexue wenhua suzhi shi bashi niandai funu yundong xin tedian zhi yi' ('Improving Women's Scientific and Cultural Quality Is a New Characteristic of the Women's Movement of the '80s'), *FNGZ*, September, pp. 14–15.

JUDD, ELLEN (1990) 'Alternative Development Strategies for Women in Rural China', *Development and Change*, Vol. 21, No. 1, pp. 23–42.

JUDD, ELLEN (1994) *Gender and Power in Rural North China*, Stanford, California, Stanford University Press.

KELLIHER, DANIEL (1992) *Peasant Power in China: The Era of Reform, 1979–1989*, New Haven and London, Yale University Press.

MIES, MARIA (1982) *The Lace Makers of Narsapur: Indian Housewives Produce for the World Market*, London, Zed Press.

NEE, VICTOR and SU SIJIN (1990) 'Institutional Change and Economic Growth in China: The View from the Villages', *Journal of Asian Studies*, Vol. 49, No. 1, pp. 3–25.

NMRB, 8 March 1985.

NMRB, 12 June 1986.

NMRB, 17 July 1986.

NMRB, 17 May 1988.

OI, JEAN (1989) *State and Peasant in Contemporary China: The Political Economy of Village Government*, Berkeley, University of California Press.

POTTER, SULAMITH and POTTER, JACK (1991) *China's Peasants: The Anthropology of a Revolution*, Cambridge, Cambridge University Press.

QI QUANMU (1993) 'Tingyuan jingji – zhi fu de jin' ('The Courtyard Economy – A Goldmine'), *Shehui* (*Society*), No. 1, pp. 24–6.

RAI, SHIRIN (1992) '"Watering Another Man's Garden": Gender, Employment and Educational Reforms in China', in RAI, SHIRIN, PILKINGTON, HILARY and PHIZACKLEA, ANNIE (Eds) *Women in the Face of Change: The Soviet Union, Eastern Europe and China*, London and New York, Routledge, pp. 20–40.

RMRB, 27 January 1985.

RMRB, 31 October 1986.

SHANXISHENG HUAIRENXIAN FULIAN (The Women's Federation of Huairen County, Shanxi Province) (1984) 'Tingyuan zi you zhi fu lu' ('The Courtyard Itself Is a Way to Get Rich'), *FNGZ*, September, pp. 24–6.

SHUE, VIVIENNE (1988) *The Reach of the State: Sketches of the Chinese Body Politic*, Stanford, California, Stanford University Press.

SUMMARY OF WORLD BROADCASTS, 5 October 1988, FE/W0046/A/1.

WAN SHANPING (1988) 'The Emergence of Women's Studies in China', *Women's Studies International Forum*, Vol. 11, No. 5, pp. 455–64.

YOUNG, MARILYN (1989) 'Chicken Little in China: Some Reflections on Women', in DIRLIK, ARIF and MEISNER, MAURICE (Eds) *Marxism and the Chinese Experience*, New York and London, M.E. Sharpe, Armonk, pp. 253–68.

ZGFN, March 1979, p. 5.

ZGFN, October 1985, p. 46.

ZGFN, May 1986, p. 12.

ZGFNB, 20 June 1986.

ZGFNB, 18 August 1986.

ZGNMB, 22 May 1983.

ZHANG RUIHUA (1987) 'Nongcun tingyuan jingji chutan' ('A Preliminary Investigation of the Rural Courtyard Economy'), in *Zhongguo Renmin Daxue Shubao Ziliao Zhongxin, Fuyin Baokan Ziliao, Funu ZuzM yu Huodong* (*Press Clippings on Women's Organizations and Activities, Centre for Books and Newspaper Materials, The Chinese People's University*), No. 8, pp. 65–7.

ZHAO XISHUN (1988) *Gaige yu Nongcun Jiating* (*Reform and the Rural Family*), Sichuan, Sichuansheng Shehui Kexueyuan Chubanshe.

Chapter 9

Women, Migration and the State

Annie Phizacklea

Introduction

Over the last fifteen years or so there has been an increased recognition, amongst women researchers at least, of the need to provide a gendered account of migratory processes. Nevertheless, despite a recognition of the importance of women's role in migration, many accounts of contemporary migratory processes continue to fail to take on board what this means at an analytical level. For instance Stephen Castles' and Mark Miller's book *The Age of Migration* starts by commenting on the increased feminization of migration and how this is one of four tendencies likely to play a major role in migratory movements over the next twenty years. But the book in itself does not pursue this observation in any serious way (Castles and Miller, 1993).

In what follows I want to explore the relationship between women's migration, employment and state practice in three globalized industries – clothing, sex and the maids industry. These case studies throw light on how a world market for women's labour and services continues to be mediated by the policies of inidividual nation-states which have not only been constructed in highly masculinist ways but which contribute to the reproduction of women's subordination and dependency in traditional forms. Concerns of this kind have become increasingly unfashionable in Western feminist analyses where a poststructuralist concern with identity, difference and diversity amongst women has become more widespread. Given Western feminism's tendency to universalize the experience of Western, affluent women, a focus on the diversity of women's experiences is welcome. Nevertheless it needs to be emphasized that there are also real dangers in an emphasis on diversity if it obscures the continuing material inequalities between women in racialized hierarchies of power; these have not gone away: they may take different forms and be expressed in novel ways but they remain a significant and persistent feature in the constitution of diversity and difference amongst women at a global level. In fact one of the purposes of this paper is to highlight specific situations which raise uncomfortable and pressing questions for feminists in affluent societies. A recognition of difference and diversity does not however mean that coalitions cannot be built between women of different class, ethnic and national backgrounds. The structure of this chapter is as follows: it begins with a brief overview of the ways in which women's migration has been conceptualized and the global forces which have shaped women's migratory experiences; it then goes on to the case studies; and it concludes with a very brief consideration of organization and coalition-building.

Theorizing Migration – Voluntarist versus Structuralist Accounts

In this chapter I am not concerned with the migration of well-qualified, usually professional migrant workers whose relatively scarce skills can be sold for generous rewards on the world labour market. My concern is with those migrants (and this includes refugees) who through poverty, unemployment or war are forced to seek a livelihood outside their country of origin.

Women constitute half of the world's migrants and 80 per cent of the world's refugee population. This includes women living permanently or for long periods of time outside their country of origin as well as those migrating for relatively short periods of time on fixed-term work contracts. Others may have migrated in order to join husbands or relatives already working abroad and still others are forced to leave their home countries due to unrest, persecution and violence. But none of these women just wake up one morning and decide to migrate from their homes; rather, the causes of migration are complex, and they are very often different for men and for women.

While there is not the space here to present a literature review on women and migration, I want to suggest that there have been two main models. One I will call voluntarist, because it stresses the role of human agency and the potentially emancipatory effects of migration for women, particularly when this is related to the pursuit of increased wage-earning opportunities. The alternative structuralist model regards women's migration, whether it be individual or family-related, as determined by economic necessity and the migratory experience shaped by external forces leaving little space for 'choice' to be exercised. I want to suggest that, given the type of migratory flows that I am addressing in this chapter, the latter model is the most appropriate, and I will emphasize the role of the state in shaping migratory projects. Migration has always been and continues to be an expression of uneven economic development on a global scale. In describing South-North migrations in the 1960s, Castles and Kosack (1973) suggested that we might regard such migrations as a form of development aid to the North. With the demise of the 'communist bloc' and rapid capitalist development in many south-east Asian countries our binary shorthands of 'North-South' or the always pejorative notion of First, Second and Third World have limited value even at a descriptive level. Some of us have now started to refer simply to affluent and poor countries of the world, though it is important to remember the historic linkages which explain why some are affluent and some are poor. The unevenness was established in its clearest forms under colonization by European nation-states from the fifteenth century onwards. Colonization meant the enrichment of the European nation-states at the expense of the colonized economy and population, often the latter's destruction and its substitution with imported slave labour. The European colonial powers went on to impose their domination onto large tracts of the world. In many cases the colonized, dispossessed of their land either through compulsory acquisition or changes in communal land holding, were forced to work on estates or in mines producing food and raw materials for export. Political independence from the colonizer rarely brought with it economic independence because the legacy of colonialism was economic underdevelopment, a distorted economy, degraded land and structural unemployment. These same countries continued to be economically dependent on their ex-colonizers and other affluent developed countries through the presence of multinational companies, external debt and a dependence on export-led growth.

The economic and social dislocation which arises from this distorted development process is not gender-neutral – deprived of traditional subsistence activities on and around the land it is often women who become a 'relative surplus' population in the poorer, 'developing' countries of the world. Up until the end of the 1970s women's migration from poor countries was very often bound into these colonial linkages as they migrated in search of work to the affluent metropolitan society.

From the mid 1970s this pattern began to change as multinational companies in the affluent countries began to site more and more of their production in the poor countries themselves. This change is often referred to as the move to 'capital to labour' rather than 'labour to capital'. Most affluent countries introduced strict immigration controls on the entry of new workers by the mid 1970s as their need for migrant labour was reduced. Nevertheless the demand for low-waged female labour in manual service jobs has remained and many countries have permitted the entry of family members if those workers already in the migration setting can prove that they are able to support their families without 'recourse to public funds'.

At the same time the demand for manufacturing workers increased in newly industrializing countries such as Hong Kong, South Korea, Singapore, Malaysia and Taiwan. Dispatched to earn cash in the world market factories located in urban areas, young women have been targeted by multinational companies for their cheapness, vulnerability and supposed 'nimble fingers' since the 1960s (Hancock, 1983). In their search for foreign investment, developing country governments have encouraged this, as a brochure from the Malaysian government in the early 1970s demonstrates:

The manual dexterity of the oriental female is famous the world over. Her hands are small and she works fast with extreme care. Who therefore could be better qualified by nature and inheritance to contribute to the efficiency of a bench-assembly production line than the oriental female? (quoted Hancock, 1983)

This rural-urban migration is often the first step in what becomes an international migration because many poor, developing country governments encourage their surplus population to work abroad and send home remittances to ease internal poverty and help service foreign debt.

In addition the Gulf States began to recruit large numbers of personal service workers. In countries such as Kuwait the rapid increase in the numbers of professional and managerial women has been paralleled by an equally significant rise in demand for maids, the vast majority of whom migrate from southern Asia, particularly Sri Lanka. The demand for personal service workers has risen throughout affluent societies (Anderson, 1993).

Often it is very difficult to distinguish between what may be considered to be 'individual' choices governing migratory decisions and economic factors. For instance, migration may be regarded by some women as offering the possibility of escape from oppressive patriarchal cultures where notions regarding appropriate behaviour for women are strictly defined. But Morokvasic has shown the greater number of divorced, separated and widowed women in labour migrations in comparison to men with those statuses (Morokvasic, 1983). Women have greater difficulty surviving economically with that status or changing it, thus while the migratory decision may appear to be an individual's 'choice' it is underwritten by economic necessity. In many cases it is women who are left behind as heads of households in war zones. Family men may have left to fight or been killed, resulting in the situation where 80 per cent of the world's refugee populations are now female (Forbes-Martin, 1991).

State Masculinism

The vast majority of women migrating from poor, usually formerly colonized, countries are not entering an ideological vacuum when migrating to affluent parts of the world. A major feature of the colonization process was the development of an ideology alleging the innate inferiority of the dominated. Within this context, women from poor countries are stereotyped as illiterate beasts of burden, the bearers of many children and the guardians of 'tradition' (Morokvasic, 1983). As such national states impose restrictions on these women in order that they do not challenge the normalizing discourse of state masculinism. All women migrating legally as workers are controlled by the work permit system which not only stipulates the type of work but usually the actual employer. In cases where the woman has entered as the spouse of an employed male or 'mail-order' bride she may be bound to an unhappy, even violent marriage by immigration laws which render her right of residence dependent upon her husband (Potts, 1990). If a woman in this situation divorces she is liable to deportation. The legal entry of spouses and dependants is only allowed if a sponsor can provide evidence that he or she can support and accommodate them without recourse to 'public funds'. Not only is the family then forced to settle without state support, in many cases there is a waiting period before legal access to the labour market is granted. This forces many migrant women into unregistered work such as homeworking. They cannot work in registered jobs because they do not have a work permit. Even when they do have a legal right to work, racial discrimination and disadvantage may still confine migrant and immigrant women to low-paid homeworking jobs as we shall see in the clothing industry case study. These stereotypes also have serious implications for women in other areas of their lives. For instance, unsafe methods of contraception, such as Depo Provero, abortion and sterilization have often been forced on migrant women in the name of 'emancipation' (Bryan, Dadzie and Scafe, 1985).

As we have seen, racial discrimination often further constrains the labour market and therefore the earning opportunities of migrant women. This in turn is reflected in the kind of housing migrants can afford and the increased likelihood of overcrowding. But again this is not just a reflection of low incomes; in Europe at least there is plenty of evidence to show how the differential access to employment, housing, education, social and health services which is experienced by immigrants as compared to European nationals can be traced to institutionalized racism (Kofman and Sales, 1992).

It is within this context that we consider three specific cases of women's migration and the role of the state in shaping their migratory experience.

The Sex and Marriage Industries

Over the last twenty years we have witnessed the rapid growth of the sex-related entertainment industry in affluent and newly industrializing countries. Prostitution and other forms of sex-related 'entertainment' have become very big business for many countries where the industry has become an integral part of tourism. While women from many parts of south-east Asia and Africa have been deceived and 'trafficked' by the sex industry, now women from Eastern Europe and the former Soviet Union are finding their way into the clubs and brothels of north-west Europe in particular. The traffic in women is largely illegal and undocumented. Many women are recruited as entertainers, but when they arrive in the migration setting they realize that the only entertainment they are expected to provide is sex. Others indebted in their home country may be trafficked as bonded labour, but because they are very often illegal migrants any attempt to break free of the trafficker or pimp will result in deportation (Truong, 1990; Truong and del Rosario, 1994).

A related growth industry is that of 'mail-order' brides. Whereas in the past women from south-east Asia were 'favoured' for their 'submissiveness', now Eastern European women are being promoted on cost grounds (Truong and del Rosario, 1994) as the following extract from a German newspaper indicates: 'whereas a Thai is unprepared for cold German winters – one has to buy her clothes – a Pole brings her own boots and fur coat. And she is as good in bed and industrious in the kitchen' (*Bild*, 9 January 1991, cited in Morokvasic, 1991).

Following Brown (1992), Truong and del Rosario (1994) put forward a compelling theoretical framework with which to analyse the nature of power relations governing the lives of trafficked women, but I would want to argue that it has a broader applicability to the situation of migrant women generally and particularly all those who are undocumented or who have gained entry to the migration setting as a spouse.

They argue that the state is pivotal to such power relations in so far as it encompasses so many institutionalized dimensions of masculinism including the juridical-legislative, the capitalist, the prerogative and the bureaucratic dimension. Brown's argument is that the juridical-legislative dimension of the state is based on a public/private distinction placing the family, and women's place within it, firmly within a male-regulated private domain (Brown, 1992, p. 20). Troung and del Rosario argue that this has serious implications for the way that trafficked women in the sex industry and mail-order brides are treated by the state. To reiterate, trafficked women are often deceived or coerced into an illegal migration and remain under the physical control of procurers in the migration setting. If they come to the notice of the state, deportation is likely to be the result for the worker as an illegal alien while the procurer may hide behind the many different forms of legal sex-related services (Truong and del Rosario, 1994, p. 5). The burden of proof is shifted to the woman; in the eyes of the state she is an undesirable alien. In the same way if a mail-order bride wishes to leave the relationship which secured her entry into the migration setting, she too will be liable to deportation. In this way Truong and del Rosario argue that 'state practices buttress the interests and power of individual men as husbands, fiances or pimps' (Truong and del Rosario, 1994, p. 11). As they point out, once women are shifted out of the private sphere it is immigration law which determines their status, not family law or the laws against trafficking. The capitalist dimension of the state restricts the level of state intervention and regulation of the sex and marriage industries which are regarded as being part of the private domain in any case. Exactly the same 'logic' applies to the state's attitude to the maids industry.

The Maids Industry

By the early 1980s it was estimated that less than 15 per cent of families in the US conformed to the idealized notion of breadwinning husband, housewife and 2.4 children. The vast majority of households either contained dual-earner couples or were single-headed (Andersen, 1988). Other affluent societies have followed suit and the reality of the working mother and a diminishing role for the state in the care of the very young and the elderly has resulted in a massively increased demand for domestic workers in affluent societies. In the US the work of Hertz (1986) and Hochschild and Machung (1989) indicates very clearly that more affluent women can buy their way out of performing many reproductive tasks traditionally associated with women's 'role' in the private sphere by employing poorer (often undocumented) migrant women to perform them instead.

Anderson's work shows how in the Gulf States and in Britain also migrant domestic workers are treated by the state as members of households: they have no immigration status in their own right. This non-recognition as an employee leaves such workers, virtually all of whom are women, vulnerable to all sorts of abuse, physical, mental and material. Just as we saw in the previous case study, they are trapped by an immigration law which ties them into what can be a wholly unsatisfactory, even physically dangerous relationship with their employer. If they leave their employment they will be liable to deportation (Anderson, 1993).

Thus women from poor countries such as Mexico, Sri Lanka and the Philippines allow women in affluent countries to escape the drudgery of housework in conditions which sometimes approximate a contemporary form of state-facilitated slavery. In the final case study we examine some of the experiences of migrant women in the clothing industry.

Making Clothes

To reiterate, by the late 1970s we had witnessed a changing pattern of female migration in affluent societies. Rather than manufacturing industries in the higher-wage countries importing labour, they began to export certain labour-intensive stages of production to lower-wage poor and newly industrializing countries instead. While the electronics industry pioneered this trend, the clothing industry was quick on its heels, seizing the opportunity of reducing labour costs by shifting production to 'off-shore' sites. There were a number of incentives to do so, such as tax holidays, unrestricted repatriation of profits, and laws restricting the organization and bargaining power of trade unions, though lower labour costs were the biggest incentive.

In 1980 the English-language version of the influential study by Frobel, Heinrichs and Kreye, *The New International Division of Labour*, was published. They argued that the majority of clothing firms in what was then West Germany had relocated their production to low-wage countries to reduce labour costs in an industry where further mechanization was deemed too risky (Frobel, Heinrichs and Kreye, 1980). While their thesis is compelling and the trend towards a global relocation of labour-intensive manufacturing a continuing reality, there remain national differences which I would want to argue are closely related to differing immigration policies. A comparison between Britain and what was then the Federal Republic of Germany makes this clear (Phizacklea, 1990).

By the early 1970s both the British and German clothing industries were faced with declining profitability and both looked to subcontracting as a way of reducing labour costs. While Germany subcontracted abroad, British firms found new domestic subcontracting sources in the growing number of small, often 'family' dominated, inner-city factories run by ethnic minority entrepreneurs and labour.

While Germany had tied its migrant workers to specific jobs, had restricted the right of foreigners to set up businesses and had discouraged family re-union, Britain had imposed no such restrictions on migrant workers from ex-colonies entering prior to the restrictions of 1962. But the situation has been very different since then with even family re-union becoming increasingly difficult. The entry of spouses and family is only allowed if a sponsor can provide evidence that she or he will not have recourse to public funds. To reiterate, this forces many families to settle in poverty; it forces migrant women to find whatever work is available. In a 1990 study of homeworking in the English city of Coventry, my colleague Carol Wolkowitz and myself found that not only was the Asian-dominated clothing industry the only manufacturing growth industry in the city, it was also a major employer of Asian immigrant women, many of whom work for very low wages in their homes assembling garments. When we asked these women if they preferred to work at home, virtually all of them responded that working at home made them neither 'happier' nor 'unhappier'; they felt that they had no other choice (Phizacklea and Wolkowitz, 1995).

What the case studies indicate is, firstly, the extent to which the structural model of women's migration continues to have very real explanatory power and, secondly, the continuing importance of state immigration policies in shaping the migratory experience of women from poor countries.

Organizing

Within the context of an unashamedly structural analysis I hope to have indicated not only the diversity of migratory experiences but also what that means in terms of the persistence of inequalities between women on a global scale. One of the most pressing questions this leaves us with is what the possibilities are of organization and coalition-building between women of different classes, ethnic groups and nationalities when these categories represent hierarchies of power and privilege.

Self-organization and activity has often been forced upon migrant workers. In many cases organizations representing particular nationality groupings have been set up initially with a social function. Yet it is these very organizations which have shown themselves capable of transforming their role through networking to take on a political campaigning function, for example Filipina women's organizations in Europe. In 1979 the Commission for Filipino Migrant Workers was set up to support Filipino migrants in Britain, many of whom are maids and totally isolated. In the words of one woman, 'I went back to normal. Before when I was alone, I didn't trust anyone. My experience with my employers meant that I couldn't speak up. It makes you silent and not open. When I began to talk to people in similar situations and I saw that I was not alone, I realised that the problem was not just to do with me, that it was the Philippines and Britain and the government in those countries' (quoted in Anderson, 1993, p. 59).

Women who escaped from abusive employers, whatever their nationality, have been helped by the Commission, but it became increasingly clear that a campaign to change the immigration law relating to the position of domestics was vital. Kalayaan was formed, representing a coalition of migrant and immigrant groups, trade unions and concerned individuals who have campaigned to change the law as well as providing practical help for migrant domestic workers in Britain (Anderson, 1993).

The National Group on Homeworking in Britain (which now has links with homeworking groups worldwide) represents another coalition campaigning in the interests of homeworkers. While the National Group has campaigned for years to achieve employee status for all homeworkers it recognizes that if the majority of homeworkers are to achieve something approximating equal opportunities then many structural obstacles must be tackled such as racist and sexist immigration legislation and the opening up of real alternative employment possibilities for homeworkers, in some cases looking towards successful initiatives established by casualized women workers in poor countries. Swasti Mitter has examined a number of organizations including the Self-Employed Women's Association in India (SEWA) as models. SEWA was set up in 1972 as a workers' association for homeworkers and petty traders and vendors. As a trade union it organizes campaigns around conditions of work and childcare; it provides leadership training and has encouraged the formation of women's savings banks and producer cooperatives. As Mitter emphasizes, perhaps the most important role that SEWA has carried out is in bringing the plight of casualized workers to the notice of national and international policy-makers (Rowbotham and Mitter, 1994).

In the Netherlands local women's groups have taken up the cause of illegal migrant sex workers who would face deportation if they were to personally publicize and campaign against the bonded conditions under which they work (Truong and del Rosario, 1994). There are many other instances of coalition-building amongst diverse groups which only go to underline the point that a recognition of diversity and difference does not preclude collective organization across class and ethnic boundaries that challenges state practices and ideology.

Bibliography

ANDERSEN, M. (1988) *Thinking about Women: Sociological Perspectives on Sex and Gender*, New York, Macmillan.

ANDERSON, BRIDGET (1993) *Britain's Secret Slaves*, Anti-Slavery International.

BROWN, W. (1992) 'Finding the Man in the State', *Feminist Studies*, Vol. 18, No. 1, pp. 7–34

BRYAN, BEVERLEY, DADZIE, STELLA and SCAFE, SUZANNE (1985) *The Heart of the Race*, London, Virago.

CASTLES, S. and KOSACK, G. (1973) *Immigrant Workers and Class Structures in Western Europe*, OUP.

CASTLES, S. and MILLER, M. (1993) *The Age of Migration*, London, Macmillan.

FORBES-MARTIN, SUSAN (1991) *Refugee Women*, London, Zed Press.

FROBEL, F., HEINRICHS, J. and KREYE, O. (1980) *The New International Division of Labour*, Cambridge, Cambridge University Press.

HANCOCK, R. (1983) 'Transnational Production and Women Workers' in PHIZACKLEA, A. (Ed.) *One Way Ticket*, London, Routledge.

HERTZ, R. (1986) *More Equal Than Others*, Berkeley, University Of California Press.

HOCHSCHILD, A. and MACHUNG, A. (1989) *The Second Shift*, New York, Viking.

KOFMAN ELEONORE and SALES, ROSEMARY (1992) 'Towards Fortress Europe', *Women's Studies International Forum*, Vol. 15, Nos. 5/6, pp. 29–40

MITTER, SWASTI (1986) *Common Fate, Common Bond*, London, Pluto.

MOROKVASIC, MIRJANA (1983) 'Women and Migration: Beyond the Reductionist Outlook', in PHIZACKLEA, A. (Ed.) *One Way Ticket: Migration and Female Labour*, London, Routledge.

MOROKVASIC, MIRJANA (1991) 'Fortress Europe and Migrant Women', *Feminist Review*, No. 39 (Winter), pp. 69–84

PHIZACKLEA, ANNIE (1990) *Unpacking the Fashion Industry: Gender, Racism and Class in Production*, London, Routledge.

PHIZACKLEA, ANNIE and WOLKOWITZ, CAROL (1995) *Homeworking Women: Gender, Racism and Class at Work*, London, Sage.

POTTS, L. (1990) *The World Labour Market*, London, Zed Press.

ROWBOTHAM, S. and MITTER, S. (1994) *Dignity and Daily Bread: New forms of organization amongst poor women in the third world*, London, Routledge.

SEN, GITA and GROWN, CAREN (1988) *Development Crises and Alternative Visions: Third World Women's Perspectives*, London, Earthscan.

SHAH, NASRA, AL-QUDSI, SULAYMAN and SHAH, MAKHDOOM (1991) 'Asian Women Workers in Kuwait', *International Migration Review*, 25 (3), pp. 464–86.

TRUONG, THANH-DAM (1990) *Sex, Money and Morality: Prostitution and Tourism in Southeast Asia*, London, Zed Press.

TRUONG, THANH-DAM and DEL ROSARIO, VIRGINIA (1994) 'Captive Outsiders: Trafficked Sex Workers and Mail-Order Brides in the European Union', in WIERSMA, J. (Ed.) *Insiders and Outsiders: On the Making of Europe II*, Kampen, Pharos.

TYREE, ANDREA and DONATO, KATHERINE (1986) 'A Demographic Overview of the International Migration of Women', in SIMON R.J. and BRETELL C.B. (Eds) *International Migration: The Female Experience*, New Jersey, Rowman and Allanheld.

Notes on Contributors

Anne Marie Goetz is a Fellow at the Institute of Development Studies, Sussex University. Her research and publications centre on empirical and theoretical investigations into gendered power relations in public administration, the way they shape public policy, and the impact of development policies on women. Her work focuses in particular on field-level development workers in rural credit programmes in Bangladesh. She is currently analysing the new governance policy agenda in terms of the place of gender concerns and poverty issues in discussions of accountability and the role of civil society.

Maria Holt has worked extensively as a researcher and consultant for non-governmental organizations concerned with Anglo-Arab relations.

Tamara Jacka is a lecturer in Chinese Studies at the School of Humanities, Murdoch University, Australia. She has written extensively on Chinese women and work, and on Asian feminist perspectives on women's studies. Her research interests are gender and division of labour, and women's employment in China.

Geraldine Lievesley lectures in Latin American politics at Manchester Metropolitan University. Her research interests include Peruvian politics and the Latin American left. She is the author of *Democracy in Latin America: Mobilisation, Power and the Search for a New Politics* (Manchester University Press, forthcoming)

Malika Mehdid was born and grew up in Algeria. She is a lecturer in the Department for Cultural Studies at Birmingham University. Her research interests are the sexual politics of North African and Middle Eastern societies. She is the author of *Tradition and Subversion in North African Feminist Writing* (Zed Press, forthcoming).

Annie Phizacklea is a Professor of Sociology at the Department of Sociology. University of Leicester. Her research interests are migration and female labour. She is currently writing *Migration and Globalisation: A Feminist Perspective* (Sage, 1996). She is author of *Unpacking the Fashion Industry:*

Gender, Racism and Class in Production (Routledge, 1990), and (with C. Wolkowitz) *Homeworking Women: Gender, Racism and Class at Work* (Sage, 1995).

Shirin M. Rai is a lecturer in Politics at the Department of Politics and International Studies, and also teaches in the Centre for the Study of Women and Gender at the University of Warwick. Her research interests include Chinese politics, gender, representation and the politics of development. She is the author of *Resistance and Reaction: University Politics in Post-Mao China* (Harvester Wheatsheaf, 1991), and the editor (with H. Pilkington and A. Phizacklea) of *Women in the Face of Change: The Sovier Union, Eastern Europe and China* (Routledge, 1992), and (with G. Griffin, M. Hestor, and S. Roseneil) of *Stirring It: Challenges for Feminism* (Taylor and Francis, 1994).

Ann Stewart is a senior lecturer at the School of Law, and also teaches in the Centre for the Study of Women and Gender at the University of Warwick. She is the author of *Housing Action in an Industrial Suburb* (Academic Press, 1981) and *Rethinking Housing Law* (Sweet and Maxwell, 1996). She is completing ESRC-funded research on the Power of Law in Municipal Politics jointly with Davina Cooper. She also specializes in the area of feminism and the law, particularly in relation to the Third World. She is editing a book on *Gender, Law and Justice* and has organized international seminars on women and law for the British Council.

Georgina Waylen is a lecturer in Politics at the Department of Politics at the University of Sheffield. Her main research interests are gender and politics and development primarily in Latin America and the Caribbean. She is the author of *Gender in Third World Politics* (Open University Press, 1996) and is currently working on a project examining gender and simultaneous political and economic liberalization in comparative perspective.

Index

abortion 112–13
Acker, J. 131
Ackerly, B. 121
agriculture 147–8, 151–2, 157–9
Algeria 63, 78–9, 80, 82–7, 89, 91–2,
    94, 96–8, 100–1
  Family Code 86–8
  National Transitional Council
    93–6
  National Union of Algerian
    Women 83
  Person Status Code 87
  Revolution 11, 92
Alianza de Mujeres del Peru
    (Alimuper) 55–7
Alianza Popular Revolucionaria
    Americana (APRA) 52–3
All-China Women's Federation
    146–7, 154, 156
Alvarez, S. 58, 104
Amal 72, 75
Andreas, C. 51, 54
Angelo, G. 106, 108
'anti-politics' 49
apertura 47
Arafat, Yasir 61
Arteaga, A. 105
authoritarianism 45

Bangladesh 118–43
Bangladesh Rural Advancement
    Committee (BRAC) 120–1,
    124–5, 129–30, 134–9
Bangladesh Rural Poor Programme

(RPP) 120, 124–5, 130, 135–6,
    139
Barrie, M. 50, 56
Blondet, C. 50
Booth, D. 47
Boserup, E. 156
Botswana 23–4, 27, 35
  1984 Citizenship Act
Bryson, V. 58
Buvinic, M. 119

Catholic Church 48–50
  and Chile 112
  and Peru 52
Cedamanos, G. 51
Charlton, S. 104
Child and Mother Welfare
    Association (Lebanon) 73
Chile 103–18
China 143–62
Christian Democracy 105–7, 110,
    112–13
citizenship 24, 35, 84
  naturalization 24
civil society 2, 14, 16–18, 28, 85, 89,
    91, 105, 138–9
clan 23, 31, 92
  elders 31
  practice 23
class 14–15, 46–7, 54, 56, 79, 103,
    119, 121, 123, 126–8
  origins 2, 13
clientelism 49–51
collectivization 144